Punitive War

Punitive War

Confederate Guerrillas and Union Reprisals

Clay Mountcastle

University Press of Kansas

Published by the University Press of Kansas (Lawrence, Kansas 66045), which was
organized by the Kansas Board of Regents and is operated and funded by Emporia State
University, Fort Hays State University, Kansas State University, Pittsburg State
University, the University of Kansas, and Wichita State University

Library of Congress Cataloging-in-Publication Data

Mountcastle, Clay.
  Punitive war : confederate guerrillas and union reprisals / Clay Mountcastle.
      p. cm. -- (Modern war studies)
  Includes bibliographical references and index.
  ISBN 978-0-7006-1668-8 (cloth : alk. paper)

  1. United States—History—Civil War, 1861-1865—Underground movements. 2. Counterinsurgency—United States—History—19th century. 3. Guerrilla warfare—United
States—History—19th century. 4. Guerrilla warfare—Confederate States of America.
5. United States. Army—History—Civil War, 1861-1865. 6. Guerrillas—United States—
History—19th century. 7. Guerrillas—Confederate States of America. I. Title.
  E470.M73 2009
  973.7′3—dc22

                                                                    2009011965

British Library Cataloguing-in-Publication Data is available.

Printed in the United States of America
10 9 8 7 6 5 4 3 2 1

For the American soldier,
past and present

Contents

Acknowledgments   *ix*

Introduction   1

1. The American Antebellum Experience with Guerrilla Warfare   8

2. Proving Ground for Punishment: Pope, Halleck, and Schofield in Missouri   21

3. A Remedy for All Evils: Retaliatory Destruction on the Mississippi   56

4. War and Individual Ruin: Sherman's Campaigns of 1864   85

5. The Valley Aflame: Punitive War in Virginia   103

Conclusion   138

Notes   *147*

Bibliography   *181*

Index   *193*

Acknowledgments

There is no possible way that this book would have ever made it to publication without the aid of many. For the past five years, I have been the beneficiary of the patience, kindness, and support of several people and agencies, to all of whom I owe a tremendous debt.

The generous guidance I received from a number of colleagues in the History Department at Duke University provided me with much-needed direction. Alex Roland was instrumental in helping me craft and refine the argument that formed the basis of this book from raw ideas. His patience and persistence were incredibly helpful and will always be greatly appreciated. Duke professors Margaret Humphreys and Laura Edwards were kind enough to provide invaluable insight on the people and character of the Civil War South. Their astute observations brought me to the realization that a traditional operational history would not be an effective fit for my argument. Professor Richard Kohn from the University of North Carolina at Chapel Hill provided much-needed advice as I began my research and continued throughout the writing process. One cannot say enough about everything Dick has done for the scores of military officers he has helped to become military historians over the years.

The faculty and staff of the Department of History at West Point were the best cheerleaders that a budding historian and author could hope for. Colonels Ty Siedule and Matthew Moten were incredibly supportive and never let me give up on my hopes of earning my doctorate and publishing a book. It was truly an honor to work with such professionals and world-class scholars.

While conducting my research, I greatly benefited from the superb support offered by the staff at the U.S. Army Military History Institute at Carlisle, Pennsylvania. Colonel (ret.) Conrad Crane, Louise Arnold-Friend, and many others devoted more time than they should have on assisting me in my several trips to MHI throughout the years. Together, they preside over what I believe to be the nation's greatest single asset available to the military history community in terms of research. Just as supportive was the staff at the Library of Congress Manuscripts Division, who were undaunted by my trips to the front desk seemingly every five minutes.

The delightfully helpful staff at University Press of Kansas made the process of publishing this book both easy and rewarding. Mike Briggs's enthusiasm for the project was inspirational. As one of the few publishing houses still truly committed to the publication of military history, I applaud UPK for their courage to do so.

No single person was more instrumental in the publication of this book than Professor Joseph Glatthaar. He is, without a doubt, the finest Civil War historian I know and an even better friend. Joe was kind enough to read the manuscript and talk with me at length about the nature of my argument and ways to improve it. He and his lovely wife, Jackie, were extremely gracious and provided Sally and me with a home away from home whenever we visited Chapel Hill over the years. I cannot thank them enough and eagerly look forward to more visits in the future.

A special note of thanks goes to my parents, and especially to my father, Jack Mountcastle, who long ago set me on the path that led to this book. He imbued in me a great love and appreciation for our history and for the soldiers who have provided our freedoms throughout the centuries. I will always look back on the many days spent walking Civil War battlefields with my dad as some of the most worthwhile times of my childhood. This book is the direct result of his teaching, mentorship, and assistance throughout the years.

Finally, I would like to thank my wife, Dr. Sally Mountcastle, whose patience and understanding were more helpful than she could ever possibly know. Sally had to work around my numerous research trips and multitude of hours spent writing, all of which she took in stride. She never allowed me to rest on my laurels and constantly reminded me that something worth doing is worth doing well. She is always right.

Despite the wealth of assistance I received on this project, any errors found in the writing or context of this book are mine and mine alone.

Punitive War

Introduction

As the late summer sun settled over the Mississippi River on the evening of 25 August 1862, what was left of the small town of Randolph, Tennessee, still smoldered in the fading daylight. Earlier that day, a regiment of Ohio Infantry debarked from a steamer just below the town, marched into Randolph, and began burning every house. The soldiers did not engage in combat with any Confederate forces because none were there. They did not seize any military supplies or ammunition stores because the town did not possess any. Instead, the Ohioans moved quickly and efficiently from house to house, setting them aflame. Then, as quickly as they had arrived, they departed—a dark cloud of smoke rising behind them. A single house was left standing, the only evidence that Randolph ever existed.

It was easy for the destruction of one small town to become lost amidst the cataclysmic swirl of battles and sweeping campaigns that racked the nation in the second year of the Civil War. After all, it was only a single town. But the burning of Randolph was not an isolated incident, not an aberration. Throughout the occupied South, similar scenes sprang up increasingly as the war wore on. Entire towns, sometimes cities, were destroyed and the inhabitants forced to flee even though these locations had no real operational or strategic value. It was what Union cavalryman William Porter Wilkin referred to as "the ravages of war" when he surveyed the destruction of barns, mills, and houses in western Virginia in early 1862.[1] These ravages, however, were not pointless or wanton. Nor were they merely the unavoidable byproduct of a prolonged, desperate conflict. There was a distinct purpose for the brand of deliberate destruction seen in the burning of Randolph, and a specific cause.

It is not surprising that four years of extensive fighting and occupation took a disastrous toll on the once prosperous South, and by the spring of 1865, much of it lay in ruins. Atlanta, Columbia, and Richmond remained little more than blackened chimneys and smoldering ash. Countless miles of railroad were either destroyed or extensively damaged. Agriculturally rich expanses such as the Mississippi Valley and Virginia's Shenandoah Valley were left decimated and devoid of crops or livestock as Union armies lived off the countryside and worked to destroy the Confederate Army's ability to sustain itself. Tens of thousands of displaced civilians worked to reestablish their homes and mend their broken lives. For the people of the defeated Confederacy, the Civil War brought devastation the extent of which they had never before seen, nor would they see again.

In truth, however, the war's most blatant displays of aggression toward noncombatants and their property had little to do with feeding soldiers or starving the opponent. Instead, they were about punishment. The Union waged a punitive war against the people of the South in conjunction, if not always in concert, with its efforts to defeat the Confederate Army on the battlefield. It was an element of the war that was not fully orchestrated, nor at times, even planned. And yet, punitive war became an integral part of the Union war effort. By 1864 it evolved into a powerful and decisive force and it ultimately enabled the Union to achieve victory.

A number of factors contributed to the Union's adoption of punitive war, which can be described as the use of military force for the sole purpose of punishment or retribution. The frustration of a prolonged contest, the overt defiance displayed by Southern civilians, and the belief by many that increased severity would hasten the end of the war were just some of these factors. None of these, however, were as influential as the vexing problem caused by guerrilla warfare waged in the South. Throughout the conflict, Union troops were faced with the threat of attacks by guerrillas in varying forms and degrees. Beginning in the war's first months, Federal troops often met with deadly resistance by armed and violent Southerners who fought the war on their own terms, usually far from a battlefield. At times, the danger seemed to press the Union soldiers from all sides, whether marching in column or alone on picket duty. It was an almost intangible threat, one that was interwoven with the Southern population and landscape. Guerrillas in the South were, as one angry Federal soldier described, "Thieves and murderers by occupation, rebels by pretense, soldiers only in name, and cowards by nature," and they were as hard to identify as they were to kill or capture.[2] Because of this, guerrillas presented the Union Army with a distinct tactical problem that altered the Union perception of Southern civilians and the rules of warfare. Where it flourished, this guerrilla problem touched all ranks, from the most influential generals down to the most common foot soldier, and the response was almost always punitive war against civilians and their property. Therefore, when considering the extensive damage done to the South during the Civil War, it is necessary to realize that much of it was caused either directly or indirectly by the guerrilla problem.

The complexity surrounding the term *guerrilla* makes it difficult to establish exact definitions of every Southerner who conducted irregular warfare against the Union Army. As historian John Ellis once noted, guerrilla warfare is not an "absolutely discrete phenomenon . . . it merges into many other types of military activity."[3] Such was the case in the occupied South. Those who conducted guerrilla warfare against the invading Union Army fit many different definitions. There were Confederate cavalrymen, such as Nathan Bedford Forrest and John Hunt Morgan, who practiced evasive hit-and-run-style tactics as part of organized and sanctioned Confederate raid operations. So-called partisan rangers, who often wore Confederate uniforms but enjoyed complete autonomy from the conventional force, preyed on Federal railroads, telegraph lines, and supply wagons. There were bushwhackers who, in the guise of innocent civilians, waylaid Union pickets for the mere purpose of robbery or murder. Perhaps the most difficult class of guerrilla to define, although quite prevalent, was that which attacked simply for the sake of resisting the Union invaders.

Within the guerrilla problem, however, tactics were the constant. While their appearances and objectives may have varied, the manner in which Southern irregulars fought was quite similar. They usually conducted surprise attacks, or ambushes, against a vulnerable, outnumbered enemy. These quick attacks were frequently followed by a rapid retreat, and they seldom took prisoners. This type of fighting often led Union soldiers to equate Southern guerrillas with Indian or Mexican foes from previous wars. In the words of one Union general in 1861, "Scalping their victims is all that is wanting to make their warfare like that which seventy or eighty years ago was waged by the Indians against the white race on this very ground."[4] And just as the colonists struggled to solve the problems inherent to this type of warfare, so too would their Yankee descendents.

When examining the Confederacy's use of guerrilla warfare, as a number of recent studies have done, it is indeed important to adhere to the various distinctions between irregulars.[5] When focusing on the Union response to the guerrilla problem, however, it is not. In fact, it is crucial not to make such distinctions, for the very important reason that Union officers and soldiers normally did not differentiate among the various types of enemy irregulars, or as historian Mark Grimsley put it, they usually did not "carefully distinguish" between them.[6] Indeed, this study suggests that Union soldiers and their leaders almost never did so. Those who practiced any fashion of guerrilla-style tactics against Union forces were universally considered to be guerrillas or bushwhackers, regardless of their background, organization, or uniform. Union (and many Confederate) soldiers generally despised their shadowy style of fighting, which flew in the face of widely accepted nineteenth-century norms for combat. Such was the sentiment of Sergeant John Anderson of the 2nd Massachusetts Infantry, who referred to guerrillas as "desperadoes who enlist in neither army, but carry on a warfare on their own account for the sake of satisfying their desire of revenge for fancied wrongs, or thirst for adventure and plunder."[7] No matter what their objectives were, or whether they donned a uniform or not, all irregular combatants presented essentially the same tactical problem for the Union occupiers and were therefore viewed as part of the same, distinct challenge. Primarily occupied with the burden of defeating the Confederate Army in the field, the Federals had neither the time nor the inclination to analyze this guerrilla threat to any greater extent.

The fact that the Union Army encountered the guerrilla problem in the Civil War is, in itself, neither surprising nor particularly noteworthy. After all, American armies faced similar threats in their previous conflicts. What made the guerrilla problem significant in the Civil War was the potent effect it had on Union attitudes toward Southern civilians and their property. As these attitudes changed, so did the very nature of the war. As most Civil War historians would likely concede, the conflict witnessed a drastic change in its character from beginning to end, particularly seen in the Union's prosecution of the war. According to Russell F. Weigley, as the war progressed the United States adopted a "new mode of war" defined as "war against peoples" and not just against enemy armies. This transition centered on the Union's willingness to abandon conciliatory policies and include civilians in the hardships of war. Charles Royster, author of *The Destructive War: William Tecumseh Sherman, Stonewall Jackson, and the Americans*, argued that Union operations in the war's later years reached an "extent and severity of ruin" that was decidedly new to American warfare. Stephen V. Ash came to a similar conclusion in *When the Yankees Came*, stating that the North shifted from a "conciliatory and conservative policy" to a "punitive and radical one that brought destruction, disruption, and suffering" on the people of the South.[8] Of course, a number of elements combined to make the Civil War harder on civilians. The widely accepted practice of foraging, the caustic issue of emancipation, and mounting Union frustration over losses on the battlefield all amounted to suffering for the people of the South. None of these elements, however, offer a reasonable explanation for the burning of homes and forced evacuation of entire communities, which happened more often than most general histories of the Civil War admit. Nor can they explain the willingness of Union troops to carry out the devastating campaigns seen in Georgia, South Carolina, and Virginia in the last year of the war.

A detailed consideration of the most influential leaders and events in the evolution of Union military policy reveals a common link—experience with facing a guerrilla threat. And yet this is a contentious issue with Civil War historians. While some, such as Grimsley, have argued against the notion of guerrilla warfare having played a major role in the Union's abandonment of its conciliatory approach, others see it as paramount. Grimsley credited guerrilla warfare for, at the very most, having "placed a strain" on Union policies, but not breaking them. The most emphatic denial of the guerrilla problem's effect on Union policies to date was presented in Mark Neely's recent book, *The Civil War and the Limits of Destruction*, in which the author dismissed the idea of guerrillas having much of an effect on Union conduct.[9] Andrew J. Birtle disagreed, claiming that "the political and military disruption created by the guerrillas and their civilian sympathizers" was the single most important factor in causing the Union to "stiffen its pacification policies" during the first two years of the war.[10] Along these same lines, Ash argued that "the burgeoning guerrilla violence in the countryside" did the most to convince Union soldiers to wage a war of reprisal against the South.[11] As such, there exists a significant disagreement on the importance of guerrilla warfare's role in the Union's abandonment of conciliation in favor of a more vigorous treatment of the South's infrastructure and its people. As for the minute number of studies that specifically address guerrilla warfare in the Civil War, the most extensive of these being Robert Mackey's *The Uncivil War: Irregular Warfare in the Upper South, 1861–1865*, they are primarily confined to operational and tactical narrative. While arguing that the Confederacy "fought and lost" an unconventional war in addition to the conventional one, Mackey did not attempt to define guerrilla warfare's influence on Union attitudes to any great extent.[12] While these and other works have gone far to introduce the topic of guerrilla warfare in the Civil War, they alone do not provide enough depth of detail to fully illustrate the relationship between the guerrilla problem and the changes in Union attitudes and action during the war.

The purpose of this book is to provide those necessary details. What follows is not so much a study of guerrilla warfare in the Civil War, but rather, a study of the Union Army's response to it. This book examines the guerrilla problem and punitive war dynamic from its roots in America's antebellum experience and then traces its progression from the Western Theater in 1861 to its apogee in the East in the last two years of the war. Much like the guerrilla problem itself, the story does not follow a straight chronological path, but rather, moves from one operational theater to the next to illustrate how the problem grew throughout the South at varying times and in varying degrees. From Missouri to the Lower Mississippi Valley, across Mississippi and Georgia, and ultimately into Virginia, the causal relationship between the guerrilla problem and the increasing brutality of the war became more evident with each passing year. By war's end, the Union Army had adopted retaliatory measures that challenged the sensibilities of even the most hardened soldiers. It was what historian Gerald Linderman called "a warfare of frightfulness," the kind that was not easy to prosecute, much less understand.[13] While there were indeed other facets of the war that pushed the participants to greater measures of severity, nothing eroded the barrier between the soldier and civilian spheres more than the guerrilla problem.

Some readers may be disappointed to see that the following pages contain little to no discussion of large-scale engagements such as Shiloh, Antietam, or Gettysburg. The reason for this is quite simple: the guerrilla problem had little to no effect on their conduct or outcome. With the exception of Sherman's campaigns in 1864, I have intentionally avoided detailed descriptions of the war's larger conventional battles and campaigns in order to focus on many smaller, lesser-known developments and incidents that filled the spaces in between. When taken as a whole, these events paint a telling picture of the punitive side of the Union war effort heretofore untold, and serve as a poignant reminder that much of the Civil War was fought far away from the battlefield.

Perhaps the greatest challenge for this book is to argue a point centered on the gradual evolution of thoughts, attitudes, and actions rather than just a sequence of events. Saying that the Union Army was enticed into using punitive war because of frustration brought on by guerrilla violence requires the examination of thoughts and words as much as action. It is impossible to appreciate the psychological and moral effect that Southern guerrilla operations had on Union troops (and the Southern people) solely based on the number of Union soldiers killed, the total dollar value of equipment destroyed, or the percentage of soldiers deployed to guard against guerrillas compared to those in the field. This is only part of the story, and the least important at that. Scholars who have dismissed the relevance of the guerrilla problem based on these simple criteria miss the forest for the trees.[14] While quantitative analysis can be useful in gauging guerrilla warfare's tactical influence on Union military operations, it does little to illustrate the mounting frustration that led to significant changes in the way the Union Army viewed, and dealt with, the Southern population and the conflict itself, which was the guerrilla problem's most meaningful contribution to the war.

What can be proven is the frequency with which Union officers and soldiers pointed to the guerrilla problem, and the Southern peoples' presumed support of it, as justification for their use of punitive war. Enough evidence exists to establish a credible cause-and-effect relationship between Southern guerrillas and the Union's espousal of punitive war that exceeds other explanations for the change. Not only can the most irrefutable examples of Union hard war policy, such as Order Number 11 in Missouri, be directly linked to guerrilla activity, but so can the lesser-known events, such as the directed destruction of entire towns up and down the Mississippi shoreline in 1862 and 1863. When juxtaposed with the abundance of Union rhetoric about the need for a severe response to the guerrilla problem, the Army's use of punitive war illustrates a clear causal relationship between the two. Evidence of this relationship in the words and deeds of Union officers and soldiers is so substantive that it goes beyond circumstantial correlation and offers as viable an explanation for the destructiveness of the Civil War as any other.

Punitive War is not designed to condemn the Union's use of punitive war or to condone it. Nor does it seek to assign a measure of success to Confederate guerrilla operations in the Civil War. It is certainly not aimed at passing moral judgment on either subject. It is designed, instead, to remind the reader that the American Civil War was a complicated affair waged with passion and, at times, great frustration. Those who participated, from the youngest private to the most seasoned general, shaped the character of the war with their thoughts, words, and deeds, and the result was often devastating, especially for civilians in the South. Given the proven durability of guerrilla tactics and strategy throughout the centuries, it is worthwhile to realize just how susceptible a large, professional fighting force like the U.S. Army can be to the powers of frustration and anger, which traditionally accompany a guerrilla threat. The American Civil War provides a superb example from which to learn.

CHAPTER ONE

The American Antebellum Experience with Guerrilla Warfare

*An invasion against an exasperated people, ready for all sacrifices
. . . is a dangerous enterprise.*
—Baron Antoine Henri Jomini, *The Art of War*

The Union Army's experience with the guerrilla problem in the Civil War had its precedents. In 1990, historian John D. Waghelstein posed the apt question, "Why has [American] history been so full of difficulties in dealing with irregulars, partisans, and guerrillas when so much of our military experience is in just this type of conflict?"[1] On the eve of the Civil War, Union and Confederate military leaders should have been familiar with guerrilla warfare and its many complexities. Americans had dealt with irregulars of some form in every conflict the nation witnessed prior to 1861. Throughout the American Revolution, Indian wars, and the Mexican War, the developing American army fought either as guerrillas or against guerrillas. As a result, by the eve of the Civil War there existed a substantial amount of empirical evidence on the subject. With this, the North and South could have better prepared themselves for the uncertainties involved with fighting an unconventional enemy and dealing with a hostile population. When the first shots were fired on Fort Sumter, however, both armies were focused solely on what they believed would be a quick, conventional war fought in the classic European style. They envisioned the two armies engaging in a single, decisive engagement and returning to their homes in a matter of weeks. They were tragically wrong not only about the duration of the impending conflict, but also about its simplicity. As historian Russell Weigley concluded, America's military leaders were totally unprepared for "the full dimensions of the Civil War."[2] One of these dimensions would involve the task of facing armed and violent civilians and responding to them. Had they looked to the past, they would have realized that the guerrilla problem was unavoidable.

During the colonial era, Americans were introduced to irregular warfare during their numerous conflicts with the Indians. Tactics differed markedly from those practiced on the battlefields of Europe between conventional armies. Anglo-Indian clashes were characterized by surprise raids, ambushes, hand-to-hand fighting, and the targeting of enemy settlements and food supply. In describing warfare under "American conditions," one historian wrote, "The formal tactics of the Old World were replaced by forest tactics which approximated those of the Indians themselves."[3] King Philip's War (1675–1676) and the French and Indian War (1754–1760) both revealed the need for colonists to augment their rigid line formations and tactics with more unconventional, fluid ways of fighting. In some cases, the use of Indian auxiliaries became necessary. The objectives of warfare changed as well, becoming total and all-encompassing. The limits of European-style warfare did not fit the unconventional nature of frontier war. When the colonists became frustrated by the guerrilla-like tactics used by their Indian opponents, according to John Morgan Dederer, they had "little alternative in their fight for self-preservation but to try and destroy the Indians as a people."[4] This included the destruction of entire Indian villages, livestock, and crops. In doing so, the colonists were the first of many generations of Americans to resort to punitive policies in response to the frustrating problem posed by guerrilla warfare.

During the American Revolution, the colonials themselves waged a vigorous guerrilla campaign throughout the southern colonies to frustrate the British Army and to deplete its supply base. In early 1780, the Continental Army was contained to the northeast and therefore the burden of the South's defense fell upon those who took up arms to fight as irregulars. Francis Marion, the fabled "Swamp Fox," was perhaps the most successful of America's partisan leaders, along with Thomas Sumter, the heralded "Gamecock" of South Carolina. Under the command and supervision of General Nathanael Greene, Marion and Sumter conducted what one historian referred to as a "shadowy sort of *maquis* warfare," engaging in ambushes and hit-and-run attacks against British supply lines, stores, and outposts.[5] The effort often worked. The victory scored by colonial partisans at the Battle of Huck's Defeat in 1780 diminished British control of the region and marked a significant change in momentum in the southern colonies.[6] In May 1781, Marion's capture of Fort Watson and Fort Motte outside of Charleston and Sumter's effective harassment of British supply lines running toward Columbia convinced Britain's Lord Rawdon to abandon his secure position in Camden, thereby playing into Greene's strategy of getting the British out in the open and on the move.[7] Although effective, partisan attacks did not bring about a British defeat on their own. Their cumulative effect did, however, seriously hamper Lord Cornwallis's movement and dashed his hopes of putting down the rebellion in the South.

In response, Cornwallis adopted punitive measures such as executing prisoners and threatening the destruction of entire towns. But neither Cornwallis nor his officers were ready to embrace the ruthlessness of punitive war whole-heartedly. Although Cornwallis believed that retaliation was necessary, it wore on his conscience. As historian Piers Mackesy described, "In an auction of terror, the rebels could always outbid him."[8] Thus, while treating the civilians in the colonies with an increasingly harsh hand, the British never resorted to the level of retaliation that the Americans would employ in future wars.

Despite the effectiveness of guerrilla operations conducted by the likes of Marion and Sumter, the experience did not translate to any strong American faith in irregular warfare. The guerrilla tactics used in the southern colonies were largely the result of strategic necessity based on the Americans' inability to compete conventionally with the professional British Army. While some historians have attributed Cornwallis's defeat in the South to Greene's coop-eration with local guerrillas, the general himself never viewed the operations of partisans or guerrillas as paramount to victory.[9] He did indeed employ a form of guerrilla strategy to defend the South, but the role of irregulars came second to the importance of the conventional army. This fact is not so surpris-ing when one considers that for every one of the relatively few unconventional victories scored by colonial partisans or militia during the Revolution, such as King's Mountain on 7 October 1780, there were an equal number of embar-rassing defeats, such as Long Island and Camden. Therefore, the potential for guerrilla warfare as a worthy strategy on its own was dubious. At war's end, many influential leaders in the new United States, including George Wash-ington, were convinced that future wars could be won only by trained con-ventional forces and not by disorganized militia or irrepressible partisans.[10] Guerrilla warfare had served its purpose for the Revolution, but it did not factor into the military vision for a new America. As Weigley observed, "The later course of American military history, featuring a rapid rise from poverty of resources to plenty, cut short any further evolution of Greene's type of [guerrilla] strategy."[11] In fact, the American Revolution marked the last time that the U.S. Army would rely on a guerrilla strategy. Thereafter, guerrillas were the enemy. Unlike the Confederacy, the invading Union Army had no need for such a strategy in the Civil War.

As the U.S. Army developed into a more professional fighting force in the early nineteenth century, attentions turned from preparing for a threat from Europe to dealing with Indian problems on the frontier. As William B. Skelton noted, it was "a time of crisis" for American regulars engaged in wea-risome frontier duty that "offered few chances for martial glory and raised disturbing moral questions about their professional role."[12] An exercise in frustration ensued, one that showcased the clash between European conven-tional tactics and primitive, irregular war. As seen during the Colonial pe-riod, in almost every location along the frontier where whites settled, tensions with Indian tribes arose and often erupted in violence. Examples include the Creek War of 1813 and the Black Hawk War in 1831. In these conflicts, the Indians maintained their traditional methods of war making. They fought in classic guerrilla fashion, attacking in small groups and quickly dispersing, to avoid decisive engagements. Their irregular, hit-and-run tactics were in stark contrast to the linear, European-style tactics embraced by the still developing American Army. In no other conflict was this disparity more apparent, and problematic, for the American troops, than in the wars with the Seminole Indians in Florida.

During the Second Seminole War, fought between 1835 and 1842, the U.S. Army marched deep into the swamps of Florida in an attempt to subdue the Seminoles who, led by the pugnacious Osceola, had attacked a number of white settlements. On 28 December 1835, a war party of Seminoles wiped out two companies of American soldiers under the command of Major Francis Dade in what would come to be known as the Dade Massacre. This sparked the U.S. military into action. Initial operations, commanded by General Winfield Scott, were strictly conventional in nature and designed to cow the Indians with, according to Waghelstein, "the weight and sight" of Scott's trained professionals.[13] They were not successful. As Scott and others soon learned, the Seminoles were not easily intimidated and were very good at avoiding an open fight with the army. The more the U.S. soldiers searched, the further back the Seminoles retreated into the impassible hammocks, choosing to attack outposts and small detachments of soldiers when the odds favored them. Even a significant increase in troop numbers failed to help the situation, as it brought difficulties with logistics and troop management.[14] The attempts by Scott and his fellow officers to score victories against the Seminoles using conventional tactics, while unproductive, were not without reason. According to Weigley, "When Indian opponents could be brought to stand in battle, the best way to crush them was to pour a heavy fire into them and then assault them with a disciplined charge."[15] The problem was that the elusive Seminoles could rarely be brought to battle.

The Battle of Okeechobee, fought on Christmas Day in 1837, marked the one instance that the Seminoles made the mistake of facing the soldiers in a full-scale conventional fight, and they ended up paying for it dearly. American forces under "Old Rough and Ready" General Zachary Taylor conducted a determined charge against the loosely arranged Seminole defenses, forcing them out of their positions and deeper into the swamp, where Taylor's men were able to pursue and capture or kill most of them. Not only was Okeechobee the bloodiest battle of the Seminole War, but it reinforced a false faith in the utility of conventional tactics against Indians.[16] For those who refused to concede the effectiveness of the line formation and the bayonet charge, it was a vindication. Even so, Okeechobee was not decisive. The war would continue for another five tedious years, with the U.S. soldiers struggling to catch the tenacious remnants of the Seminoles, who became increasingly difficult to bring to battle, and according to Francis Prucha, had to be "ferreted out almost one at a time."[17]

The series of failed attempts to corner the Seminoles in the tangled swamps of Florida left U.S. commanders thoroughly frustrated and resulted in the U.S. Army resorting to the destruction of Indian villages as a means to force the Seminoles into submission.[18] The most aggressive and effective commander at this practice was Colonel William J. Worth, who, upon taking command of the army's operations in Florida, directed a campaign aimed at destroying Seminole crops and settlements during the exceedingly hot summer of 1840. The desired effect on the Indians was achieved. As the winter months approached, much of the remaining Seminole tribe suffered from starvation.[19] By the end of 1841 the majority of remaining Seminole parties submitted to removal from Florida. On 14 August 1842, with approval from the government, Worth declared an end to the war. But it was an end only in word, as a number of small groups of Seminoles remained in the swamps for decades, refusing to submit to U.S. authority. It was a lackluster victory for the small army, brought to conclusion only because the army declared it was over, not because it had won.

The Second Seminole War was a costly affair, with more than 1,500 U.S. soldiers killed out of a total force of approximately 40,000.[20] The U.S. government invested more than $20,000 dollars on what one historian described as the "bitterest episode in the annals of the frontier army," in which "after more than six years of fighting under conditions that no soldier was trained or equipped to meet, the futile contest was declared over."[21] Most significant, however, was the extent to which lessons from Florida would seem to go unheeded by the U.S. Army in the years following. The fact that U.S. troops had struggled when faced with an enemy who refused to stand and fight was all but forgotten. As Weigley concluded, "The experience should have served as a standing warning against the difficulties of guerrilla war," but it was a warning that went unheeded.[22] The very few conventional victories, like that earned at Okeechobee, dominated the American military memory of the conflict.

As a result, no significant changes were made in military instruction or tactical training to address the difficulties experienced during the Seminole War. And while the lessons of failed conventional tactics seem to have been forgotten, the memory of the effective targeting of Seminole settlements was not. American military leaders and theorists deemed this indirect approach to dealing with the guerrilla problem effective as well as perfectly acceptable,

Painting depicting the burning of a Seminole village by American forces. (Library of Congress)

given the perceived cultural inferiority of the enemy. While the act of destroying settlements in response to Indian attacks may have been controversial, it did not lead to any significant or notable protests from the leadership or the white population. Since the enemy Indians were viewed primarily as savages, less than human, traditional rules of war were considered inapplicable.[23] What is clear is that the American experience with the Seminoles did not lead to significant changes in the American consideration of guerrilla warfare. As Waghelstein put it, "Despite seven years of guerrilla warfare experience, the American Army emerged from this war no better prepared to fight a guerrilla war than when it started."[24] Many veterans of the Seminole Wars, such as Scott, Taylor, and Worth, were soon afforded the opportunity to learn the lessons of guerrilla warfare once again.

In the years 1846–1848, the American military would test Jomini's principles regarding wars of invasion, believing his theory that "it is better to attack than to be invaded."[25] During America's war with Mexico, the U.S. Army encountered sporadic, sometimes extensive, resistance from Mexican guerrilla bands. While the war was, by most accounts, primarily a conventional war fought in the classic European style, certain campaigns such as Winfield Scott's in 1847 were often frustrated by guerrilla attacks on supply and communication lines. These attacks were described by one historian as "the most worrying aspect of the war" for the Americans considering the relative ease with which they defeated the conventional Mexican Army.[26] In fact, by the summer of 1847, the threat facing the American occupiers was primarily that posed by decentralized guerrillas rather than regular forces. Lieutenant Ralph W. Kirkham stated as much in a letter home in May 1847, as his regiment occupied the remote village of Perote between Jalapa and Mexico City. "The Mexicans have resolved on a guerrilla mode of warfare and [we] will not again meet a large body of troops," he wrote, adding that the Mexicans intended to "cut off small parties wherever they find an opportunity."[27] For Kirkham and his fellows the conflict would become increasingly more difficult to define and prosecute.

The Mexican reliance on guerrilla action came on the heels of a string of battlefield defeats. Palo Alto, Resca de la Palma, and Cerro Gordo did little to bolster Mexico's confidence in its regular army. Immediately after Scott's convincing victory over General Antonio López de Santa Anna at Cerro Gordo on 18 April 1847, one Mexican general realized the futility of further conventional operations and issued a proclamation calling for the formation of guerrilla bands to take up a "war of vengeance" against the Americans and to "attack and destroy the invaders in every manner imaginable."[28] Admitting that guerrilla warfare was a "cruel method," Mexican politician, journalist, and ideologue Carlos Maria de Bustamante claimed that it was inevitable. As an example, Bustamante offered the American use of irregular warfare in its own War for Independence.[29] Many emboldened Mexicans answered the call. In the summer and fall of 1847, Scott's army was besieged by guerrilla attacks all along the route of march from Veracruz to Mexico City, often having to slow its advance due to burned bridges or the detachment of soldiers to garrison the main roads. Once Mexico City was captured, the burgeoning guerrilla threat spread to locations previously pacified by the Americans such as Puebla and Veracruz, thereby offering the U.S. Army a bitter introduction to the difficulties associated with the role of foreign occupier.

The campaign in Northern Mexico, commanded by General Zachary Taylor, however, was the most disrupted by the attacks of Mexican guerrilla bands. Similar to his experiences with the Seminoles in 1837, Taylor's conventional battlefield successes in Mexico were followed by months of frustration dealing with irregulars. During the first year of the war, Taylor's army endured a rash of guerrilla attacks on outposts, supply lines, and smaller detachments of soldiers. These attacks most often resulted in a handful of dead U.S. soldiers and rising anxiety in the ranks concerning the security of the army. While not devastating, they were enough to prompt a young officer to write late in the war, "Though hostilities have nominally ceased, still we have to exercise the same precautions in going from one place to another as before. The guerrilla parties are as numerous and kill and rob the same as ever. This puts a great hindrance to traveling."[30] By March 1847, Taylor was so preoccupied with the problems caused by the attacks on his supply line between Buena Vista and Monterrey that he personally led antiguerrilla expeditions in the area, with little success.[31] Early attempts to search out guerrilla bands operating in the region usually proved fruitless, with most efforts yielding the killing or capture of but a few individuals whose complicity with guerrillas was often in question.

Not only did U.S. officers have to deal with the dangers of guerrillas harassing their flanks, but they were also forced to keep their own soldiers from committing unchecked violence against the Mexican citizenry and thereby fueling the fire for resistance. Cities such as Matamoras, Monterey, and Jalapa witnessed periods of destructive mayhem waged by the occupiers. More so than the regulars, volunteer soldiers were prone to disorder that amounted to, at best, drunken mischief and, at worst, outright atrocities against noncombatants. In Monterey, one officer estimated that as many as 100 citizens were unjustifiably murdered by U.S. soldiers over the span of a few days.[32] In a few cases, local commanders were compelled to resort to imprisoning, or even shooting, their own soldiers in response to depredations or criminal acts.[33] General Scott later admitted that concerns about the potential damage caused by his errant soldiers "weighed me to the earth." He expressed as much in a letter to the Secretary of War on Christmas Day, 1847. "The success of the system . . . depends on our powers of conciliation," he wrote, "disorders and crimes . . . may destroy the best-concerted plans by exasperating the inhabitants, and rendering the war, on their part, national, interminable, and desperate."[34]

It was not until the U.S. Army combined aggressive counterguerrilla campaigning with a system of collective responsibility, holding the local population responsible for attacks, that significant progress was made in dealing with the guerrilla threat. In late 1847, officers in both Scott and Taylor's commands began to achieve success in pursuing and breaking up guerrilla bands that harassed U.S. supply lines. Examples include Brigadier General David E. Twiggs and Brigadier General Joseph Lane, "by far the best American antiguerrilla leader" of the war, according to historian Jack Bauer. What qualified Lane as the best was his aggressiveness in dealing with the local citizenry. It was the same type of ruthlessness that earned William J. Worth recognition against the Seminoles in Florida ten years prior. Nonetheless, intensified American cavalry patrolling succeeded in halting the majority of guerrilla attacks on major supply routes by the summer of 1848.[35]

When many local U.S. commanders, such as Brigadier General John E.

General Winfield Scott.
The hero of the Mexican
War dealt with the guerrilla
problem during his advance
on and occupation of
Mexico City. (Library of
Congress)

Wool, began to hold communities responsible for guerrilla activity, often levying fines for attacks, support for guerrilla bands began to dry up. American officers often gave Mexicans the choice of handing over the guerrillas or reimbursing the army for damages. When officials in the village of Salinas failed to offer up any guerrillas, they were fined $500 for their assumed cooperation with attacks against Wool's soldiers.[36] The practice of imposing taxes on entire communities was a tricky business, however, and neither Scott nor Taylor utilized the option liberally for fear of stoking anti-American sentiment.

Mexican guerrillas found even less support from the local citizenry when U.S. soldiers, acting under orders, destroyed buildings and the homes of those suspected of complicity in attacks against Americans. While still cautious of inciting insurrection, Scott embraced the punishment of communities for guerrilla depredations. In a few instances, a frustrated Scott appeared to throw caution to the wind. In response to guerrilla attacks along the National Road between Veracruz and Mexico City, for example, according to Andrew Birtle, Scott "used the torch with such liberality" that the road "was marked by a black swath of devastation several miles wide."[37] By confiscating either money or homes, the U.S. Army had discovered a program that was able to finally exert some form of control over the guerrillas and bring the problem to a manageable state.[38]

Fortunately for the Americans, localized political disputes throughout

Mexico combined with effective American policies to purchase goods from the local community resulted in growing internal discord between guerrilla leaders in late 1847, a fact that certainly limited their capability.[39] Also, the relatively short duration of the occupation prevented any prolonged exposure to guerrilla resistance. The Mexican War lasted just twenty-six months, significantly shorter than Napoleon's occupation of Spain or British operations in America during the Revolution. It is likely that a longer stay in Mexico would have meant a continuation, and perhaps an increase, of guerrilla resistance from a restive population.[40]

Despite a wealth of information describing the guerrilla problem in Mexico, particularly after Scott captured Mexico City, incidents of guerrilla activity, and especially those that resulted in substantial loss of life or materiel were rarely reported in military correspondence or in newspaper accounts of the war.[41] This can partially be attributed to the fact that U.S. soldiers did not recognize Mexican irregulars as legitimate combatants. Seldom interested in their motives or rationale, U.S. troops normally viewed guerrillas, in the words of one scholar, "as vagabonds and highway men."[42] As such, they were considered unworthy of serious attention. Regardless of the U.S. Army's problems, and at times significant problems, with Mexican guerrillas, the immediate American memory of the war primarily focused on the seemingly perfect victory of the regular army. Members of Congress proclaimed it to be a shining triumph gained through the use of "uniform gallantry and good conduct."[43] Texas and California were secured, the professional army was vindicated, and its leaders returned as heroes. Amidst the elation over the perceived flawless victory, the frustrations of Mexico were quickly forgotten.

If the experience of previous wars failed to prepare the United States for the difficulties of guerrilla warfare in the Civil War, the formal training of the army, and its officers in particular, did little to remedy the shortcoming. The vast majority of the senior leadership for both the Union and Confederate armies attended the U.S. Military Academy at West Point.[44] At the academy, these future leaders of America's armies were exposed to a curriculum heavy in engineering and mathematics but short on strategy or tactics. Cadets spent a great deal of their time at the academy studying fortifications, artillery, and army organization rather than the tactical lessons of the Indian frontier or Mexico.[45] When their studies did turn to strategy, the focus was primarily on the European wars in the Age of Napoleon, not American conflicts.

The most influential military theorist in West Point teachings was Henri, Baron de Jomini, whose writings served as the foundation for military instruction at the academy. Jomini was a French-Swiss veteran staff officer of Napoleon's wars in Spain, and his theories were the dominant voice of Napoleonic studies in the West Point curriculum. "In American eyes, Jomini was nothing less than Napoleon's St. Paul," according to Weigley. "[He] wrote nostalgically of the polite forms to which war had adhered before the French Revolution and to which he hoped to return."[46] In Jomini's principal text studied by cadets, *The Art of War*, he stressed the strategic initiative, the importance of interior lines, and the need to concentrate firepower at the decisive point. Jomini's description of war was one of principles and guidelines, which if followed correctly, as had Napoleon, would provide sure success on the battlefield. In essence, Jomini made war seem organized and reasonable, downplaying the human, psychological element. One group of scholars would later claim that Jomini "never fully realized that with the [French] Revolution and Napoleon a new age had dawned in warfare," adding that Jomini had "actually set military thought back into the eighteenth century," which made the professional soldiers of the time both "comfortable and safe."[47] Nevertheless, Jomini was the preeminent theorist of his time and the academy embraced his approach.

The central figure in the military training of those who went on to become the Civil War's leadership was Dennis Hart Mahan, professor and head of the engineering department from 1832 to 1871. In addition to industrial drawing and architecture, Mahan taught military science and fortifications. His *Advanced Guard, Out-Post, and Detachment Service of Troops*, commonly referred to as *Outpost*, served as the primary textbook for military science courses at the academy during the mid-nineteenth century. One scholar claimed that Mahan's text "probably had more impact upon American military concepts than any other single publication of the time."[48] In it, Mahan echoed many of Jomini's principles of warfare and included practical instructions for the construction of field fortifications, picket duty, marches, and patrols. Very much akin to Jomini, Mahan warned against waging an offensive campaign in hostile territory. In his limited discussion of partisan warfare, Mahan mentioned the potential dangers of "an exasperated population, waiting but the opportunity to rise and throw themselves" upon an invader.[49]

Despite making particular mention of *petite guerre* (meaning "small war") in his book, Mahan couched the subject in conventional terms of detachments and ambushes, rather than discussing the unconventional methods seen in guerrilla warfare. Although he did adjust his course to include a brief discussion of warfare with Indians, his proposed solutions offered the simple guidance of relying on superior firepower to overcome the difficulties of Indian tactics. "This was pitifully little," according to James L. Morrison, considering the scope of the army's requirements on the frontier at the time.[50] Mahan's focus was almost entirely on conventional war. *Outpost* reminded its readers that war was "based upon settled principles," and when combined with a firm knowledge of military history, adherence to such principles would most often lead to success on the battlefield.[51] Though Mahan attached the utmost importance to the study of Napoleonic campaigns, he made very little mention of Napoleon's troubles in Spain with guerrillas. This fact is perhaps not surprising considering the heavy Jominian flavor of Mahan's theories.

Opinions on the amount of influence that Jomini and Mahan had on the conduct of the Civil War are mixed. Many historians have made the case that the lessons taught at West Point were not solely responsible for the course of the Civil War. According to one historian, "most antebellum regular officers had neither the opportunity nor the inclination to study."[52] Some have suggested that it was "the arresting image of Napoleon" rather than the actual study of strategy or tactics that most influenced the mind of the U.S. Army during the war.[53] However, some evidence of Jomini and Mahan making a mark on the war does exist. An example was provided by Major General William T. Sherman, who, despite later denying that Jomini influenced his actions in the war, posted an order in 1862 demanding that all of his officers be familiar with Jomini and Mahan's principles or risk "a lasting disgrace."[54] Officers such as George B. McClellan and Henry Wager Halleck, who would both rise to the highest level of command in the Union Army, placed a great deal of faith in the military teachings of West Point. Halleck, one of Mahan's star pupils, echoed much of what Mahan had to say about Jomini and Napoleon in his own strategic study produced in 1846, *Elements of Military Art and Science*. Like *The Art of War* and *Outpost*, Halleck's *Elements* made little mention of guerrilla warfare. In his view of modern warfare, guerrillas and partisans, such as those faced by Napoleon in Spain or Scott in Mexico, were not legitimate combatants and, if captured, could be "punished the same as freebooters and banditti."[55] Halleck would be forced to revisit the issue in much greater detail in 1861 when Confederate guerrillas became a serious problem for the Union Army.

Much about the Civil War came as a surprise to the U.S. Army and the nation as a whole. The conflict's duration and cost in materiel and human lives far exceeded any previous American experience and most expectations. As historian Charles Royster described, "Americans surprised themselves with the extent of violence they could attain" during the war.[56] As the new volunteer armies of 1861 marched off to battle, they carried with them a simplistic understanding of war, reflective of the eighteenth-century roots of American military thought. It was generally accepted that war was "a gentlemanly enterprise," according to one historian, "rooted in Napoleonic tradition."[57] And as James McPherson described it, "many Americans had a romantic, glamorous idea of war."[58] The war also had to be waged carefully according to the most influential strategic minds of the time. General Winfield Scott warned against waging a war of conquest for fear of creating an unmanageable peace at war's end.[59] Despite popular support in the North for a campaign that would punish the secessionists, this call for restraint from the hero of the Mexican War made sense to many. Military thought of the day, backed by the teachings of Jomini, Mahan, and Halleck, held that the destructiveness of war should be limited to the conventional armies on the field. Such a policy was "an easy course to follow," according to one scholar, "because military practice for nearly two centuries had aimed at avoiding the hostility of civilians."[60] The memories of the colonial wars with the Indians had receded, only to be replaced by a Victorian view of warfare that did not include everyday citizens.

Events, however, would soon demonstrate that the Civil War would not be as limited as those previous. It was to be a war characterized by massive mobilization efforts on both sides, destruction of resources and property on an immense scale, and the development of punitive practices and policies toward civilians. The very definition of military necessity would be changed from its mid-nineteenth-century understanding. The measures that the Union Army would employ in response to the guerrilla problem in the South would highlight the transition to a new, more severe, era of warfare in America.

The U.S. Army was destined to learn again the frustrations of irregular warfare. It had been an advantage for Americans in the Revolution. The army had then fought against it in the Seminole Wars and in Mexico, both times adopting punitive policies directed at noncombatants. Leaders of both the Union and Confederate Armies predicted swift victories, which after the war seemed tragically naïve. The scene was set for a rude awakening. Once again, the Americans would come to realize the frustrating difficulties in dealing with guerrilla warfare and its powerful potential for altering the character of the entire war. If nothing else, they should have predicted a more complex and destructive war, one that would eventually involve civilians to some extent. But it was not to be. As described by one scholar, Union soldiers eventually became "frustrated by what they had expected to do and could not do and horrified by what they were sure they would never do and then began to do."[61] And what they did do was profound.

This failure to predict the depth of the coming storm, however, does not fully explain how or why the Union Army eventually came to make war against civilians and their property during the Civil War. For that we have to look to the hills of Missouri, the banks of the Mississippi River, and the mountains of western Virginia in the tumultuous years of 1861–1865. Throughout all reaches of the Confederacy the guerrilla problem erupted in sporadic, unpredictable fashion ensuring that the Federal occupation of the South would not go according to plan. For the officers and soldiers of the Union Army, it was a problem that they had to solve.

CHAPTER TWO

Proving Ground for Punishment: Pope, Halleck, and Schofield in Missouri

*The first dead men I saw while in the army were eight
Missouri farmers murdered by guerrillas and left lying in the hot
sun and dust at the roadside. The sight moved me as no great
battle did afterward.*
—Major Samuel H. Byers, *With Fire and Sword*

The seeds for punitive war were planted in the West. For those who lived in the politically divided state of Missouri and the young "Free State" of Kansas, the beginning of the Civil War in 1861 was hardly the beginning of violence. Stretching back to the establishment of Kansas as a free territory by the Kansas-Nebraska Act of 1854, the border region endured a ruthless political war marked by intimidation, coercion, and murder. This period, commonly referred to as "Bleeding Kansas" or "The Long Agony," witnessed the struggle between gangs of Border Ruffians supported by the government of pro-slavery Missouri and the Jayhawkers of abolitionist Kansas.[1] Fueled by a maniacal hatred for the opposition, both groups conducted vengeful raids across the border to bully, terrorize, and sometimes kill their enemies. Those involved were not trained soldiers but armed citizens, self-proclaimed defenders of their cause, conducting violent surprise attacks that often targeted civilians. Perhaps the most memorable of such attacks took place on the night of 24 May 1856 near Pottawatomie Creek, Kansas. A small war party of abolitionist zealots led by John Brown brutally butchered five proslavery citizens in front of their families.[2] Such acts served only to enflame the already potent animosity between abolitionists and the supporters of slavery. The events at Pottawatomie eventually triggered a "terrible guerrilla war," according to historian Stephen B. Oates, in which "armed bands of men . . . prowled the countryside, shooting at one another and looting enemy stores and homesteads."[3] Although support for slavery was mixed throughout Missouri, with the strongest antislavery sentiment residing in the northern portion of the state, the majority of the population was strictly opposed to outside influence in what they considered a state affair. On the other side of the border, Kansans were quick to defend their abolitionist ideals against resistance from the East, with the rifle if need be. According to one observer, "armed men who balked not at the crimes of assassination, arson and robbery" wielded the most power despite the fact that they made up a minority of the region's population.[4]

Bleeding Kansas set the stage for a difficult occupation for the Union Army during the Civil War. T. J. Stiles, the biographer of Confederate guerrilla turned famous outlaw Jesse James, claimed that "The bloodshed in Kansas proved to be both a precipitating factor in the outbreak of the Civil War and a first skirmish in the conflict between North and South." In addition, "it created a hardcore of militants who championed the state's Southern identity, battling a prevailing sense that Missouri was more West than South."[5] These militants, veterans of the violence of Bleeding Kansas, made up the core of guerrilla bands that terrorized the border region during the Civil War.

When the turmoil of Bleeding Kansas bled into the beginning of the Civil War, a residual lawlessness and disorder pervaded Missouri, affecting the operations of both the Union and Confederate armies. In 1861, the number of active guerrillas in Missouri far exceeded that in any other state remaining in the Union. Missouri's guerrilla situation was unique in that by the time the war began, many of the belligerents already had years of experience with guerrilla war. Commonly referred to as either guerrillas or bushwhackers, those who adopted the tactics of hit-and-run and ambush for the purpose of suppressing Union loyalists or harassing U.S. Army operations were also labeled marauders, bandits, armed rebels, or murderers by Federal troops. Whatever they were called, they answered to no authority but their own. According to historian Michael Fellman, the author of the most extensive study of the guerrilla war in Missouri, one of the greatest challenges for the occupying Union Army was the undefined and intangible character of the insurgency it faced. "This was a war of stealth and raid, without a front, without formal organization, and with almost no division between civilian and warrior," Fellman described, noting that the guerrillas "acted more on the caprice of moments than according to any overall scheme."[6] And while a number of guerrillas in Missouri aligned themselves with the Confederate cause and at times cooperated with the Missouri State Guard led by Major General Sterling Price, their actions usually served to advance their own purposes of revenge or personal gain rather than to enhance the chances of Confederate victory. Military analyst Don Bowen described Missouri's guerrillas as part of a "relatively spontaneous, organizationally unstructured, ideologically rudimentary, social movement." For this reason, they created great difficulty for Union troops.[7] Not only was it hard to identify the guerrillas, it was hard to plan against an enemy that often lacked its own sense of organization or purpose.

Civil War Missouri

Union commanders were forced to confront this freebooting warfare as they conducted operations in St. Louis and across the northern half of the state in the summer of 1861. Led by the fiery brigadier general Nathaniel Lyon, a fervent abolitionist and proponent of the war, 8,000 Union troops marched quickly into the center of the state in order to drive out fledgling Confederate forces under Governor Claiborne Jackson and Sterling Price. By August, the only organized Confederate threat in Missouri was confined to the southwest corner of the state, while the rest of the region remained embroiled in local-ized violence between Union and Confederate sympathizers. In an attempt to pacify secessionist aggression, the newly installed (not elected) governor, Hamilton R. Gamble, published a conciliatory proclamation to the people of the state. Gamble's message, which was endorsed by President Abraham Lincoln, promised little military intervention into citizen affairs, amnesty for any person previously involved in aggression toward Union forces, and no interference with the institution of slavery.[8] The tone of this proclamation, emphasizing a careful approach toward dealing with civilians and their property, matched that of similar policies instituted by Union commands in the East at the time. Predictably, Gamble's proposition did little to quell the growing resentment within the pro-Southern populace, who now found itself under an unwelcome Federal occupation. The state's downward spiral into instability continued, and guerrilla activity escalated.

Into the mounting maelstrom strode Brigadier General John Pope, whose harsh policies would serve to stoke the fires of insurgency rather than quench them. Primarily remembered for his dismal loss at Second Manassas a year later in the war, Pope was the first Union commander to take overt steps to include civilians in Union antiguerrilla policies and practices during the war. In Pope, punitive war had its first high-level champion.

Pope was a graduate of West Point, a career officer, and a veteran of the Mexican War, where he experienced the challenges that came with pacifying a hostile population.[9] Upon assuming command of the Department of North Missouri in July 1861, Pope was alarmed by the violence and chaos running rampant in the region. Just a week before arriving in St. Louis, Pope predicted that "a vigorous campaign of a week will settle secession in North Missouri."[10] The situation awaiting him proved much more dire. "It was impossible for any man living in the country, away from considerable towns, to avoid taking arms up against somebody," Pope would later write. "War was precipitated on the people of Missouri by their own leaders; not war in the open field and by armies duly marshaled for battle, but war by one neighbor against another."[11]

Nowhere was the violent lawlessness more rampant than along the railroad that connected Northwestern Missouri with the government headquarters in St. Louis. During the months prior to Pope's arrival, small groups of pro-Southern guerrillas attacked the lines to Springfield and points west with impunity, tearing up the tracks and felling trees along their path to hamper Union supply trains. Reports of "bushwhackers" firing into passing trains were common as well. Frustrated Union officials in St. Louis blamed the damaged railroad for the inability to resupply Lyon's army stalled in Springfield, and Lyon himself reported on 17 July, "The want of supplies has crippled me so that I cannot move, and I do not know when I can."[12] It was apparent that something needed to be done to protect the railroad, or military operations to ensure Union control of the state would be jeopardized.

In his first action as commander, Pope issued a warning to the population of northern Missouri on 21 July, announcing the demise of conciliation in the region:

It is very certain that the people living along the line of the North Missouri Railroad can very easily protect it from destruction, and it is my purpose to give them strong inducements to do so. I therefore notify the inhabitants of the towns, villages, and stations along the line of this road that they will be held accountable for the destruction of any bridges, culverts, or portions of the railroad track within 5 miles on each side of them. If any outrages of this kind are committed within the distance specified . . . the settlement will be held responsible, and a levy of money or property sufficient to cover the whole damage done will be at once made and collected.

It has been impossible heretofore even to ascertain the names of the criminals engaged in this kind of work, although they were well known to everybody in the neighborhood. If people who claim to be good citizens choose to indulge their neighbors and acquaintances in committing these wanton acts, and to shield them from punishment, they will hereafter be compelled to pay for it . . . I therefore expect all law-abiding citizens at once to take measures to secure the safety of the North Missouri Railroad in their vicinity.[13]

At the center of the new policy was the issue of assessments, taxes to be levied on those citizens deemed guilty of supporting or tolerating guerrilla attacks on the railroad. If Pope could not catch the offenders, and he did not believe he could, he would then make the local population pay for damages or be expelled from the region. Because the guerrillas were so elusive, Pope explained, "The systematic pursuit of these small bands by detachments of soldiers would have carried disorder and dismay into every part of the country." Therefore, it was necessary to make it "impossible for [guerrillas] to commit any overt act without the most serious consequences being at once visited on their friends and relatives."[14] At the time, these "most serious consequences" were to come in the form of fines, sometimes as much as $5,000 to $10,000 per town. If charged citizens failed to pay the fines or give up the guilty parties, they were then arrested and their property confiscated.[15]

Pope's strict decree was legally perilous. His willingness to take military action (in the form of exacting money or property) against civilians in a *Union* state was unprecedented as well as unsanctioned by his commander and those in Washington. If placed before a Missouri civil court, Pope could have been prosecuted for criminal conduct. The new department commander, however, viewed the policy as absolutely necessary to combat Missouri's "lawless parties of marauders." In his memoirs, Pope made it clear that he saw little difference between active armed rebels and the civilians who supported them or failed to take action against them. Acknowledging that his policy introduced "methods which any American would shrink from applying," Pope insisted that the only remedy for guerrilla activity was "to make the whole population along the line of these roads directly responsible for the acts of the irresponsible parties of outlaws who were perfectly known to the whole community."[16] Necessary or not, such a policy made it particularly difficult to adhere to Governor Gamble's calls for military forbearance in civilian affairs.

Although his policies were controversial, Pope had little to fear in the way of condemnation from peers or superiors. After all, the act of holding civilians responsible for guerrilla attacks was not unfamiliar to veterans of previous American wars. All Pope was doing was revisiting policies that were upheld by William J. Worth in the Second Seminole War and by John E. Wool in the Mexican War in which Pope participated. Indeed, the general concept of taking forceful military measures against a hostile population, to include civilians, was nothing new.[17]

Pope also had a sympathetic audience of subordinates. Junior officers who had grown accustomed to the guerrilla depredations in Northern Missouri believed that the time for stern measures had come for both the guerrillas and their sympathizers. In *Inside War*, Fellman argued that once introduced to the threatening climate in Missouri, many Federal troops soon developed contempt for the local population and considered them the enemy.[18] By August 1861, Major John McDonald of the Eighth Missouri Volunteers was so angered by guerrilla activity around the small town of Saint Genevieve that he threatened to "retaliate in the most summary manner" if the town's citizens failed to prevent future attacks on Union troops. Frustrated Union officers did not entertain the citizens' claims of neutrality. "It will be no excuse that they [townspeople] did not assist the rebels," McDonald warned, "they must prevent any outrages on Union men or take the consequences." When the attacks continued despite the warning, McDonald's men took $58,313.58 from the town bank.[19]

Some officials questioned Pope's policy, believing the effort to directly kill or capture guerrillas seemed a more appropriate response to the problem. In a letter to his friends on 14 August 1861, a frustrated Union railroad official lamented, "I am tired of receiving blows. I want to see the war offensive on our part," adding that continued guerrilla attacks, if left unanswered, would "soon ruin our cause before the world." This same official appealed for action, bemoaning Pope's focus on the civilian population rather than on the guerrillas themselves.[20] Pope, however, was convinced that the active pursuit of bushwhackers was wasted effort. In a report to Major General John Frémont he argued, "The system of pursuing the perpetrators of these outrages can lead to no good results while so large a body of people sympathize with them." Pope added, "It is a war which can only be ended by making all engaged suffer for every act of hostility committed."[21] Years after the war, Pope echoed this sentiment, claiming that Union attempts to find guerrillas in Northern Missouri most often ended "without successful result."[22]

A further demonstration of Pope's commitment to place the burden of the guerrilla problem squarely on the shoulders of the people was his effort to establish Committees of Public Safety in every town throughout his district. In his Order No. 3, published on 2 August 1861, Pope instructed his subordinate officers to spread through the various counties and to order the most "respectable citizens" of each town to maintain the peace or face military taxation and seizure of property. Pope believed that "once the secessionists are made to understand that upon peace in their midst depends the safety of their families and property, we shall soon have quiet again in North Missouri."[23] The problem with Pope's rationale was that the dangerous climate of the region forced citizens to focus primarily on self-preservation rather than preservation of property.[24] Most citizens in Missouri feared guerrilla vengeance more than harsh Union policies, for the guerrilla brand of punitive war was far worse.

Despite Pope's initial warnings, orders, and mandates, sporadic attacks against the Hannibal and St. Joseph Railroad increased in the late summer of 1861.[25] On 16 August, a train carrying a regiment of Union volunteers was heading west from the town of Palmyra in Marion County when guerrillas hiding in the brush alongside the tracks fired upon the passing cars. One Union soldier was reported killed, and one wounded. In his report on the incident, Pope claimed, "This county of Marion has been the principle [sic] seat of disturbances in North Missouri, and it is my purpose immediately to inflict such punishment as will be remembered."[26] The following day, a detachment of Federal troops visited Palmyra bearing a message from Pope to the local citizens:

> You are hereby notified and required to deliver up to the military authorities of this brigade, within six days from the date of these presents, the marauders who fired upon the train bound west on the Hannibal and Saint Joseph Railroad on the evening of 16th instant, and broke into the telegraph-office. If the guilty persons are not delivered up as required, and within the time herein specified, the whole brigade will be moved into your county, and contributions levied to the amounted to $10,000 on Marion County and $5,000 on the city of Palmyra.
>
> By order of Brig. Gen. S. A. Hurlburt, Under direction of John Pope, Brigadier-general, commanding North Missouri.[27]

If Federal troops did not collect the assessments as quickly as directed, their commanders were admonished. Such was the case in Marion, and Pope's second in command curtly reminded a colonel in the Illinois cavalry

Major General John Pope.
A pioneer of punitive war
policies in the Civil War,
Pope dealt with guerrillas
in Missouri and Virginia.
(Library of Congress)

that he was there "to punish the people of Marion County for their conniv-
ance in the various outrages committed within their limits." Hurlburt then
threatened to have the officer arrested if he did not comply with the order.[28]
There was little room for sympathy-driven reluctance. Pope was in earnest.

Anticipating that his superiors in St. Louis or Washington would probably express doubt about his severe treatment of Palmyra, Pope defended it
to Frémont. Such actions were absolutely necessary, Pope claimed, and he
predicted that failure to pursue his course would result in an outbreak of
armed resistance throughout Northern Missouri. As part of his justification,
Pope touched on the very essence of the guerrilla problem. "When so large
a portion of the population sympathizes with the authors of the atrocious
acts of guerrilla warfare which have hitherto disgraced North Missouri,"
Pope argued, "it is impossible to apprehend the perpetrators of such outrages." Therefore the reachable civilians would have to pay, literally.[29] Given
their experience that summer, the citizens of Palmyra were not likely to take
Pope's threats lightly. Previous visits from Union detachments had resulted

in extensive arrests, harassment, and looting.[30] This time, when no guerrillas were offered up, Pope's troops quickly began confiscating civilian property. One officer even ordered that a well-known secessionist be lashed to the top of a train engine as it prepared to travel to Macon.[31] As Pope viewed it, the people of Marion County had chosen to test his resolve and Palmyra was his answer.

Just as Pope anticipated, however, his immediate supervisor and famous American explorer, Major General John C. Frémont, expressed concerns about his antiguerrilla policies and the vigor with which his men were carrying them out. Recently appointed to the region, Frémont was not yet willing to endorse such a hard-line approach. In his memoirs, Pope blamed "unfounded representations" from "unwise counsels" for convincing Frémont to order a temporary suspension to Pope's system of assessments in Northern Missouri.[32]

Despite Frémont's call for restraint, reports of continued attacks on trains and Union outposts by small groups of armed rebels filled the telegraph lines in the following days. In the words of one scholar, "North Missouri was soon in a state near anarchy."[33] On 19 August, a railway official reported another attack along the Hannibal Line and complained about the lack of Union response to the guerrilla threat. Two days later, a Federal supply train traveling from St. Louis to Rolla detonated a powder keg that had been placed under the track by saboteurs, and portions of track were discovered missing for the suspected purpose of derailing troop transports.[34] In Frémont's own words, the armed resistance had reached a point at which guerrillas infested "nearly every county of the State," creating a situation of "sufficient urgency" that required a broad, immediate action.[35]

In response to the growing problem, Frémont proclaimed martial law throughout Missouri on 30 August, an act that eventually jeopardized his tenure as the commander of the newly established Western Department. Pope applauded the action. In his mind, martial law was the next step in the "logical sequence" of punitive measures taken against the population in Northern Missouri.[36] In a proclamation announcing the new policy, Frémont argued that it was born of necessity, claiming that "the severest measures" were required to "repress the daily increasing crimes and outrages" perpetrated by "bands of marauders and murderers." In the order, Frémont threatened that any person found with arms in their possession would be tried by court-martial and executed upon being found guilty. Those caught damaging rail lines, bridges, or telegraph lines would suffer "the extreme penalty of the law." The property of those deemed disloyal or supportive of guerrillas was subject to confiscation, and those found absent from their homes would be assumed guilty of aiding the enemy. Frémont's decree demanded not only "acquiescence" but also "active support" from the local population. Placed inconspicuously within the middle of the proclamation was the statement that would ultimately cost Frémont his command: slaves belonging to those opposing the Union authority in Missouri were declared free.[37]

It was a seminal moment in Missouri, and in the war. By authorizing the trial and execution of civilian prisoners by military commission in a Union state, Frémont set a precedent that would eventually find its way deep into the occupied South. Not only had Frémont declared martial law without prior consent from Washington, he did so without suspending habeas corpus.[38] As historian Mark Neely described, Frémont's decree "dangerously broadened military authority over civilians."[39] Just weeks before, the provisional governor of the state publicly promised that Union forces would not interfere in any way with the peculiar institution.[40] At a time when the control of the Border States was still in contention, Frémont's proclamation was potentially damaging for the Union. An alarmed President Lincoln immediately requested that the general rescind it. He also informed Frémont that no captured citizens were to be executed without his prior consent.[41] On both issues, Frémont remained stubborn, claiming his emancipation order was "right and necessary," and that the shooting of those who attacked his soldiers, even after being captured, was "a necessary measure of defense" as well as "entirely according to the usages of civilized warfare." Lincoln would have none of it. He curtly ordered Frémont to overturn the proclamation.[42]

Frémont's proclamation was more than just a case of a maverick abolitionist seizing on an opportunity to free slaves.[43] At its core, it was a reaction to the dangerous environment that pro-Southern guerrillas had created in the region. According to Frémont's biographer, the purpose of the proclamation was to "quell guerrilla warfare and to penalize disloyal slaveowners in the North."[44] Whereas the order to consider freeing the slaves certainly created political rancor, it was Frémont's authorization to execute citizens in arms that prompted the most virulent response from Confederates. Days after Frémont's proclamation, Confederate Brigadier General M. Jefferson Thompson threatened to "Hang, draw, and quarter" numerous Union soldiers or their supporters for every Southern "citizen in arms" shot under Frémont's order. "I intend to exceed General Frémont in his excesses," Thompson warned, "and will make all tories that come within my reach rue the day that a different policy was adopted by their leader . . . I will retaliate tenfold, so help me God!"[45] Not only had Frémont's declaration of martial law been met with trepidation and ultimately overruled by his own commander in chief, but it also served to aggravate the exact disorder and chaos that it was intended to subdue.[46]

Within a matter of weeks, Lincoln had seen enough. The controversy surrounding Frémont's proclamation, combined with news of incompetence and corruption in the Western Department, prompted Lincoln to send a commission from Washington to investigate. What they found in Missouri was a military department in disarray and an arrogant commander who appeared incapable of effective leadership. In the commission's final report, the references to Frémont were not flattering, with one commissioner going so far as to label him a nincompoop. The commission's scathing report ensured that Frémont was relieved.[47] Major General David Hunter, who later became an avid practitioner of punitive war in Virginia, temporarily replaced him. Because of the strong support Frémont enjoyed from radical Republicans in Washington, however, Lincoln chose to make the politically secure move of appointing him to another command back East, a decision he would later regret.[48]

Two major reverses on the battlefield accompanied Frémont's political downfall. First, at Wilson's Creek in August and at Lexington in September, greatly outnumbered Union forces were battered by Sterling Price's Missouri State Guard, which advanced as far north as Springfield. By the time Frémont was replaced by Hunter on 3 November, the Confederates threatened a good section of western Missouri, and Union forces were distributed throughout the central and southeastern parts of the state, trying to prevent the loss of any more territory. The Union's operational hold on Missouri was tenuous at best.

The contest between Lincoln and Frémont that summer reflected the diverging perspectives of Washington and many Federal commanders in the field. While Lincoln and his advisors still hoped for conciliation at the end of 1861, officers and soldiers in the Western Department began to conclude that conciliation was realistically impossible, and they acted on this conclusion. At the time, George C. Burmeister, an infantryman from Iowa, noted how "everybody seems to follow his own inclination and numerous depredations are committed upon persons and property which pass on unnoticed."[49] For Burmeister and his fellows, emancipation was not the salient issue. They were more concerned with making the people of Missouri fear the consequences of contributing to the ever-increasing guerrilla problem. As if to underscore that very point, a detachment of vindictive Union cavalry rode into the small border town of Dayton, Missouri, on the last night of the year and set fire to all but one of the forty-seven houses in the town.[50]

The end of 1861 brought a change of Union leadership in Missouri. The most notable of these changes was the exit of Pope, who was given orders to move his army to the southeast corner of the state for the winter. There he performed admirably leading the Union's capture of Island Number 10 on the Mississippi River in April 1862. Despite this success, Pope left behind a legacy of failure in dealing with the guerrilla violence that gripped Northern Missouri. After the war, Pope admitted that the policies he had enacted in Missouri had failed to "get rid" of the guerrilla problem, as he had intended. He attributed this failure to the lack of strong civil government in the state. "Missouri could have been spared the larger part of these sufferings by ordinary faithful and manly conduct on the part of the state officials at the beginning," Pope would later write, adding that the chaos of guerrilla warfare was "simply an illustration of what the natural, savage instincts of men will lead to once the restraints of law are abandoned."[51] For Pope, his service on the Mississippi was to be a short sojourn into the realm of guerrilla-free operations. He would again encounter the problem in the East. Even though Pope departed Missouri in early 1862, the elements of punitive war that he helped to establish remained. His successors inherited a tumultuous situation and looked for more severe ways to retaliate.

It was during this time that two of punitive war's greatest proponents, Ulysses S. Grant and William T. Sherman, first expressed their doubts about conciliation and the need to get tough with the Southern people. Both were stationed at posts in Missouri, Sherman in St. Louis and Grant in command of the Southeastern District. The seemingly unending reports of guerrilla activity convinced them that the population was not to be trusted and should pay a price. On 9 January 1862, Sherman wrote to his brother claiming that many Missourians pretended to be peaceful farmers but became active insurgents "when a bridge [was] to be burned." As a solution, Sherman recommended forcing the people from their farms and imprisoning them wholesale.[52] Two days after Sherman penned his letter, bushwhackers attacked four Union pickets near the southeastern town of Bird's Point. Grant immediately ordered one of his subordinates, Brigadier General Eleazer Paine, to arrest every man, woman, and child within a six-mile radius of the town and to hold them "under penalty of death and destruction of their property." Paine complied with the order, and within a day, nearly a hundred citizens were taken from their homes and placed under Union guard.[53] Such measures were just a glimpse of what was to come. Neither Grant nor Sherman spent much time with the guerrilla problem in Missouri, but it was enough to make a lasting impression. The situation was potent enough that it invaded their minds, and as with Pope, it would continue to shape Grant and Sherman's attitude toward the Southern people when the two moved east.

During the first year of the war, the Union use of punitive war in Missouri was primarily limited to civilian arrests and assessments. This was short-lived, however, and Union efforts soon became more lethal. By early 1862, they relied increasingly on summary executions to eliminate known or suspected bushwhackers and strike fear into their would-be supporters.[54]

Federal troops of all ranks viewed guerrilla attacks against soldiers, citizens, or other "outrages" and "depredations" against Union property such as trains or transport ships as justification for summary punishment.[55] One Federal commander ordered his troops to be on the lookout for a band of guerrillas operating along the Kansas border, telling them to "execute at once any you may find."[56] In a separate incident, Colonel C. C. Marsh directed the relatives of a suspected guerrilla leader to write a warning to their kin: "The Colonel says that if you attack Commerce to-night [sic] he will hang us." The Union officer attached his own missive confirming the warning. "If you injure the people of Commerce or their property I will hang them," he wrote, "and take bitter revenge on you in other respects." When reporting the incident to his commander, Marsh reasoned that the pursuit of armed rebels was futile and that the men he held were guilty of actively supporting guerrillas in the area. Marsh also reported that his actions had the desired effect by preventing any attack on the town.[57]

While some threats of execution were just that, others were often carried out. In October 1862, Major General John McNeil, commanding Union troops in Palmyra, oversaw the execution of ten prisoners suspected of burning bridges and firing on Federal troops. After hearing of the execution, one observer reported that "persons who engaged in guerrilla warfare in the rear of the lines without uniforms . . . were regarded by most of the Union generals as a kind of land pirates and not entitled to treatment of prisoners of war." He added, "General McNeil was not the only Federal officer who ordered their execution when they were caught."[58]

Lieutenant John Boyd of the Sixth Missouri Militia executed ten suspected guerrillas and ordered the burning of twenty-three houses near the small Missouri town of Rolla, located in the center of the state. An adjutant general's investigation of the incident revealed that Boyd believed himself to be following the "special instructions" of his commander, a Captain Murphy, who had given the detachment the order to "clean them out." Boyd also claimed that the men were killed trying to escape and that the houses burned had been vacant. Ultimately, the investigator in the case concluded that "Lieutenant Boyd acted correctly, and for the good of the service."[59] While the incident demonstrated that Union commanders sometimes questioned the execution of suspected guerrillas, it also showed that not much in the way of justification was needed.

The legality of guerrilla warfare and the Union's response to it became a key issue during the command of Major General Henry Halleck, who replaced Hunter as commander of the Department of the Missouri on 9 November 1861. Halleck, a veteran of the Mexican war, former lawyer, and according to his biographer, "one of the most famous military men of his time," was also an accomplished scholar on the international laws of war.[60] A graduate of West Point in 1839, Halleck had been thoroughly influenced by the teachings of Antoine Henri Jomini.[61] Halleck's works, *Elements of Military Art and Science* (1856) and *International Law, Or, Rules Regulating the Intercourse of States in Peace and War* (1861), served as two of the very few existing texts on the legal aspects of land warfare. Halleck was among the most knowledgeable officers on the laws of war of the time, a reputation that earned him favor in military circles. However, "Old Brains," as subordinates often called him, was more impressive as an organizer of armies than as a commander of troops.

Upon assuming command of Union forces in Missouri in late 1861, Halleck was confronted by the increasing guerrilla problem that threatened to destabilize western and northern Missouri. One of Halleck's first actions was to reestablish the authority for martial law in the state. Within a week, he sent numerous messages to General George B. McClellan, then commander-in-chief of the U.S. Army, requesting written authorization to establish martial law. According to Halleck, no legal authority had been established for it under the previous commander. The order was critical, Halleck argued, because "the mass of the people here are against us." He believed that "the authorities at Washington do not understand the present condition of affairs in Missouri," but he wanted to avoid a repetition of Frémont's cavalier usurpation of authority.[62] The authorization eventually came from Lincoln via the pen of Secretary of State Seward, who wrote:

> GENERAL: As an insurrection exists in the United States and is in arms in the State of Missouri, you are hereby authorized and empowered to suspend the writ of *habeas corpus* within the limits of the military division under your command, and to exercise martial law as you find it necessary, in your discretion, to secure the public safety and the authority of the United States.[63]

Armed with this authorization, Halleck was free to deliver his General Order No. 34 on the day after Christmas, reinstating martial law and stressing the need for strict control of the population in the areas surrounding Federal railroads throughout the state.[64] The order did not authorize its application throughout the entire state, only in those areas with frequent guerrilla attacks and an openly disloyal population.

Halleck also revamped the program of levying assessments on active secessionists. On 7 January 1862 he issued Special Order No. 18, which established a new collection board that oversaw the collection of military taxes primarily in the St. Louis area. When targeted sympathizers did not pay the mandated amount, their property was seized by Union troops as payment. In all, more

Major General Henry W. Halleck. Introduced to the guerrilla problem in Missouri in 1861, Halleck went on to become the chief of staff of the Union Army and a strong proponent of punitive war. (Library of Congress)

than $10,000 in money or property was collected in a matter of a few weeks from alleged secessionists in St. Louis. When his subordinates initiated their own assessment programs in their local areas, Halleck required them to get his approval before continuing their collection of fines.[65]

Although Union soldiers' frustration and anger with the rebellious people of Missouri increased throughout the winter of 1861–1862, commanders did not abandon restraint completely. A few clear examples exist of Union officers endeavoring to keep the vengeful tendencies of their soldiers in check. When the "Jayhawker" Brigade of the Seventh Kansas Cavalry went on a destructive binge in late September 1861, destroying the homes of secessionists along the border region and completely wiping out the town of Osceola, Halleck was alarmed. He directed Pope to force the unruly Jayhawkers out of Missouri, or arrest them. Their ruthless and vindictive behavior was a disgrace to "the name and uniform of American soldiers," Halleck declared, warning that such behavior threatened to further ignite anti-Union sentiment in the region and dash "all hopes of a pacification of Missouri."[66]

Another example of Union restraint was seen in February 1862 when

Union soldiers under the command of Brigadier General Samuel R. Curtis occupied the small village of Mud Town, just across the Arkansas border. A number of Curtis's troops became sick and one officer died after eating food left behind by fleeing Confederates. Poisoning was suspected. Although his soldiers were enraged, Curtis quickly posted orders warning against any action directed toward the citizens of the town. "It is my earnest desire to prevent damage to private property," he informed his subordinates. "Restrain your troops from acts of cruelty and folly."[67] In this case, Curtis's troops acquiesced and the town was spared. Recurring and frequent reports of guerrilla attacks throughout the department, however, ensured that similar restraint would become increasingly scarce. Those Union officers who were reluctant to target civilians and their property were left to stem the growing tide. Captain James D. Thompson of the First Iowa Cavalry was one of those. When he witnessed Union soldiers kill a number of citizens and burn their houses near the town of Warrensburg in retaliation for guerrilla attacks, Thompson bemoaned such "nefarious business" and urged the commanding general to take action against the "wanton destruction of life and property."[68] In essence, Captain Thompson and his fellow officers were involved in two separate battles: one to defeat the guerrilla menace and one to keep their angry, frustrated soldiers from engaging in atrocities. The longer the war waged on, the more difficult each battle became.

It became increasingly clear that soldiers would act out of anger and frustration regardless of the efforts their officers took to contain them. Not surprisingly, letters or diaries sometimes contained evidence of punitive war measures taken up by soldiers that were not detailed in official reports. As the years dragged on, and punitive war policies became more widely accepted by Union authorities, such reports became more frequent. As late as the fall of 1862, however, it was still not uncommon to have significant events go unreported, only to be outlined in detail by the soldiers involved. One vivid example of this involved the small town of Keetsville, which was nestled in the southwestern corner of Missouri, just 10 miles north of the Arkansas border and 20 miles east of Kansas. It was a location suited for bushwhackers, who frequently fired upon Union troops moving past the town. It did not take long for the bushwhacking to provoke a punitive response from angry soldiers. In his diary, Iowa infantryman Benjamin McIntyre wrote, "Our men had bourne these outrages until forbearance could not longer be indulged and our soldiers burned nearly the entire place." McIntyre estimated that the town was almost completely destroyed by the burning. The destruction was not limited to Keetsville, but spread to the surrounding area. "Along the entire distance we have came today nearly ever dwelling had been destroyed," he noted. "The inmates claimed strong proclivities for the Union yet had harbored rebels who practiced their murderous warfare."[69] Despite McIntyre's description of extensive burning, little to no mention of it was made in official reports at the time. The only official recognition of the incident was buried in the middle of a report made by Major General Samuel Curtis nearly two years later in which he mentioned the "ruins of Keetsville."[70] It was not the first, and certainly not the last time that a Missouri town went up in flames in response to guerrilla activity. Much more was to come. The burning of Keetsville underscored the fact that, despite official attempts to restrain Union troops, spontaneous instances of punitive war erupted from time to time. It was a thorny challenge that faced Halleck and his successors, made all the more difficult by the political leadership in Washington that was still, at the time, railing against the "wanton, useless destruction of property" by Union officers in the field. Lincoln was adamant that the Union army would not bring undue loss or suffering upon the people.[71]

The conventional war rolled on, a fact that the political and military instability in Missouri often overshadowed. In the first days of March 1862, nearly 11,000 Union soldiers under the command of then brigadier general Samuel Curtis crossed from Missouri into Arkansas and took up a defense position behind Little Sugar Creek near Bentonville. There, they were met by Confederate Major General Earl Van Dorn's Army of the West, some 16,000 strong, and the Battle of Pea Ridge ensued. Two days of back and forth fighting left Van Dorn's force short on supplies and unable to contend with a series of attacks made by Curtis's divisions. On March 8, the exhausted Confederates fell back and limped south to Fayetteville. Van Dorn was then ordered to move what was left of his army east to Tennessee. The conventional Confederate threat to Missouri was effectively over. Although Sterling Price would conduct an ill-fated raid into the state two years later, it posed little threat and was rapidly defeated. For the remainder of the war, the greatest danger facing Union forces in Missouri were the small groups of Confederate deserters and proslavery guerrillas who attacked rail and telegraph lines and targeted Union detachments. As Brigadier General Thomas Ewing described to Halleck weeks before, "These marauding bands are now the great mischief to Missouri."[72] The unpredictable nature of their attacks, combined with the continued futility of active counterguerrilla patrolling by Union cavalry, left Halleck increasingly baffled as to how to alleviate the damage being done. In one of his first official orders of 1862, Halleck made his intentions clear:

I am satisfied that nothing but the severest punishment can prevent the burning of railroad bridges and the great destruction of human life. I shall punish all I can catch, although I have no doubt there will be a newspaper howl against me as a blood-thirsty monster. These incendiaries have destroyed in the last ten days $150,000 worth of railroad property, notwithstanding that there are more than 10,000 troops kept guarding the railroads in this State . . . This is not usually done by armed and open enemies, but by pretended quiet citizens, living on their farms. A bridge or building is set on fire, and the culprit an hour after is quietly plowing or working in his field. The civil courts can give us no assistance, as they are very generally unreliable. There is no alternative but to enforce martial law. Our army here is almost as much in a hostile country as it was when in Mexico.

I have determined to put down these insurgents and bridge-burners with a strong hand. It must be done; there is no other remedy. If I am sustained by the Government and country, well and good; if not, I will take the consequences.[73]

The significance of Halleck's message should not be overlooked. Halleck was not calling for a more vigorous prosecution of the conventional war. The target for Halleck's proposed "strong hand" were not the "armed and open enemies" but rather "pretended quiet citizens" found on farms or working in the field. Halleck was, in essence, targeting anyone who *might* have been guilty of guerrilla activity. He was injecting a level of ambiguity into the definition of noncombatant, stating that those who appeared to be innocent could very well be the enemy. Without actually saying it, Halleck suggested that appearances meant very little. "If you could not identify the enemy, all civilians became enemies," Fellman suggested, adding, "It was up to the field officers to interpret this policy, to decide who was a true noncombatant and who a belligerent outlaw."[74] It was this sort of ambiguity that plagued Union commanders and soldiers, not only in Missouri, but throughout the occupied South during the war. Unfortunately for the common soldiers in the field, and the civilians living in an area where guerrillas were active, proof of guilt or innocence was rarely certain.

The day after his warning, Halleck stressed the need to get tough with the disloyal people in Missouri. "The time for conciliation, I am sorry to say, has passed," Halleck wrote to a citizen in St. Louis, claiming that only "military power" would pacify the state.[75] The importance of this statement was in its timing. Here was the future U.S. Army general-in-chief openly declaring the futility of conciliation a full six months before the Union Army would suffer its major defeats in the summer of 1862. Although Halleck was speaking specifically of Missouri, his statement certainly contradicts claims that he was an ardent advocate of conciliation until much later in the war.[76]

Halleck acknowledged that his approach, or specifically, the establishment of martial law throughout Missouri, might be met with trepidation by his own government and countrymen. Although his actions might be controversial, according to Halleck, they were both justified and perfectly legal. He drew upon his personal understanding of law and history to make his case. In his General Order No. 1, Halleck explained that "insurgents, not militarily organized under the laws of the State, predatory partisans, and guerrilla bands . . . are not legitimately in arms, and the military name and garb which they have assumed cannot give a military exemption to the crimes which they may commit." He added that guerrillas were "in a legal sense, mere freebooters and banditti, and are liable to the same punishment which was imposed upon guerrilla bands by Napoleon in Spain and by Scott in Mexico."[77] What exact punishment Napoleon and Scott had used upon guerrillas, Halleck did not specify, but death might be inferred. Nor could one find an exact definition of insurgent, partisan, guerrilla, freebooter, or banditti in Halleck's order. Such distinctions would come later in the war.[78] For the time being, soldiers were left to make those determinations on their own. During his six-month command in Missouri, "Old Brains" Halleck never completely eschewed the need for restraint in regard to the truly innocent, once declaring, "Retaliation has its limits, and the innocent should not be made to suffer for the acts of others over whom they have no control."[79] The Confederate loss at the Battle of Pea Ridge, however, resulted in a stream of defeated Missourians returning to the state to, in the words of one scholar, "lurk in the woods" and terrorize Union troops.[80] In addition, Halleck heard of Confederate authorities authorizing guerrilla activity in Missouri. To this, he offered a pointed warning to the state's citizens: "All persons are hereby warned that if they join any guerrilla band they will not, if captured, be treated as ordinary prisoners of war, but will be hung as robbers and murderers. Their lives shall atone for the barbarity of their general."[81]

Soldiers of all ranks shared Halleck's hardened opinion. By the spring of 1862, it was clear that the U.S. War Department was not terribly concerned with the legalities surrounding the execution of captured guerrillas. In response to reports of guerrilla attacks in western Virginia, assistant secretary of war P. H. Watson compared those responsible to "pirates and buccaneers" and suggested that they "be hunted and shot wherever found." Watson predicted that summary executions would quickly bring an end to the "barbarities" being committed by Missouri's guerrillas.[82] The imprecise wording of Watson's message, however, suggested that anyone conducting any form of irregular warfare was worthy of being shot upon capture. Proof of guerrilla involvement was neither necessary nor important, as pointed out by one scholar, "Those shot on the spot were men whom Union soldiers declared to be guerrillas," often resulting in the execution of "men who were neither guerrillas nor their supporters."[83] And while President Lincoln was too guarded to ever authorize individuals being "hunted and shot," he was willing to leave the mess in Missouri to firebrands such as Watson.

Major General Samuel Curtis and Brigadier General Benjamin Loan, both Union commanders in Missouri, were strong believers in the need for executions. After two years of enduring chronic guerrilla attacks in Missouri they expressed the need for a severe remedy. "The contest for the supremacy of this state must be a war of extermination," Loan wrote to Curtis. In his view, the government in Washington, "in its zeal to conciliate the rebels and traitors . . . allows the loyal citizens to be deliberately murdered by the allies of the rebels, the guerrillas." Curtis was both quick and blunt in his reply: "Death to bushwhackers is the order. Have a commission ready to try, determine, and execute immediately, if they are unfortunately taken alive."[84] This "no quarter" policy found its way into the dealings of local provosts. In one case, a Union soldier expressed pity for a number of men arrested for attacking a Union forage train near White River because, in his words, "The Provost Marshall shows no mercy to such men." With the situation as brutal as it was by the start of 1863, mercy on either side was increasingly hard to come by.

Even so, reports of bushwhackers or guerrillas captured throughout Missouri outweighed reports of summary executions, although the latter did commonly occur.[85] Many guerrillas were reported killed in action or trying to escape. Explicit mention of execution in official correspondence was rare, and the details were usually ambiguous. For example, on 28 June 1863 a Union captain reported an engagement with a group of nearly thirty bushwhackers and added that he was "sorry" to report that his command was "forced" to take guerrillas prisoner, but went on to mention that all guerrillas had been captured, and one had been killed.[86]

Following escalated guerrilla campaigns in Missouri in 1863, the Union practice of killing those suspected of being guerrillas was more accepted within the ranks and rarely condemned.[87] As the guerrilla problem continued to fester, blatant references to executions became more common in official reports. They eventually became so routine that the killing of captured guerrillas required little to no justification in dispatches. As late as January 1865, Brigadier General Clinton Fisk reported that his soldiers "captured and killed the guerrilla Captain Childs . . . three of his men share his fate." Fisk's report added, "The troops in Platte County killed two guerrillas Saturday last."[88] The matter-of-fact nature of Fisk's statements illustrated the hardened attitude that Federal officials and soldiers in Missouri developed when dealing with the guerrilla problem.

Union execution of captured guerrillas or arrest of those suspected of aiding them did not go unchallenged; certainly not by Confederates. In response to news of Union troops killing captured guerrillas, one Confederate commander in Missouri exclaimed, "The perversion of the war for the Union to a war of extermination forces upon us retaliation . . . and if another Confederate soldier or citizen is executed without due process of law five Union soldiers or citizens shall with their lives pay the forfeit."[89] Hearing of McNeil's ordered executions in Palmyra, Confederate President Jefferson Davis himself threatened to execute the same number of captured Union officers should such practices continue.[90]

The legal and moral dilemma presented by the execution of prisoners was not lost on the legally astute Halleck. After a short stint as field commander during the Battle of Corinth, Halleck was promoted to the position of commanding general of the U.S. Army in July 1862. He took his Missouri experience to Washington, where he immediately encountered other complaints from angry Union officers describing guerrilla activity throughout the occupied regions of the South. Union armies in Kentucky and Tennessee were being harassed daily by guerrilla attacks on their supply lines, and Federal troops in Arkansas and Louisiana were under constant threat of bushwhacking. Just three months before, the Confederate government in Richmond had passed the Partisan Ranger Act, authorizing the formation of independent partisan companies.[91] Union officials, to include Halleck, saw this as an inexcusable open call for guerrilla warfare—one that required a response. Within a month of his arrival in Washington, Halleck solicited expert legal advice on the matter from an old acquaintance.

Dr. Francis Lieber was a German-born veteran of the Napoleonic Wars and an accomplished scholar of political philosophy. Because of a shared interest in international law, he and Halleck became friends during the early years of the war. Just prior to the outbreak of the war, Lieber attempted, unsuccessfully, to have a course on the laws of war added to the curriculum at West Point.[92] Knowing that Lieber had devoted substantial time and effort to the study of guerrilla warfare, Halleck petitioned him in August 1862 for his insight on the matter. "The rebel authorities claim the right to send men, in the garb of peaceful citizens, to waylay and attack our troops, to burn bridges and houses, and to destroy property and persons within our lines," Halleck wrote, and requested that Lieber provide his views on the legitimacy of guerrilla warfare and the execution of those who practiced it.[93] Lieber's reply came in the form of an essay entitled "Guerrilla Parties Considered in Reference to the Laws and Usages of War." In it, Lieber stressed the historical ambiguity surrounding the term *guerrilla*, using examples from European wars to differentiate freebooters, bandits, partisans, guerrillas, armed rebels, and others. According to Lieber, the intentions of the offender largely determined their protection under law upon capture. For example, Lieber considered "partisans" to be those who practiced guerrilla or irregular tactics against the enemy. Although organized independently, they were still "part and parcel of the army," and therefore entitled to the protections of the laws of war. On the other hand, the "armed prowler or bushwhacker" who, while wearing no form of uniform or badge, conducted surprise attacks against unwitting Union troops or civilians, was guilty of "homicides which every civilized nation will consider murder" and deserved to be shot when captured. The intent to deceive, Lieber claimed, was the distinguishing factor between a bushwhacker and a member of the *levée en mass*, who wore no uniform but fought overtly, and was therefore protected by law.[94]

Perhaps most importantly, Lieber acknowledged the ambiguity surrounding irregular warfare. "Indeed, the importance of writing on this subject is much diminished by the fact that the soldier generally decides these cases for himself," said Lieber. "The most disciplined soldiers will execute on the spot an armed and murderous prowler found where he could have no business as a peaceful citizen." Despite its detailed definitions, Lieber's essay did not address the specific guerrilla situations in Missouri or other parts of the occupied South. Nor did it provide a formula by which to prove the guilt or innocence of those captured. The broad nature of his wording meant that readers could interpret the essay in many different ways.[95]

Halleck immediately ordered 50,000 copies of Lieber's essay to be printed and distributed throughout the Army.[96] In the meantime, Halleck continued to rationalize the need for a more punitive approach to waging the war. The following November, he made his views clear to one Union commander, stating that a "vigorous and strong policy" was needed, claiming that his own policies in Missouri had been "most beneficial" in dealing with a hostile population (although, in truth, they had achieved little). He instructed the commander to target citizens "who persevere in offense" and to "let the guilty feel that you have an iron hand; that you know how to apply it when necessary."[97] Halleck's push for a more severe prosecution of the war coincided with key events in fall of that year, such as Lincoln's Emancipation Proclamation and continued Union setbacks on eastern battlefields.[98] In the words of his biographer, Halleck realized that "the days of chivalric war were over" and that a need had developed for new regulations and rules to guide the army as the conflict intensified.[99]

Halleck again called upon Lieber, and together with a board of four politically minded generals, set to work producing guidelines for the conduct of Union armies in the field. The result was General Orders 100, *Instructions for the Government of Armies of the United States in the Field*, published by the Department of the Army on 24 April 1863. The "Lieber Code," as it was commonly referred to, would eventually become one of the most noteworthy

Dr. Francis Lieber. A leading mind in the realm of the laws of war, Lieber crafted the basis for General Orders 100 at the behest of Halleck. (Library of Congress)

developments in American legal history. Scholars have described the Lieber Code as "the first code of rules for land warfare ever adopted by any nation," and "the final product of the eighteenth-century movement to humanize war through the application of reason," which would ultimately have a "profound effect on the international law of land warfare."[100] The order was divided into ten sections, the fourth of which was devoted to the explanation of the different classes, or categories, of irregulars in warfare. Lieber's definitions did not vary much from his previous essay on the subject. Partisans were described as those who wore a uniform and fought as auxiliaries to the regular army, although they were "detached" from the main army for the purpose of "making inroads" into Union territory. As "soldiers armed and wearing uniforms," they were to be protected by the law of war if captured. The "armed prowler" was identified as the independent rogue who targeted railroads, telegraph wires, and communications. Members of this class could be shot if captured. The most vague category of irregular was that of "men or squads who commit hostilities." In this grouping, Lieber left much to the personal interpretation of the reader: "Men or squads of men who commit hostilities, whether by fighting or inroads for destruction or plunder or by raids of any kind without commission without being part and portion of the organized hostile army . . . are not public enemies and therefore if captured are not entitled to the privileges of prisoners of war, but shall be treated summarily as highway robbers or pirates."[101]

Most, if not all, of the guerrillas operating in Missouri against the Union military fit into Lieber's definitions of armed prowlers or "armed enemies not belonging to the hostile army." Although other sections of General Orders 100 specifically addressed issues other than guerrilla warfare, the guidelines primarily provided rules for dealing with a hostile population. For instance, in the section considering insurrection, the order directed commanders to "throw the burden of war" on the "disloyal citizens" of an occupied area. In a discussion of prisoners of war, the order warned that those who fought in uniforms of the enemy without distinctive markings deserved "no quarter."[102] The last line of General Orders 100 reminded the reader that "armed or unarmed resistance by citizens of the United States" against the Federal Army amounted to treason and was therefore punishable by death.[103] Historian Andrew Birtle argued that the code "considered the relationship between soldier and civilian to be reciprocal in nature," and that according to Lieber, "military necessity required that the Army adopt stern measures" if local citizens turned against the Army with armed resistance or support for guerrillas.[104]

Lieber's Code was not a handbook for fighting and winning conventional operations in the field. Instead, it offered guidelines for an occupying army that faced the moral and ethical challenges inherent to suppressing an unruly population. Like Lieber's initial essay, it was vague and permitted troops to apply the rules as they saw fit. According to historian Richard Hartigan in his study of Lieber's Code, the inexplicit wording of the order enabled the Union soldier "to justify extreme severity toward the enemy" if he chose to do so.[105] If the reader of General Orders 100 was an advocate of conciliation, Lieber's call for restraint would resonate. If the reader believed that harsher measures were required to combat the guerrilla problem (as did Pope and Halleck) then they could point to the order's authorization of "direct destruction" and other strict measures to ensure the "speedier subjection of the enemy."[106] The exact purpose of the code has been the subject of historical debate. Neely claimed that the true intent of the code was to "codify and publish rules to limit the destructiveness in war," although nothing in Halleck's initial request to Lieber indicated that he sought to limit the response to the guerrilla problem.[107] In reality, Halleck wanted Lieber to put his specialized stamp of approval on Halleck's own view of the illegitimacy of the Confederate authorization of guerrilla warfare. Historian Harry T. Stout recently argued (overzealously) that the code was, in essence, "a blank check" for Union commanders to use in their "new war that would deliberately invade civilian lives and properties."[108] And while the image of a blank check might not match Lieber or Halleck's intent for the order, it could certainly apply to the manner in which some Union leaders in the field chose to interpret it. Given its ambiguity and broad definition of military necessity, the Lieber Code did not provide a practicable solution for the guerrilla problem, and in some ways, it made it more complex.

The production of General Orders 100, however, was evidence of the changing dynamic of the war. No longer could U.S. political or military leaders assume wars were to be conducted strictly according to chivalric codes of honor or nineteenth-century definitions of the fair fight. If nothing else, the code suggested that war could be waged legally with either the utmost restraint or with extreme severity. In essence, the very fact that the code was deemed necessary was just as significant, if not more so, than the guidelines it contained. Had resistance in the South been negligible, the Union Army would not have gone to the trouble to produce and distribute Lieber's original essay on guerrilla parties. Nor would General Orders 100 have been deemed necessary. As it was, however, the guerrilla problem was fomenting punitive war, and the Lieber Code was an attempt to codify and control it.

Although General Orders 100 would eventually prove instrumental in the development of U.S. land war policies later in the nineteenth century, the Lieber Code's impact on the conduct of the Civil War was quite limited. Field commanders ignored it, were not familiar with it, or chose to interpret it to suit their own purposes. Specific mentions of the order in official correspondence and dispatches during the remainder of the war were extremely rare. When it was mentioned, it was primarily in reference to the exchange of prisoners; not the treatment of guerrillas or their noncombatant supporters. In a rather rare and ironic case, General Orders 100 was used to exonerate a Confederate general accused of destroying government property when he surrendered a post in Alabama. According to one scholar, "Most regulations throughout the remainder of the war seem to have been in harmony" with the Lieber Code, but did not necessarily abide by it to the letter.[109] It was not hard to stay within the broad parameters of the code. If most Union regulations were in harmony with it, it was more coincidence than consequence.

Even so, the process by which the Lieber Code came about was indicative of the fact that the guerrilla problem had become something that the U.S. Army would be forced to address in an official capacity (as well as the issues of foraging, treatment of prisoners, and other elements inherent to a military occupation). Its publication was, in a way, an admission that a very real problem existed. It all began with Halleck's own frustrating experiences in Missouri combined with his outrage at the Confederate Partisan Ranger Act, which resulted in Lieber's pamphlet on guerrilla warfare, and ultimately General Orders 100. The stress that the guerrilla problem was placing on the existing rules of warfare could now be seen on paper.

The evolution of punitive war policies continued as the war raged on further to the East. On the conventional front, Missouri offered little. As the Union and Confederate armies bludgeoned one another at Gettysburg and Vicksburg in the summer of 1863, the security situation in Missouri became more and more of an afterthought. Nonetheless, what transpired in the state for the remainder of the war closely mirrored events that occurred anywhere in the South where the guerrilla problem could be found. Missouri's situation was unique only because the guerrilla problem greatly eclipsed all other issues facing the Union occupiers. Unlike their counterparts fighting in the Eastern Theater, who had the specter of extensive, costly campaigns to distract them from the monotony of occupation duty, officers assigned to Missouri had just the daily menace of bushwhacking to worry about. The unfortunate inheritor of the problem was Major General John M. Schofield, who took command of Federal forces in St. Louis following Halleck's departure to Washington. By May 1863, Schofield commanded the entire Department of the Missouri. During his tenure overseeing what Schofield himself called a "scene of unsoldierly strife and turmoil," he established several punitive policies that further demonstrated the powerful impact of the guerrilla problem in Missouri.[110] Faced with the unenviable task of pacifying the troubled state and receiving little to no guidance on how to do so from Washington, Schofield eventually (and predictably) resorted to increasingly severe measures, including what historians have described as "the most drastic measure taken against civilians during the Civil War prior to General Sherman's march to the sea," and "the harshest treatment ever imposed on United States Citizens under the plea of military necessity."[111] In doing so, he would establish himself as one of the Union's greatest advocates and practitioners of punitive war.

Schofield, a graduate of West Point and former instructor of philosophy at the academy, spent the majority of the first two years of the Civil War becoming intimately acquainted with the brutal nature of the conflict in Missouri. He fought under Nathaniel Lyon at Wilson's Creek and supervised Federal military operations in the state while Halleck commanded at Corinth in April 1862. In his memoirs, Schofield described the false assurances he received from Halleck in relation to the guerrilla problem as he took command in St. Louis: "[Halleck] informed me with evident satisfaction that north Missouri was cleared of rebels, and that the war was ended in that part of the State! In fact," continued Schofield, "the guerrillas 'flushed' like a flock of quail by

Pope's advanced guard, had taken to the bush . . . and then were found feeding again on their old ground."[112] He clearly did not share Halleck's optimism about the demise of the guerrilla threat.

Schofield spent the summer of 1862 trying to round up or exterminate the remaining small groups of guerrillas plaguing the Missouri countryside. It was both a frustrating and burdensome task; more than fifty thousand Union troops were assigned to hunt for an estimated three or four thousand scattered bushwhackers.[113] Despite a brief lull in reported guerrilla attacks during the winter of 1862, the campaign was ultimately unsuccessful, as an eventual increase in violence toward the summer of 1863 demonstrated. Schofield then renewed the practice of exacting taxes from communities deemed disloyal or in support of guerrilla operations. In each town, a committee of Union-supporting citizens administered the levies upon the suspected citizens. These committees, according to Fellman, "frequently acted on unproven suspicions and out of a desire for revenge," which only served to agitate local resistance to Union authority.[114]

While major campaigns in the East and on the Mississippi River were shifting the tides of the conventional war in 1863, the military and political situations in Missouri remained mostly the same. This rapidly eroded Schofield's patience and tolerance, and his rhetoric took on a bitterness similar to that previously voiced by Pope and Halleck. Like his predecessor, Major General Samuel Curtis, Schofield sought to "create a wholesome fear" amongst the disloyal population.[115] It was at this time that punitive war in Missouri moved well beyond assessments and the summary executions of suspected guerrillas and entered the realm of retaliatory burnings. Up to this point, the Union use of the torch aimed against noncombatants had been limited and sporadic. The towns of Dayton, Osceola, and Keetsville, which were destroyed in response to guerrilla activity, were three of the few early examples. But under Schofield's watch, the people of Missouri would become much more familiar with the sight of barns, houses, and public buildings in flames. The guerrillas themselves contributed to the incinerations, sometimes carrying out more burning than the Union soldiers, which just added to an already chaotic climate that denied local citizens any kind of refuge.

One of the incidents to mark a new era of destructiveness in Missouri occurred on 23 June 1863 in the small town of Sibley, located on a lazy bend in the Missouri River 15 miles east of Kansas City. A detachment of six companies under the command of Captain Samuel Flagg of the Fourth Missouri was engaged in a two-day search for guerrilla parties that reportedly "infested" the area when it came upon Sibley early in the morning. A quick skirmish ensued, with Union troops being fired upon by guerrillas from some of the houses in town. After sustaining a number of casualties, the guerrillas

Major General
John M. Schofield.
Schofield presided
over the strife in
Missouri in 1863,
to include the
execution of Order
No. 11. (Library of
Congress)

fled, leaving Sibley in the hands of angry Union troops. Flagg ordered the town burned, claiming that it was a haven for bushwhackers targeting Union vessels on the river. His soldiers went to work, destroying all but two of the houses in the town. When Flagg's commanding officer, Brigadier General Thomas Ewing, received the report of the action he seemed to support it. "I think it probable that it was for the good of the service that the town was burned," Thomas wrote, even though he expressed a desire to investigate the incident in order to "ascertain the character of the people, and their conduct" as well as the "circumstances under which the town was burned."[116] It is unlikely that such an investigation took place. It was a situation of burn first and ascertain later, a practice that became the hallmark of punitive war not only in Missouri, but in other areas plagued with the guerrilla problem.

   The destruction of Sibley was quickly overshadowed by what would become the darkest chapter in the violent history of the Missouri-Kansas border, and one of the darkest in the Civil War. Up until the summer of 1863,

Missouri's greatest significance within the larger context of the guerrilla problem and the evolution of punitive war was its influence on key Union leaders, such as Halleck, Grant, and Sherman, who were destined to take the lead in the Eastern Theater in the latter years of the contest. During that summer, however, Missouri's operational path of significance diverged away from the rest of the war, and the state became somewhat of a military and political backwater. While those in Washington paid little attention to the ongoing strife in the state, they were forced to deal with it from time to time. Half-hearted attempts were made to bolster the security situation and prevent the guerrilla problem from eroding Union control in the state. Nothing, however, could prepare the people in Missouri for what happened along the Kansas border in the late summer of 1863. Two bloody weeks introduced the region to a level of violent vindictiveness never before seen. The events that took place sparked outrage and alarm all across the country and left John M. Schofield searching for a "most radical remedy" for the guerrilla problem.[117]

That remedy was General Order No. 11, which was triggered by the most infamous guerrilla attack in the region, and perhaps the entire country, during the war. On 19 August 1863, a band of over 400 Confederate guerrillas from Missouri led by William Clark Quantrill crossed the border into Kansas with the intent to "kill every man and burn every house" in the abolitionist stronghold of Lawrence. Quantrill, a former teacher who once lived in Lawrence, had amassed a small army of some 450 partisans devoted to killing Jayhawkers and stomping out Union sentiment on the border. Although more organized, and certainly larger, than most of the bushwhacking bands operating throughout Missouri, Quantrill's group employed the same ruthless hit-and-run tactics for the same vengeful, and profitable, reasons as the others. By attacking Lawrence, many of Quantrill's men felt they were avenging what they believed to be the intentional killing of a number of their women relatives by their Union captors.[118] However, given the town's known connection to Free-Soil leaders, such as Senator Jim Lane, it is likely that Quantrill had envisioned the attack months before.

On the night of 20 August, Quantrill's column rode anxiously through the night toward their target, their excitement and bloodlust growing with each hour that passed. In the early morning of 21 August, just as the sun was rising over Lawrence, the raiders struck. Catching the community completely by surprise, the guerrillas tore through the town, ruthlessly carrying out their vengeful mission. Men and boys were dragged into the streets where they were shot and their bodies burned. Shops, offices, and houses were quickly set aflame. No building was safe from looting, damage, or outright destruction. When the grisly work of Quantrill's men was done, at least 180 men and boys (all unarmed) were dead, and most of the town's stores and a quarter of the private homes had been burned to the ground. According to one scholar, Quantrill's Raid left Lawrence "almost wiped from the map." In the words of another, it was "the most horrible atrocity of the entire Civil War."[119] There can be little doubt that Quantrill's Raid was a massacre, in the truest sense of the word. The ruthlessness displayed by its perpetrators was on par with any seen previously in the nation's history. It was a scene that made Union punitive efforts before and after seem pedestrian.

While some Southern newspapers hailed the guerrilla attack on Lawrence as both "a perfect success" and "a gallant and perfectly fair blow to the enemy," reaction in the North was, predictably, one of outrage. The call for immediate retribution was raised by apoplectic Kansans who blamed the entire population of Western Missouri for the attack. An alarmed President Lincoln directed Schofield to explain what happened in Lawrence and to prevent the impending "indiscriminate slaughter" on the border through use of "very judicious action."[120] Spurred on by the political pressure and a potential uprising on his hands, Schofield approved a plan initially developed by Major General Thomas Ewing weeks earlier. All citizens in four Missouri border counties suspected of harboring the likes of Quantrill's guerrillas would be driven out and all sources of food and subsistence destroyed. Schofield reasoned: "I am pretty much convinced that the mode of carrying on the war on the border during the past two years has produced such a state of feeling that nothing short of total devastation of the districts which are made the haunts of guerrillas will be sufficient to put a stop to the evil."

In Order No. 11, Schofield declared that the citizens of Cass, Jackson, Bates, and Vernon Counties were "determined to harbor and encourage a band of scoundrels whose every object is plunder and murder. This state of things cannot be permitted longer to exist, and nothing less than the most radical remedy will be sufficient to remove the evil." The order called for every citizen within the four counties, with the small exception of those living in the immediate vicinity of a Union military post, to vacate their property within fifteen days, at which time "all houses, barns, provisions, and other property" would be destroyed by the Union Army to prevent their use by guerrillas. In essence, the order was designed to leave the counties barren, uninhabited, and useless. Schofield added: "The commanding general is aware that some innocent persons must suffer from these extreme measures, but such suffering is unavoidable . . . A district of country inhabited almost solely by rebels cannot be permitted to be made a hiding-place for robbers and murderers, from which to sally forth on their errands of rapine and death."[121]

The mention of "innocent persons" having to suffer demonstrated that Schofield now believed that it was absolutely necessary to visit punishment upon noncombatants in order to defeat the guerrilla problem. Their

Quantrill's Raid on Lawrence, Kansas (*Harper's Weekly*)

association with guerrillas had made it "unavoidable" in his words. Even so, historians have debated the punitive nature of the order to a great extent. At least one historian has argued that the order was "not a punitive measure," but rather, a previously planned action occasioned by the raid on Lawrence. Another, while admitting that the order was "very cruel" by standards of the time, also claimed that it "helped prevent much worse" by satiating the lust for revenge on the part of Kansas Jayhawkers.[122] It is impossible to know what the enraged Kansans would have done to the border counties in Missouri had Thomas and Schofield not done it for them. Nevertheless, Schofield's discussion of Order No. 11 suggested that depopulation of the region was conducted more out of passion and anger than a sense of military necessity. It is true that the seeds of the order had been planted well before the sacking of Lawrence, but even then the initiating cause had been the aggravating disadvantage Union troops were placed in by guerrillas and their supporters. In fact, Schofield later claimed that the "utter impossibility of deciding who were guilty and who innocent" made the collective nature of the order necessary.[123] His willingness to indiscriminately drive all the citizens out of their homes went beyond the mere military pragmatism of denying the enemy guerrillas subsistence and extended to the unabashed punishment of their supposed supporters, who Schofield clearly considered enemies as well. The notion that Schofield and Thomas actually did the people of western Missouri a favor by evicting them from their homes and destroying their farms and thereby keeping the Jayhawkers at bay is implausible at best.

What distinguished Order No. 11 from previous punitive policies produced by Pope, Halleck, or other commanders in Missouri was its magnitude and its thorough execution. Union troops, most of them from Kansas, carried out the order methodically and completely, destroying the vast majority of homes and barns in the named counties and creating some 20,000 refugees. Historians have debated the exact numbers, but according to one scholar, "The death toll of innocent and guilty alike was well into the hundreds and the property loss far into the millions."[124] As directed, the offending population was removed and the counties desolated—almost nothing was left untouched. The report of a lieutenant colonel in the state militia confirmed that the strict nature of the order was being enforced and finding resonance within the ranks. Upon sweeping through Jackson County, he recommended sending "every citizen, man woman and child" out of the country and using or destroying all the forage that could be found. "Every farmer there, with one or two exceptions, favors and feeds the bushwhackers, and the quickest way to destroy them is to destroy their subsistence and remove their friends."[125] The widespread destruction carried out along the border resulted in the region quickly becoming known as The Burnt District, a term that would endure well after the war ended. In fact, the damage was so extensive, that the counties affected would be, in the words of James McPherson, "a wasteland for years."[126] Whereas previous policies under Pope and Halleck had exacted money from communities and targeted those suspected of being guerrillas for execution, Schofield took the extra step of actually forcing nearly 20,000 civilians from their homes and then burning their barns and property. It was an unprecedented move, and although several other punitive measures with similar characteristics were employed throughout the remainder of the war, none matched the scope and magnitude of Order No. 11.[127]

Despite lingering outrage from Quantrill's Raid on Lawrence, the destruction of the border counties was so complete that it raised eyebrows in the North to include those in Washington. Even Halleck, who had taken a hard line with the people of Missouri, expressed concern with the severity of the order. In his monthly report for November 1863, Halleck admitted that the "outlaws from civilized society" who practiced guerrilla warfare in Missouri and were aided by the population created an "extraordinary condition of affairs" that called for "the application of a prompt and severe remedy." The report included a word of caution, however, about Schofield's action in Missouri. "Such measures are within the recognized laws of war; they were adopted by Wellington in Portugal, and by the Russian armies in the campaign of 1812, but," Halleck warned, "they should be adopted only in case of overruling necessity." Citing these concerns, Halleck agreed with the suspension of Order No. 11, hoping that it would not be necessary to renew it.[128] The physical and psychological damage had been done, however, and the region was permanently scarred. The memory of Quantrill's Raid and the retaliatory Order No. 11 faded over time, eclipsed by the magnitude of events in the Eastern Theater. With the exception of those living in the border region between Kansas and Missouri, it became one of the most amazingly overlooked incidents of the Civil War and all of American History.

As destructive as it was, Schofield's order achieved little in bringing the guerrilla problem to an end in Missouri. The winter of 1863 saw the normal dip in bushwhacking, and any bands of irregulars forced out of the affected counties simply moved to the interior of the state.[129] In fact, the following year witnessed a marked increase in the level of violence throughout the state. For the remainder of the war, Union troops were besieged by the continued ambushes of guerrillas and their attacks on the railroads, and the Federals responded with more punitive measures on civilians. As before, most attempts to round up the guilty individuals failed, and the practice of exacting fines on the populace remained popular. The typical aggravation felt by Union officers and troops at their inability to pacify the region was evident in the words of one officer's report in late 1864: "The guerrillas thus far scatter and concentrate so as to elude our forces. Our movements . . . are discovered by the bushwhackers' friends and revealed from one to another. The citizens at home are our secret and most dangerous foes," he lamented, adding, "How shall these guilty people be brought to repentance and good works? And what punishment, short of extermination, is mete for their treachery and encouragement of a warfare more barbarous than that practiced by the savages of the plains and frontier?"[130] Bushwhacking raged throughout the state in the early months of 1865, until news of Lee's surrender at Appomattox arrived. And while the majority of guerrilla parties chose to lay down their weapons and return home, the defeat of the Confederacy failed to extinguish all violence and bushwhacking in Missouri.[131]

The Union army's effectiveness in Missouri during the war, particularly with the guerrilla problem, was poor at best. Militarily, the Union Army had been able to keep regular Confederate forces, such as those commanded by General Sterling Price, from gaining control of the state. Politically, the fragile Union state government avoided collapse and the state remained in the Union for the duration, despite widespread support for secession. At no time, however, was the army able to suppress the rampant guerrilla problem, despite the claims of numerous Union commanders to the contrary. The policies and measures aimed at civilians in response to bushwhacking did little to stem the steady stream of attacks on railroads, Union troops, and Union loyalists throughout the state. As John Pope described after the war, Union attempts to "save" Missouri from guerrilla warfare "fell to the ground."[132] Neely described the Union conduct in Missouri as an abject failure for an otherwise effective wartime Lincoln administration. "Missouri proved from start to finish to be a sorry blemish on the administration's record . . . it became a nightmare for American civil liberties."[133] It had also been nightmarish for those citizens caught in the middle of the conflict, for whom neutrality was not possible.

While acknowledging Missouri's problems, many historians have dismissed them as a chaotic anomaly, a sideshow with no link to the mainstream war. Mark Grimsley rightfully claimed that examples of punitive policies in Missouri, such as Order No. 11, were both "unusual" and "as harsh as anything the war would see." The most emphatic dismissal came from Neely, who claimed that the guerrilla warfare in Missouri "had little effect" on the conduct of the war.[134] Events in Missouri, however, did not happen in a military or political vacuum. Dismissals such as Neely's seem foolish when considering the words and *actions* of those who dealt with guerrillas in Missouri later in the war. Experiences and attitudes from Missouri, particularly in regard to Southern civilians, traveled with Union troops and leaders as they were sent to other theaters. They were not left behind. James McPherson made the apt observation that "most of the Union commanders who subsequently became famous as practitioners of total war spent part of their early Civil War careers in Missouri." McPherson also claimed that these leaders' experiences in the state "helped to predispose them" to severe treatment of Southerners. While McPherson made specific mention of Grant, Sherman, and Sheridan (all of whom will be discussed in subsequent chapters), historian Daniel Sutherland argued that General John Pope was "the key" to the Union's transition toward total war in 1862.[135] If so, his experiences with bushwhacking in Missouri were instrumental in shaping the policies he instituted when faced with the guerrilla problem in Virginia. Halleck's attempts to establish a legal basis for harsh antiguerrilla measures such as tax assessments and the summary execution of guerrillas not only led to the production of General Orders 100, but also influenced his attitudes toward similar situations throughout the South. Indeed, the sheer intensity of the guerrilla problem in Missouri was unique when compared with other theaters in the war, but the Union leadership's response to it mirrored those by other Union forces in other occupied states suffering through their own struggles with the hostile population.

As described by McPherson, the early problems with guerrillas in Missouri "began a pattern whereby events in that state set the pace for the transformation from a limited to total war, radiating eastward and southward."[136]

Not only would Union punitive policies and practices spread toward the East, but they would become more systematic in their destructiveness. Much more than just an isolated backwater of the war, Missouri served as the proving ground for the Union's newfound punitive approach. Had the guerrilla problem been contained to Missouri, then perhaps punitive war would have remained there as well. Unfortunately for the Union Army and, especially, the people of the South, such was not the case. As the blue-clad armies marched deeper into the heart of the Confederacy in 1862, the problem awaited them around every bend, behind every tree.

CHAPTER THREE

A Remedy for All Evils: Retaliatory Destruction on the Mississippi

*This trying guerrilla war-fare, phoenix-like in its character,
subdued, yet, day after day rising out of the ashes of its defeat
again to menace us, inflamed itself into alarming proportions . . .*
—Colonel George E. Currie, *Warfare along the Mississippi*

In early 1862, the Union and Confederate Armies participated in a series of campaigns aimed at controlling the contested border states of Tennessee, Kentucky, Mississippi, and Arkansas. Central to these campaigns were the waterways that transected the theater, such as the Tennessee, Cumberland, and of course, Mississippi Rivers. Unlike the armies fighting in the Eastern Theater, those in the West were often separated by hundreds of miles, making river networks and railroad lines crucial for transportation and resupply.

Many within the Union leadership viewed control of the Mississippi River as the key to military victory in the West. General Samuel Curtis emphasized the river's importance to General Henry W. Halleck in early 1862, claiming that Union control of it would be "disastrous to the enemy."[1] General William T. Sherman even toyed with the idea of devoting all Union military efforts in the West to capturing the Mississippi and completely ignoring the interior.[2]

In the summer of 1862, the Union forces in the West focused their efforts on the Lower Mississippi Valley and its main strategic artery, the Mississippi River. They would soon come to find they had more than the Confederate Army to worry about. With rifles and small artillery pieces, a hostile citizenry made life on the rivers as dangerous as possible for the Federal occupiers. Faced with several weeks, and sometimes months, between major battles, Union troops in the West often found themselves on extended occupation duty. During these periods, complacency turned to frustration and anxiety as rifle shots came unpredictably from the wooded riverbanks, and the bodies of Union troops who wandered off from camp were found increasingly often, frequently horribly mutilated. Soldiers of the Union's main conventional force in the West, the Army of the Tennessee, would find themselves constantly faced with the guerrilla problem as they conducted their campaigns.

Along the bends in the Mississippi and Tennessee Rivers, Union naval and land forces blasted away at Confederate strongpoints. First, the Union captured the Confederate position in Columbus, Kentucky, and then Major General Ulysses S. Grant captured Forts Henry and Donelson to open up the Tennessee River in mid-February 1862. The next push along the Mississippi was aimed at the Confederate defenses at Island Number 10, near New Madrid, Tennessee. After heavy bombardment from Union ironclads, the fort fell into Union hands on 7 April. Less than two months later, a Union flotilla pushed its way down to Memphis and captured the key commercial center. Simultaneously, at the southern tip of the Mississippi, Union Admiral David Farragut blasted his fleet past New Orleans, and 5,000 Federal troops under the command of Major General Benjamin F. Butler occupied the city on 1 May 1862. The Union had taken control of the northern and southern ends of the Lower Mississippi Valley.

Alarmed by the string of setbacks, and realizing that the South could not match the North's firepower on the river, Confederate Secretary of War James Seddon called upon his commanders in the Mississippi Valley to encourage the local population to take up arms.[3] Likewise, political and military leaders in Arkansas and Louisiana appealed to the people in their states to mount a violent resistance to the invaders. Louisiana governor Thomas Moore proclaimed, "Let all our river banks swarm with armed patriots, to teach the hated invader that the rifle will be his only welcome." Moore appealed to "experienced woodsmen . . . with their trusty rifles and shot-guns" and claimed that every man could "be a soldier to guard the approaches to his home."[4] Such calls, however, were hardly necessary. Guerrillas had already become active throughout the Lower Mississippi Valley, targeting the flow of Union traffic up and down the river. What bushwhackers in Missouri were doing to the railroads, those along the Mississippi were doing to the river. Their ambushes were unpredictable, difficult to defend against, and aggravating. Troop and supply transports became targets of frequent attacks from the thick brush lining the banks of the river. Small bands of local guerrillas or, less often, detachments of Confederate cavalry, peppered the passing steamers with everything from musketry to artillery. In western Tennessee and northern Arkansas, Union railroads and telegraph lines were targeted daily by both Confederate cavalry raiders and disorganized bands of bushwhackers. As soon as shots were fired, the perpetrators were gone, withdrawing into the thick woods and swamps along the river.

While not terribly damaging, these unprovoked attacks often resulted in soldier and civilian casualties and enraged the Union troops. Whether or not the attackers fit the description of guerrilla, bushwhacker, or partisan was not important to Union troops; such attacks were cowardly and unjustified in their eyes. According to one historian, "distinctions did not matter," and

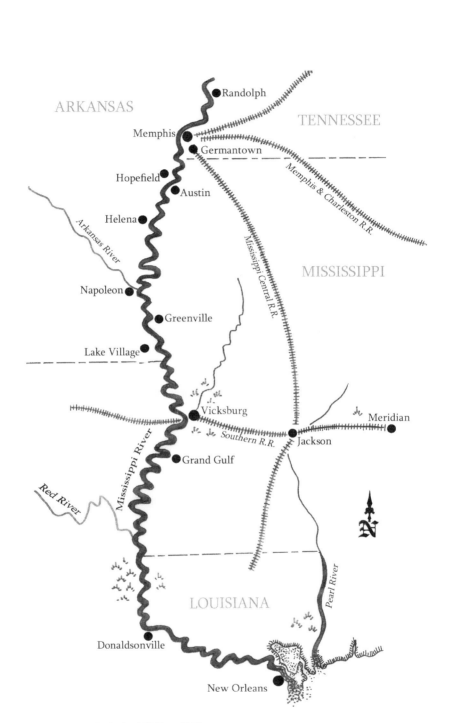

The Lower Mississippi Valley, 1862

Union soldiers "could not wait to get ashore and wreak their vengeance."[5] It did not take long for Union sailors and troops operating on the Mississippi to adopt the approach of collective responsibility, as had their counterparts in Missouri. From the spring of 1862 until the war's end the civilian population living close to the river caught the brunt of the Union's response.

It was here, in Tennessee, Mississippi, Arkansas, Alabama, and Louisiana, that Ulysses S. Grant, William T. Sherman, and their soldiers would grapple with the guerrilla problem and contemplate the necessity of taking the war to the Southern people. The frustration Grant and Sherman experienced brought the status of noncombatants into question and elicited a punitive response that would carry over into their storied campaigns of 1864. In the words of one scholar, the Union Army's antiguerrilla policies in the Lower Mississippi Valley "helped lay the groundwork for the greater hard war measures still to come."[6] Just as important, their soldiers reacted similarly to the guerrilla threat, demonstrating that punitive war had its roots from deep within the Union ranks.

An effective means of studying the Union response to the guerrilla threat in the Lower Mississippi is to first consider the changing attitudes of the Union leadership (Grant and Sherman in particular) and to then examine the events that occurred throughout the region in 1862 and 1863 that best illustrate the Union's increasing willingness to incorporate civilians and their property into the guerrilla problem. It is not surprising that the thoughts of Grant, Sherman, and other Union commanders were reflected in the punitive behavior of Union troops from Memphis to New Orleans. The most intriguing example of this fact, perhaps, was the Union Army's widespread practice of what one historian has called *retributive burning*, which was the destruction of property by fire in retaliation for perceived wrongful acts.[7] It would become the cornerstone of the Union's punitive war on the river.

In his controversial study of Sherman, *Merchant of Terror*, historian John Bennett Walters claimed that Sherman was "one of the first of the modern generals to revert to the idea of the use of military force against the civilian population of the enemy." Walters used the term "collective responsibility" to describe Sherman's practice of holding civilians responsible, and punishing them, for the "acts of those coming from outside the vicinity."[8] Benjamin F. Cooling used the term "collective punishment" to address the same practice.[9] Both authors agree, and rightfully so, that Sherman was not alone. Grant and other Union leaders shared his belief that Southern civilians as a whole were ultimately responsible for guerrilla activity. In fact, the concept of collective responsibility was in no way unique to the Union Army. Incidents throughout the war, such as the execution of Unionist guerrillas and their supporters by Confederate soldiers, were common and demonstrated that North and South shared similar attitudes on the matter.[10] The assessment programs initiated in Missouri by John Pope and Henry Halleck in 1861 were clear examples of collective responsibility in action from earlier in the war.

Historians commonly view Sherman and Grant, however, as the most significant agents in the Union's transition to a more punitive war (and some would even say total war).[11] Their campaigns in the East in 1864 and 1865 have garnered the most scholarly attention on this issue, but it was evident during their operations in the Mississippi Valley in 1862 and 1863 that both were willing to move past conciliation and get tough with the Southern people.

Many scholars have concluded that the bloody Battle of Shiloh in April 1862, in which more than 23,000 soldiers were killed or wounded, served as the tipping point for Grant.[12] Such arguments usually hinge on a single sentence in Grant's memoirs that he used to describe his reaction to the outcome of Shiloh: "I gave up all idea of saving the Union except by complete conquest."[13] The problem with this conclusion is that it does not explain how the staggering loss of life at Shiloh, a conventional battle, equated to severe measures against civilians in Grant's mind. Also, as Grimsley noted, Grant's postwar writing did not always match his "actual thinking" during the war.[14]

Other Grant scholars, such as Brooks D. Simpson, have rightly suggested that guerrillas, not Shiloh, ultimately convinced Grant to pursue a more severe prosecution of the war.[15] It was the infuriating nature of the guerrilla threat, rather than the determination of the Confederate Army, that best illustrated what Russell Weigley referred to as "the fierceness of Southern warmaking."[16] While bushwhacking provided Union troops with a certain justification for waging punitive war, losses on the conventional battlefield did not. This explanation, when compared with Grant's policies toward civilians in 1862 and 1863, makes the most sense. The forces of frustration and the mistrust of civilians, not a single bloody battle, gradually forced Grant's hard hand.

Before encountering the guerrilla problem in western Tennessee, Grant was a cautious believer in the possibilities for reconciliation. Even after the sanguinary shock of Shiloh, Grant predicted "easy sailing" for the Union.[17] Upon taking command of the District of West Tennessee two months later, his tone began to change. From his headquarters in Memphis, Grant received daily reports of guerrilla attacks on his supply lines as well as harassment from Confederate cavalry detachments under the command of General Nathan Bedford Forrest and Colonel John H. Morgan. These two cavalry chiefs conducted successful raids on Union supply and communication lines throughout the summer of 1862: Forrest in Tennessee and Morgan in Kentucky. Armies under Grant in western Tennessee and Major General Don

Carlos Buell further east found themselves immobilized, their railroads torn to pieces. The exploits of these Confederate raiders also galvanized Southern sympathy in the region, something the Northern Army sought to prevent.[18]

Recent scholarship has refrained from classifying Forrest and Morgan as guerrillas. For instance, Robert Mackey described their commands as "conventional cavalry with the specialized mission of raiding." Although these raiders sometimes disguised themselves in Union blue and incorporated surprise and ambush into their tactics, their organization and objectives largely matched those of the conventional forces, earning them the acknowledgment and approval of the Confederate high command. Nevertheless, Union soldiers and most of their leaders, with the notable exception of Buell, often considered Forrest and Morgan's irregular raiding to be the work of guerrillas.[19] The burned bridges and destroyed railroad tracks that they left behind were enough to lump Forrest and Morgan in with the other perpetrators of the guerrilla problem. In addition to their raiding operations, dispersed attacks by small groups of decentralized or independent bushwhackers plagued Union outposts throughout the region. "There is no telling when we are safe here," a young Union cavalryman stationed in western Tennessee wrote in September 1862, "The country is overrun with Guerrillas."[20]

Nobody felt the uneasiness caused by the persistent guerrilla threat more keenly than Grant. Right after taking command in Memphis in June 1862, he informed Halleck that he had insufficient cavalry forces to defend against such attacks and to protect the local population from guerrilla depredations.[21] The alternative solution to the problem was, as it had been in Missouri, to place pressure on the local civilians. On 3 July 1862, Grant issued General Orders No. 60, warning the people of Memphis that "Government collections" of personal property would be conducted in response to what Grant called "the system of Guerrilla warfare" that plagued the river north and south of the city. The order also warned that combatants not in uniform, when caught, would not be afforded the rights given to prisoners of war.[22] It was the same message Halleck had sent to the citizens of St. Louis seven months earlier: civilians were capable of stopping guerrilla attacks against Union men and materiel, and were therefore deserving of punishment if they failed to do so. Both Grant and Halleck would maintain this position on the subject for the remainder of the war.

As in Missouri, the threats of fines and confiscation of property failed to solve the guerrilla problem around Memphis, so Grant suggested a more aggressive solution. In a letter to Halleck on 28 July, he proposed expelling all Southern sympathizers from the Union lines and sending them south. "Many citizens who appear to be quiet non-combatants in the presence of our forces," Grant claimed, "avail themselves of every safe opportunity of depredating upon Union men and annoying our troops in small bodies." Therefore, as Grant argued, western Tennessee and the lower Mississippi Valley would be much more secure with such people gone.[23]

Halleck agreed wholeheartedly, and he authorized Grant to "clean out" the District of Western Tennessee and Northern Mississippi of all "active sympathizers." Using the same wording he had used in dealing with bridge-burners in Missouri, Halleck instructed Grant to handle all hostile citizens "without gloves" and to confiscate their property.[24] These communications between Halleck and Grant in late summer 1862 made it clear that the Union military leadership was rapidly becoming comfortable with the idea of including Southern civilians and their property in the war's hostilities. It would be months before similar sentiments would be officially expressed in Washington. While some might argue that Grant and Halleck's references to "active sympathizers" referred to only a small portion of the Southern citizenry, both generals seemed increasingly convinced that the majority of the population they faced were actively against them. Grant reiterated this point days later, when he claimed that the "whole state of Mississippi" appeared to be taking up arms for the Confederate cause.[25] Swarming guerrilla attacks around Corinth led one of Grant's subordinates to claim, "Every man in this State who has a gun is a guerrilla, and would shoot any of us down whenever he thought it safe to murder us without risking his own neck."[26] By the time Grant rose to command of the District of West Tennessee that included the Army of the Tennessee, Army of the Mississippi, and the Districts of Mississippi and Cairo, he and his officers had repeatedly expressed concern with the tricky nature of the guerrilla problem and campaigned for harsher measures to address it. "If the enemy, with his regularly-organized forces, attack us I do not propose to punish non-combatant citizens for it," Grant claimed, "but these guerrillas receive support and countenance from this class of citizens, and by their acts will bring punishment upon them."[27] In Grant's view, wherever there were guerrillas, there really were no innocents.

The same was true of Sherman. Like his commander, Sherman saw non-combatants as an integral part of the guerrilla problem. As such, they heavily influenced his perception of military necessity and the boundaries of war. Historian Charles Royster concluded that the pervasive guerrilla activity around Memphis in 1862 was directly responsible for Sherman's "increased severity" toward the Southern people. A few Sherman biographers have agreed with Royster, one stating that the "lawless activity" of armed resistance against Sherman's troops in and around Memphis made him seek retribution on the people. In his book, *The American Civil War and the Origins of Modern Warfare*, Edward Hagerman agreed that Confederate guerrillas played a major role in what he described as Sherman's ideological switch "from conciliation to terror." The most substantial argument linking guerrillas and Sherman's changing attitudes in the war to date was made by historian Buck T. Foster, who concluded that "his dealings with guerrillas . . . hardened his resolve toward nonbelligerents."[28] It is easier to arrive at this conclusion for Sherman than it is for Grant, primarily because of Sherman's frequent mention of the subject in correspondence and the fiery, captivating language he often used to describe his plans for the people of the South.

But language can be deceiving. Much has been written about the historical attention given to Sherman's and Grant's rhetoric during the war. Several historians have made the valid point that too much emphasis has often been placed on what these leaders said, rather than what they did. Mark Neely has accused scholars of being overtaken and fooled by Sherman's dramatic prose, and as a result failing to see "the substance" of his campaigns. As for Grant, Neely claimed that too many historians have taken for gospel that which the general said only "in temporary anger and frustration."[29] Much of this is indisputable. Sherman's and Grant's most extreme comments about waging war were, indeed, hyperbolic. A classic example was Sherman's claim in 1862 that he would "slay millions" to secure control of the Mississippi. Of course, Sherman never did, nor did he truly intend to.[30]

It would be a mistake, however, to dismiss Sherman's and Grant's frequent expressions of frustration with the hostile population as meaningless. While their words may have been extreme at times, Sherman and Grant did, in fact, take up punitive measures against civilians. Perhaps more significant is the fact that their soldiers often shared their frustrations and acted on them as well. When faced with the substantial guerrilla problem that gripped the Mississippi Valley, Grant's tough talk and Sherman's "terrible words," as Royster called them, were usually matched with terrible deeds.[31] The citizens living along the Mississippi River would come to find out that Grant, Sherman, and their soldiers were not all talk. They were committed to making the war hard on them.

The lower ranks were just as susceptible to frustrations with the guerrilla problem as were their commanding officers, and often they were the primary agents in what Grimsley referred to as an "upward spiral of violence" in which soldiers took it upon themselves to retaliate against civilian communities for guerrilla attacks.[32] Orders for restraint from their officers were often seen as unfair or naïve, and angry soldiers would ignore them. The practice of having Union troops guard civilian property against pillaging from their comrades became increasingly maligned. This type of powerful frustration was expressed in the words of one Illinois soldier who dealt, almost daily, with guerrilla harassment in northern Arkansas in early August 1862. "These people, safe in our conciliatory principles, talk their seceshism as boldly as they do in Richmond . . . I'd rather see the whole country red with blood, and ruined together than have [Southerners] conquer, or successfully resist the power of the North," he wrote; "I hate them now, as they hate us."[33] Indeed, the hostility the Southern people showed to their occupiers produced bitter resentment. In his recent study of the Army of the Tennessee, historian Steven Woodworth emphasized this point. "More than the staunch Confederate fighting at Shiloh or at the eastern battles that summer," he claimed, "what led Union men to reevaluate their treatment of white Southerners was the persistent bitter refusal of Southern white civilians to be conciliated by any means whatsoever."[34] This refusal, especially when combined with violent resistance, created a powerful provocation that was impossible for many on the Union side to ignore.

The most telling indicators of an emerging punitive war were provided by actions, not thoughts or words. It is what the Union military did, rather than what its leaders and soldiers said, that best illustrates the effect the guerrilla problem was having in the Mississippi Valley and the surrounding states. A series of events in August and September 1862 highlighted the heavy-handed approach Federal forces were increasingly adopting to deal with civilian communities along the river. They also solidified retaliatory burnings as the preferred method for dealing with the problem.

Few incidents in the Western Theater displayed the powerful influence that the guerrilla threat had upon Union soldiers better than the killing of Colonel Robert L. McCook of the Ninth Ohio Volunteers on 6 August 1862. The regiment had spent the first year of the war scouring the Kanawha Valley in Western Virginia for Confederate forces, often tangling with guerrillas in the difficult mountain passes that cut through the region. As a result, they had taken early to practicing severe measures against civilian communities. Later, in guerrilla-infested northern Alabama, the Ninth Ohio continued what one historian called their "career of mayhem" by participating in the destruction of Huntsville in retaliation for guerrilla attacks.[35] By the time the regiment, made up predominantly of German immigrants, began moving north toward Tennessee in late July 1862, they were true believers in punitive war—a powder keg waiting to explode.

On 5 August, as the regiment marched northeast from the town of Hazel Green toward the Tennessee border, its lead element was ambushed by a group of armed men led by a local partisan chief named Frank Gurley. One Union soldier classified Gurley's attackers as "a band of outlaws, or guerrillas, in the correct sense of that term, since the band was no part of the naval or land forces of the confederacy."[36] The unit's commander, Colonel Robert L. McCook, who had been injured in a previous fight, was riding in an ambulance ahead of the column when the attack occurred. The guerrillas swarmed the ambulance, shot McCook as he lay in the back, and burned three other transport carriages. Before the remainder of McCook's brigade could come to his aid, the guerrillas retreated into the woods, leaving McCook mortally wounded. He died the following day.

Upon learning of the attack, McCook's men immediately went on a punitive spree, ripping into the closest village and burning at will. The regiment was "very much enraged," Major General George H. Thomas reported, and claimed that it "burned and destroyed some four or five farm-houses."[37] John Beatty, an officer with the Third Ohio Infantry, heard of the incident and wrote about it later. "When the dutchmen of [McCook's] old regiment learned of the unfortunate occurrence, they became uncontrollable," he claimed, "and [they] destroyed the buildings and property of five plantations near the scene."[38] Eyewitness accounts from soldiers involved, however, mention even greater destruction. According to one member of the regiment, "As a revenge," the regiment burned "every house within a radius of two miles on each side of the road, and slaughtered all the stock to be found," adding, "several suspicious-looking characters had given up their lives also." Infantryman Amos Fleagle claimed that a number of the "assassins" were "hung on the spot," while "many more were taken and summarily delt [sic] with." The house of a local Baptist minister was burned because it was believed that the family cheered the guerrillas as they rode by. Union soldier Alva Griest described the aftermath by writing, "The destruction is complete, as but one house is left standing." To a reporter from *Harper's Weekly*, it was a just punishment. "Retribution—terrible retribution—is being dealt by the Ninth Ohio," he wrote. "With fire, and sword, and bayonet the scene of the foul assassination was reduced to a state of desolation from which it will not recover."[39]

As usual, Federal cavalry attempts at searching the surrounding area for the guilty guerrillas failed, leaving private homes and barns as the only accessible target for retribution. In the words of the unit historian, the "revenge taken by the regiment on the country around may have been severe, but in strict accordance with the usages of war," adding that "the citizens were in accord with the acts of the guerrilla band."[40] But the justifiability of the acts was certainly questionable. At the time, the Lieber Code had yet to be published, but once it was, it did not authorize the indiscriminate burning of property, nor burning for the sake of revenge. The code called for the cautious use of retaliation, and only after a thorough investigation into the cause of the initial offense. Even Halleck's existing *International Law and Laws of War* prohibited "barbarous or cruel" retaliation of any kind against civilians.[41] The Ninth Ohio's devastation of the town could be interpreted as barbarous or cruel, especially if the claim of the immediate executions of "suspicious-looking characters" is true. The Ohioans, however, did not see it as such. More important than their reasoning, however, was the level of agency they displayed in acting on their own. The punitive stroke was initiated and carried out by the soldiers themselves. An entire town was burned and those suspected of aiding in the attack were likely shot or hanged, all without orders from the officer ranks. Although some might view this as a predictable, if not expected, occurrence in a civil war, it certainly raises questions about the level of control that Union policy makers held over their armies in the field. If nothing else, the incident served as a potent reminder that the soldiers were human, driven by passion, fear, and anger. They were cognizant of the rules and regulations that governed the war they were fighting, but they were also capable of disregarding them when driven to do so.

The harsh nature of the Ninth Ohio's retaliation was enough to startle some members of the Union leadership and resulted in a series of orders being issued to warn against repeated destruction. A day after McCook's death, Major General Thomas issued a general order that announced McCook's passing and called upon the soldiers in his division to show restraint. "Whilst we deplore his loss," the order read, "let us be steady in our efforts to maintain such discipline as will insure to our arms a just retribution upon the dastardly foe who could take advantage of his defenseless condition."[42] Thomas's appeal was an attempt to quell the mob mentality within the ranks, but it also was a clear indicator that what the Ninth had done was well beyond the boundaries of "just retribution." In a similar case two days later, a Union cavalry detachment was sent out to search the surrounding area for those responsible for McCook's killing, but it was warned to execute the order "without permitting plunder or outrages of any kind." In addition, Major General Don Carlos Buell, commander of the Army of the Cumberland and a staunch advocate of conciliation, demanded that the "strictest injunctions" be placed on Union cavalrymen involved in hunting for guerrillas, and that "only suspicious or notoriously disloyal and hostile persons" were to be apprehended.[43] At least in Buell's case, separating the "hostile" from the rest of the population was still important. As seen in Missouri, however, the guerrilla problem made it easy for Buell's junior officers and soldiers to view the entire surrounding population as hostile. Just a day after Buell's cautionary order, one of his subordinates reported a guerrilla attack near Reynolds, Tennessee, and blamed the wealthy citizenry for aiding the attackers. Without elaborating, the Union officer claimed to have taken the "most vigorous and determined measures" against the locals.[44]

The Ninth Ohio's retaliation for the murder of Colonel McCook was a case of vengeful frustration gone unchecked. In this case, common soldiers rather than their commanders initiated the retaliatory burning of civilian homes and, quite possibly, random executions of noncombatants. Despite Buell's conciliatory leanings, his soldiers quickly took to punishing civilians for guerrilla depredations, and his junior officers did little to stand in their way. It was a perfect example of what historian Gerald Linderman identified as guerrilla warfare's ability to rapidly intensify "soldier-civilian hostility."[45] The actions of the Ninth Ohio also demonstrated the willingness of Union soldiers to respond to their frustration and rage, and not just the orders of those positioned above them. Then and for the remainder of the war, when troops resorted to destruction it was not always (and sometimes not at all) directed by the Union leadership. The guerrilla problem was creating a climate that threatened the good order and discipline so important to the army that first marched south the previous year. Revenge became a powerful motivator and tore at the shroud of restraint that officers tried to hold over their men. This was seen in the words of infantryman Hamlin Coe, who recalled in his diary the brutal killing of one of his comrades at the hands of Confederate irregulars in Central Tennessee. "He was wounded by the first fire and captured by the Bushwackers, who, to torture their captive, shot him seven times before he expired," he noted. "The affray has created a spirit of revenge among the boys, and they gone out in force to avenge the death of their comrade or lay waste the country."[46] The operations of the Confederate Army, the staggering losses on the battlefields of Shiloh or Antietam, or even the venomous words spat at them by defiant Southern women could not evoke the same type of vindictive rage in Union troops that the guerrilla problem did. It was as if the guerrillas and bushwhackers were steadily prodding at a coiled snake, one whose retaliatory strike could not be stopped even by its master.

Punitive war, of course, did not always generate from a spontaneous groundswell in the ranks. It often initiated from the top as well. An early example of this was seen in May 1862 when a train carrying Union soldiers was fired upon as it passed by the small town of Paint Rock, on the northern edge of Alabama. Immediately, a column of Union troops returned to the village. The commander of the detachment later described what happened next:

> Calling the citizens together, I said to them that this bushwhacking must cease. The Federal troops had tolerated it already too long. Hereafter every time the telegraph wire was cut we would burn a house; every time a train was fired upon we should hang a man; and we would continue to do this until every house was burned and every man hanged between Decatur and Bridgeport. If they wanted to fight they should enter the army, meet us like honorable men, and not, assassin-like, fire at us from the woods and run. We propose to hold the citizens responsible for these cowardly assaults, and if they did not drive these bushwhackers from amongst them, we

should make them more uncomfortable than they would be in hell. I then set fire to the town, took three citizens with me, returned to the train, and proceeded to Huntsville.[47]

Like so many cases that would follow, this was an example of harsh words followed with harsh action. And for many in the Union ranks, it was high time that such measures were taken. As the officer responsible noted, "General Mitchell is well pleased with my action in the Paint Rock matter. The burning of the town has created a sensation, and is spoken of approvingly by the officers and enthusiastically by the men." He went on to add, "It is the inauguration of the true policy, and the only one that will preserve us from constant annoyance."[48] This served as further evidence that "the true policy" was being inaugurated by leaders on the ground, with or without the approval of Washington. In essence, the officers and soldiers in blue were claiming it as their war to wage, and to wage in the manner that they saw fit.

Although innumerable similar incidents occurred throughout the outer reaches of the Mississippi Valley, when it came to the broad application of punitive war, no area was more affected than the banks of the mighty river itself. The guerrilla problem on the Mississippi was so virulent that by war's end a vast stretch of its shoreline lay charred and dotted with chimneys surrounded by ash. From New Orleans all the way up to Memphis, those responsible for carrying out the Union campaign for control of the river were constantly plagued by the problem. Not only did it force the Union to discover new tactics in riverine operations, but it spelled doom for the scores of lavish plantations overlooking the river as well. Forever overshadowed by the fight for Vicksburg, the Union experience on the Mississippi from 1862 to 1864 became one of the most brutal and inglorious chapters of the war.

Major General Benjamin F. Butler became infamous throughout the South for his strict policies while in command of troops occupying New Orleans in the summer of 1862. Butler ordered the execution of a New Orleans citizen, William B. Mumford, for ripping down a U.S. flag, and his threat to arrest women who were outspoken in their disloyalty to the Union earned him the nickname "The Beast." His approach toward southern guerrillas and their supporters was just as punitive as any policy he initiated against the citizens of New Orleans. Immediately after taking command in New Orleans, Butler directed one of his officers to "punish with the last severity" any guerrillas who attacked Union troops and to "burn the property of every guerrilla." Although Butler was not yet calling for the destruction of civilian property, he also did not demand proof in identifying suspected guerrillas. The following month, in a letter to Secretary of War Edwin M. Stanton, Butler suggested a radical remedy:

> We are threatened . . . with a guerrilla war, which is claimed will be interminable. I take leave to suggest that it can be terminated in a few days. A reward offered of $1,000 for each guerrilla's head and freedom to the negro who should bring it in would bring that uncivilized system of warfare to a sudden termination by an equally uncivilized remedy—"fire set to fight fire."[49]

While Butler's statement was more fiery rhetoric than actionable policy, it made clear his intentions to push the limits of "civilized warfare" when dealing with the guerrilla problem. Although Butler's proposal was never carried out, its ruthless flavor provided a prelude for his subsequent policies concerning guerrillas and their supporters. Much to the relief of the people of New Orleans, the unpopular Union commander's command of the city did not last the remainder of the year.

It did not take long for attacks on Union transports on the Mississippi to elicit a punitive response. In late May 1862, the Federal gunboat *Kineo* attacked the town of Grand Gulf, located 30 miles below Vicksburg. Having learned that there were a number of artillery positions in the woods surrounding the town that had fired upon several Union boats in previous days, the commander of the *Kineo* ordered his guns to open up on the town and the woods beyond. The official report of the engagement, made by Brigadier General Thomas Williams, described a mild action involving "several shot and shell" fired into the town followed by a short skirmish that involved "a few shots only" between Wisconsin troops and fleeing Confederates.[50] Interestingly enough, an account of the affair at Grand Gulf given by a Wisconsin soldier describes a more destructive result, with the intent of punishing the town for allowing the attacks on the ships. In his diary, Charles O'Neil claimed that the people of Grand Gulf were warned days before to prevent further attacks or suffer the consequences. When the attacks continued, O'Neil detailed the extensive shelling of both the town and the woods beyond that took place. His account continued on to describe how boats were dispatched to shore and Union troops "fired the town in several places." O'Neil's last entry has the *Kineo* steaming away from Grand Gulf "leaving the town in flames."[51] Not surprisingly, O'Neil did not make specific mention of casualties from the shelling or the number of homes that were destroyed. Considering the fact that the *Kineo* departed the scene within an hour of the commencement of the burning, it is reasonable to assume that neither O'Neil nor any of his shipmates had time enough to gather an accurate assessment of the damage done to Grand Gulf. It is also entirely possible that O'Neil, like many other eyewitnesses to war, chose to not concern himself with such details. Either way, O'Neil's description of what happened at Grand Gulf offers a distinctly different view than that provided by General Williams's report, which makes no mention of the burning of the town. Other sources tend to support O'Neil's claims. Upon seeing what was left of Grand Gulf days later, a soldier from the Nineteenth Iowa Infantry noted in his diary that the town was "entirely destroyed."[52] Very little remained to suggest that it once existed. It was a scene that would soon become familiar to Union soldiers traveling up and down the Mississippi. Abandoned plantations, overgrown barns, and deserted homes became commonplace along the shoreline. Along with these sights came increasing evidence of burning and destruction.

As seen at Grand Gulf, the U.S. Navy began to take an active role in retaliating for guerrilla attacks along the river. The approach taken, not surprisingly, was similar to that taken by the Army. Admiral David Farragut, a long-time veteran of the navy, was the most notable of the U.S. naval commanders to directly punish an entire community for the acts of a few. Throughout the summer, Farragut's steamers were continuously fired upon by small bands of guerrillas who, in the words of one scholar, took "pot-shots" at the Union vessels and then retreated into the thick swamps along the riverbanks.[53] After a number of guerrilla attacks came from the vicinity of Donaldsonville, Farragut issued a warning to the local citizens in which he threatened to retaliate if the attacks continued. Continue they did, and Farragut quickly made good on his warning. On 9 August the U.S. gunboats *Hartford* and *Brooklyn* pulled up alongside Donaldsonville and lobbed artillery shells into the town. Marines then launched a number of boats to the shore and made their way through the town's wharf, setting fires that eventually engulfed the majority of the buildings in town. At the end of the day, almost all of Donaldsonville was in ruins.[54]

As seen with Grand Gulf, the accounts of what happened at Donaldsonville vary. Farragut's biographers seem to downplay the extent of the damage. One claims that Union ships fired "a few rounds into the town" and that the burning was confined to hotels, warehouses, and a particular guerrilla leader's house. Another states that the shelling lasted only for "a brief period."[55] However, letters and diary entries of Federal sailors and soldiers involved in the attack tell of a more destructive treatment of Donaldsonville. One sailor aboard the USS *Hartford* described how "after bombarding the little village for an hour" the marines "burned the place to the ground." In another account, a young Union officer wrote, "Three gunboats came up the river and laid two-thirds of the town in ashes. But the houses left standing might well have been burned, for the soldiers Saturday and Sunday morning made wasteful havoc with the furniture and windows of those that were standing."[56] It does not appear that any specific buildings were targeted by Farragut's artillery. For the most part, the shelling was indiscriminate. Such firsthand accounts seem to undercut the attempts of Farragut's biographers to dismiss the shelling of Donaldsonville as a short, insignificant volley.

One particular casualty of the bombardment was the convent that housed the Sisters of Charity, whose Mother Superior wrote to Butler in New Orleans, complaining about the damage. Butler responded kindly, but made no apologies for Farragut's action. "The destruction of that town [Donaldsonville] became a necessity," Butler explained. "The inhabitants harbored a gang of cowardly guerrillas, who committed every atrocity." He went on to state, "I am only sorry that the righteous punishment meted out to them in this instance . . . fell quite as heavily upon the innocent and unoffending as upon the guilty."[57] In essence, Butler affirmed the notion that guerrilla warfare justified bringing the war to the people, and even those who were not actively involved with it might have to suffer as a result. Farragut, too, distanced himself from any wrongdoing when he claimed that the guerrillas alone were responsible for any retaliatory fire they provoked, and that Union forces would not be held responsible for the "death of the innocent."[58] The destruction of both Grand Gulf and Donaldsonville demonstrated that the policy of collective responsibility was not isolated to Missouri. Butler and Farragut were just as willing as Pope and Halleck to hold the local citizens accountable, and to punish them, for guerrilla attacks.

Some soldiers from the lower ranks questioned the heavy-handed nature of the Union policy in and around New Orleans. While guerrilla attacks were indeed frustrating, in the eyes of many, they did not justify the looting and burning of an entire town. In a report to his commander, U.S. naval lieutenant F. A. Roe from the gunboat *Katahdin* protested the "unsoldierly and ungallant, not to say disgraceful" razing of Donaldsonville. "I cannot further prostitute the dignity of my profession, as I conceive I have done today," Roe wrote. "It is disgraceful and humiliating to me to be ordered on guard duty of soldiers employed in pillaging ladies' dresses and petticoats." His protest, however, met with contempt from Butler. Though Butler admitted that pointless pillaging was inexcusable, so too was Roe's "improper, bombastic, and ridiculous rhodomontade of a sub-lieutenant of the Navy," he claimed.[59] Nevertheless, the disdain expressed by the young officer for the "disgraceful" conduct of the vengeful troops would soon become a common refrain amongst some in the Union ranks who found the harsh reality of punitive war at odds with their interpretation of the limits of warfare and the treatment of civilians.

Unlike the often-mentioned hard war measures taken by Sherman and Grant, the burning of Donaldsonville is absent from almost every study of Union war policy, despite its being a clear case of punitive war measures on the part of the Union.[60] A possible reason for this is the fact that the incident challenges the notion that Union armies generally maintained a temperate, guarded policy toward civilians until later in the war. Or perhaps historians have dismissed Donaldsonville as an uncharacteristic, isolated incident that amounted to little in the overall operational scheme of the war. The fact is, however, that what happened at Donaldsonville would be one of the first clear-cut examples of what would become the pattern of retaliatory behavior for Union forces operating on the Mississippi River. Had guerrilla activity like that which provoked Farragut's retaliatory strike been uncommon, perhaps Donaldsonville would truly have been an exception and unworthy of historical note. The opposite was true, however. The guerrilla problem on the Mississippi was rampant in 1862 and 1863 and many more towns and villages on the river's banks would share Donaldsonville's fate.

There is, perhaps, no period more illustrative of the Union's gradual movement toward punitive war than William T. Sherman's command of the forces at Memphis from July to December 1862. It was during his time as the military governor in Memphis that Sherman became most familiar with the guerrilla problem, from which grew his vision of a war against the Southern people. Like most Union commanders, Sherman refused to accept the actions of "ununiformed bands" of guerrillas as legitimate warfare. Soon after taking command at Memphis, Sherman wrote about the problem posed by guerrillas who would "shoot our men if they go outside our Lines, & fire on steamboats as they pass up & down the River." To him, such acts automatically justified the harshest of countermeasures.[61]

When Confederate Major General Thomas C. Hindman complained to Union authorities about the killing of captured partisans who he claimed were legitimate combatants, Sherman's response was quick and defiant. Although Sherman acknowledged "the well established rights of war to parties in uniform," he refused to extend the same protection to those who, in the guise of noncombatants, ambushed unsuspecting troops or civilians. In a telling passage, Sherman asserted his position that such actions must result in "the people" feeling "the consequence of their individual acts," and not just the offenders themselves. It had not taken long for Sherman to see *the people* as part and parcel of the guerrilla problem. He communicated this point to Secretary of the Treasury Salmon P. Chase, claiming, "All in the South *are* enemies of the North; and not only are they unfriendly, but all who can procure arms now bear them as organized regiments, or as guerrillas."[62]

Some historians have been quick to defend Sherman to a certain degree, pointing to a number of orders he made calling for restraint toward civilians. One such example happened on 7 July 1862, when Sherman's headquarters issued Order No. 49, prohibiting the "robbery and pillage" of civilian property. Sherman's order warned his soldiers that if the practice continued the

Major General
William T.
Sherman. The
Civil War's most
famous practitioner
of punitive war,
Sherman was
strongly influenced
by the guerrilla
problem on the
Mississippi River
in 1862. (Library of
Congress)

locals might "rise up and shoot us like dogs and beast."[63] On another occasion, when a number of Union troops were caught stealing mules from
civilian farms, Sherman chastised them for it. On 10 July he directed subordinates to cut down on the "petty thieving and pillaging," claiming it caused
"infinite harm" to their cause.[64] Therefore, as late as July 1862, it appears
that Sherman was not willing to endorse pointless or wanton pillaging, at
least not openly.

His restraint with the guerrilla problem, however, was limited. For the
remainder of the war, he often chose to ignore the destructiveness of his soldiers, allowing them to punish Southern communities for guerrilla attacks. As
historians such as Joseph Glatthaar have observed, Sherman rarely objected
when his men destroyed civilian property in response to bushwhacking.[65] Just
ten days after Order 49 was issued, troops from one of Sherman's regiments
marched into the small hamlet of Germantown, Tennessee, and looted and
razed all the town's stores and mills. They did so in retaliation for a guerrilla attack the day before in which two of their comrades were hanged from
trees near the town. According to a Union soldier who witnessed the looting

of Germantown, all the officers who were present, including Sherman, "did not interfere at all" with the destruction. The soldier added, "They evidently thought [the town] deserved cleaning out." A second soldier described how his comrades "took everything they wanted, and a good deal more" from the town, adding that "the officers didn't try to prevent it."[66] The permitted looting of Germantown proved that Sherman's demand for restraint from his soldiers was not absolute when enemy guerrillas were involved. The same was true for soldiers under his command. After witnessing guerrilla attacks on wagon trains and the killing of Unionists in the area, one soldier remarked, "I think we have patted the Secesh on the head hoping to conciliate them long enough." Captain William McCarty of the Seventy-Eighth Ohio Volunteer Infantry agreed. "It seems hard to destroy property wantingly [sic] or distress women and children," he wrote, "but the people of the South . . . have permitted this rebellion to come upon them by their own wickedness and imbecility and they will have to be humbled and made to cry aloud." McCarty was pleased to know that his superiors shared his disdain for the naïve notion of conciliation. In a letter home, he described how his commanding general, Brigadier General John A. Logan, looked on "rather approvingly" as the Union troops burned fences, barns, and houses.[67]

Within weeks of arriving in Memphis, Sherman made it clear to the local population that the guerrilla problem included them, and that they would answer for continued attacks on the river. In an open letter printed in the Memphis newspapers, Sherman issued a strict warning:

> The Guerillas are not Uniformed, they can if pursued disburse and mix up with the people and thereby elude pursuit, but like a few notorious men they involve the whole crowd in the punishment due the few.
>
>   If an officer is in pursuit he would be perfectly justified in retaliating on the farmers among whom they mingle. It is not our wish or policy to destroy the farmers or their farms, but of course there must be a remedy for all Evils, if the farmers of a neighborhood encourage or even permit in their midst a set of Guerrillas they cannot expect to escape the necessary consequences. It will not do for them to plead simple personal ignorance [of] . . . acts of waste and destruction which will inevitably lead to the entire devastation of the country where the Guerrillas operate.[68]

Sherman would not have to wait long to make good on his threat of "necessary consequences." For weeks, Union vessels transporting troops and supplies to Memphis had come under attack from guerrillas on the riverbanks. Often, one or two individuals would hail the steamer as it passed by, in an attempt to lure it closer to the banks where other guerrillas in hiding would open up with muskets or artillery. On 23 September the southbound Union packet steamer *Eugene* was fired into by guerrillas near the small town of Randolph, 25 miles north of Memphis. Sherman immediately ordered the Forty-Sixth Ohio Infantry Regiment, commanded by Colonel Charles C. Walcutt, to retaliate.

"The interest and well-being of the country demands that all such attacks should be followed by a punishment that will tend to prevent a repetition," he explained. Although Sherman indicated that the guerrillas involved in the attack were actually from the area of Loosahatchie some 10 miles away, he directed Walcutt to burn Randolph instead, which was the actual site of the attack on the *Eugene*. "You will destroy the place," the general ordered, "let the place feel that all such acts of cowardly firing upon boats filled with women and children and merchandise must be severely punished."[69]

Walcutt and his troops did as they were directed. The detachment quickly moved up the river on boats, landed just to the south of Randolph, and moved into the town. Walcutt's men then went to work, torching the occupied and vacated houses alike. The destruction was carried out systematically, as Sherman had directed. In his report to Grant two days later, Sherman remarked, "The regiment has returned and Randolph is gone." Confident that Grant shared his views on the growing need for punitive war, Sherman suggested that more towns share Randolph's fate if the guerrilla problem persisted.[70]

Of all of Sherman's actions while in command at Memphis, the destruction of Randolph remains the most controversial, albeit somewhat unknown. Historian John Bennett Walters used the burning of Randolph as an example of Sherman's willingness to cast aside all restraint in favor of bringing war home to the people of the South. Conversely, Mark Grimsley depicted the order as an act of military pragmatism rather than a complete departure from limited war. "The most striking feature was its almost surgical precision," Grimsley wrote. "The order reflected a sound grasp of the principles of military reprisal." While admitting that the burning of Randolph was severe, Grimsley claimed that Sherman's order was a measured response and not uncommon to other measures being taken throughout the South.[71] The truth lies somewhere in between. While Sherman did include a number of restrictions in his order limiting what Walcutt's troops could do, he also saw fit to punish a town that, as far as he knew, was likely not the home of the guerrillas responsible for the attack on the *Eugene*. The destruction of Randolph was significant not just because Sherman was holding civilians responsible for guerrilla attacks, but also because, as Grimsley put it, "his retaliatory blow would almost certainly land on the innocent," and Sherman knew it. There was hardly anything surgical about the selection of the town and nothing precise about its burning in entirety. The issue of guilt or innocence was irrelevant in Sherman's mind; everyone had to pay. In his report on the destruction of Randolph, Sherman admitted that the town "was of no importance" and yet because Sherman was angry, and because it was an easy target, the town was destroyed.[72] Of course, this was not the first such case, as seen with the previous actions against Grand Gulf and Donaldsonville further down the river that summer. For Sherman, however, the burning of Randolph was the opening act of what would become a storied career of waging punitive war.

Despite this fiery message sent by Walcutt and his troops on 25 August, the destruction of Randolph failed to prevent further guerrilla attacks on Union steamers. When the *Gladiator* and *Catahoula* were fired upon in mid-October, Sherman immediately ordered Walcutt's regiment to exact punishment once again. This time, the Forty-Sixth Ohio was ordered to destroy "all houses, farms, and cornfields" along a 15-mile stretch of the river between Elm Grove and Hopefield, Arkansas. The purpose of the order, Sherman explained, was to let it be known that "certain destruction" of the surrounding country would result from more attacks. As before, Walcutt's detachment carried out the order in full, burning a number of houses where "evidence of complicity with guerrillas" was reported.[73] In his report to Grant, Sherman acknowledged that his retaliation would "sometimes fall on the wrong head" but claimed it was the only feasible answer for the guerrilla problem. "It would be folly," he told Grant, "to send parties of infantry to chase these wanton guerrillas."[74] He made the same case to the Union commander in Helena, Arkansas. "To reach the rightful parties will be an impossibility," Sherman claimed, "and we must do something, even if every farm and plantation on the river is destroyed."[75] Although Sherman never went that far, it was becoming increasingly clear that he cared little about the guilt or innocence of noncombatants.

As an additional measure against those assumed to be supporting guerrillas, Sherman began to expel citizens from Memphis. Special Order No. 254 decreed that ten secessionist families would be evicted from the city for every Union boat fired upon by guerrillas. True to his word, Sherman forced a number of civilians to leave the city after the *Continental* and *J. H. Dickey* steamers were fired upon.[76] Further evictions, however, were limited and never came close to the massive depopulation enforced by Schofield's men in Missouri. Nevertheless, Sherman was crystal clear with the people of Memphis on his intentions should the guerrilla problem continue. In a letter to a resident penned on 6 November 1862, Sherman offered what was perhaps his most cogent explanation of the guerrilla problem and what it meant for the people of the South:

Brigadier General Charles C. Walcutt, Sherman's torch man. Walcutt commanded the burning of Randolph and extensive stretches along the Mississippi in the fall of 1862. (Library of Congress)

Mrs. VALERIA HURLBUT, *Memphis:*

DEAR MADAM,

Your letter of October—was duly received. I did not answer it at that time, as I had already instructed Colonel Anthony, provost-marshal, to suspend the execution of the order expelling certain families from Memphis, for fifteen days, to enable them to confer with the Confederate authorities upon the cause of that order, viz, the firing from ambush on our boats carrying passengers and merchandise by bands of guerrillas in the service of our enemies.

In war it is impossible to hunt up the actual perpetrators of a crime. Those who are banded together in any cause are held responsible for all the acts of their associates . . . These men have, as you know, fired on steamboats navigating the Mississippi River, taking the lives and endangering the safety of peaceful citizens who travel in an accustomed way, in no wise [*sic*] engaged in the operations of war. We regard this as inhuman and barbarous, and if the Confederate authorities do not disavow them, it amounts to a sanction and encouragement of the practice.

We must stop this, and no measures would be too severe. The absolute destruction of Memphis, New Orleans, and every city, town, and hamlet of the South would not be too severe a punishment to a people for attempting to interfere with the navigation of the Mississippi . . . Misplaced kindness to these guerrillas, their families, and adherents is cruelty to our people.

I have given them time to disavow the attack on the *Gladiator*; they have not done it. They therefore approve, and I say not only shall the families go away, but all the Confederate allies and adherents shall *feel the power of an indignant Government.*

I am, &
W. T. Sherman,
Major General[77]

To claim that Sherman embarked on a ruthless campaign of terrorism, as John Bennett Walters famously did in 1973, is to engage in the same sort of hyperbole that historians have commonly attributed to the general himself.[78] Sherman certainly wanted to intimidate the Southern population and to cow them into submission, but he stopped short of any systematic program of terror. Or did he? By letting the people "feel the indignant power of the government" through torching their towns and expelling entire families from their homes, Sherman was practicing what some historians and scholars have called terrorism. For instance, in his recent work, *The Lessons of Terror: A History of Warfare against Civilians*, Caleb Carr defined terrorism as "Warfare deliberately waged against civilians with the purpose of destroying their will to support either leaders or policies that the agents of such violence find objectionable."[79] Certainly, the type of war that Sherman adopted while in Memphis and that which he would later wage in Mississippi and Georgia would fit into Carr's somewhat broad definition. There is absolutely no doubt that Sherman was deliberate in his actions and that he targeted the will of the people. In fact, when explaining his decision to burn the town of Randolph, Sherman vowed to employ "all the terrors" necessary to protect against guerrilla attacks on the river.[80] Nevertheless, definitions are almost always subjective. It is less important to establish if Sherman's actions did or did not amount to actual terrorism than it is to simply understand their cause and effect.

It would take two years for Sherman's brand of punitive war to fully mature. While commanding at Memphis, all of his punitive strikes along the Mississippi were primarily reactive, coming only as retaliation for attacks on transports and steamers. His more proactive campaigns of destruction, those aimed specifically at civilians and their property, would not take place until 1864. Sherman had, however, established retaliatory burning as a quasi-official policy, one that would remain long after Sherman departed Memphis. Evidence of this was included in the writings of officers and soldiers like Henry A. Kircher, who traveled down the Mississippi on the Union steamer

Thomas E. Tutt at the end of 1862. "Every colonel had an order from Genr. Sherman to land immediately as soon as a boat was shot at and next to burn down the houses of the residences from which the shooting came," Kircher recorded. "So it happened that almost all the houses, with the exception of the small towns, were burned down. They generally already stood in flames or lay in ashes when we came past."[81] Undoubtedly, Sherman had left his mark on the Mississippi Valley and its people; both physical and psychological. By the end of 1862, his development into the icon of punitive war was well under way.

Sherman's successor, Major General Stephen Hurlburt, continued the practice of retaliatory burning as guerrillas continued to impede Union navigation of the river south of Memphis. When the Union tow-steamer *Hercules* was set aflame by guerrilla artillery fire on 17 January 1863, Hurlburt ordered the nearby town of Hopefield, Arkansas, burned to the ground. Four companies of the Sixty-Third Illinois Volunteers carried out the mission, destroying every home.[82] Two months later, Lieutenant Samuel Calvin Jones described what he saw at Milliken's Bend, a stopping point on the river en route to Vicksburg. "There had been a town here, but rebel guerrillas so infested the place that it was burned down by shells from our gunboats," he wrote in his diary. "At this time there is no sign that there ever was a house here." According to Jones, guerrilla attacks on the river were frequent, and he and his fellow Union troops anticipated being fired on constantly.[83] It was this way up and down the Mississippi and deep along inland routes. When the Yankee troops applied the heavy hand to one spot, the guerrillas and bushwhackers would simply appear in another. It was as if no progress was being made. Such was enough to make one exasperated Michigan infantryman stationed in Tennessee exclaim, "We are now in a country where about every family are secesh . . . I want to see them all cleaned out . . . This is great garrillia [*sic*] country." Similar frustration was expressed by Charles Weiser of the Twentieth Ohio Infantry, who had grown tired of being fired upon by guerrillas as he moved down the river toward Vicksburg. When he witnessed a number of bushwhackers captured, Weiser wrote, "If I had the say so they would be hung . . . I think the cowards should not have no mercy shown them. They are doing considerable damage lately."[84]

Unable to secure the river with detachments of regular cavalry alone, the Union Army and Navy collaborated to create a unit that could. The Mississippi Marine Brigade was a unique combined arms force formed in early 1863 to counter the guerrilla threat to Union navigation of the Mississippi. Described by historians as "revolutionary," "remarkable," "unorthodox," and "bewildering," the brigade was a 1,200-man mishmash of infantry, cavalry, and artillery soldiers, many of whom were convalescents.[85] Created from an existing Federal ram fleet, the brigade was transported up and down the river by a small fleet of steamers.

In theory, the Mississippi Marine Brigade was intended to do what Federal gunboats alone could not: to pursue guerrillas and bushwhackers as they retreated into the interior. The brigade's mission, as described by one of its chief officers, was to "chase and annihilate" the guerrilla parties that plagued the riverbanks between Memphis and Vicksburg.[86] The soldiers in the new brigade understood their mission. One wrote home about his new duty of "hunting guerrillas" and "keeping the river safe" for Union transports.[87] When passing Union steamers or transports were fired on from the riverbanks, the brigade was supposed to disembark immediately and catch or kill the perpetrators. In essence, the special unit was designed to conduct what historian Robert Mackey has described as *antiguerrilla* operations, or those operations directly aimed at capturing or killing guerrillas.[88] The *New York Herald* lauded the creation of the brigade and predicted that navigation on the Mississippi would soon be as safe as that on the Hudson.[89]

In reality, the Mississippi Marine Brigade was a poorly managed, vindictive wrecking crew that preferred the indirect (and easier) approach of burning and looting to the more difficult practice of pursuing guerrillas. Although the brigade did attempt to chase and capture guerrillas when the odds were good, the majority of its efforts on the Mississippi were devoted to ransacking and then torching the towns in close proximity to guerrilla attacks. The small groups of bushwhackers that the brigade encountered were no different than those in other regions of the South; they refused to stand and fight. Therefore, it became common practice for the Marine Brigade to attempt a half-hearted pursuit of guerrillas and then set upon the nearest town as soon as the enemy scattered. One such case was described by Josiah H. Goodwin, a Union soldier on board the USS steamer *Diana*, who wrote in his diary of a futile attempt to catch guerrillas near Richmond, Louisiana, in June 1863. Goodwin noted, "To finish the job as we always do, we set fire to all of the houses" in the nearby town, with the exception of "one little bit of a frame where an old lady was living."[90] Perhaps the most telling piece of Goodwin's entry is his reference to the regularity with which the brigade engaged in burning.

From its inauguration in February 1863 to its dissolution in August 1864, the Marine Brigade waged a destructive campaign resulting in a long list of destroyed towns and villages along the length of the Lower Mississippi. The first target was Savannah, Tennessee, where the courthouse and storehouses were destroyed on 19 April 1863.[91] At Austin, Mississippi, the brigade skirmished with, but failed to catch, a detachment of "Mississippi Partisans" that had fired on a Federal supply ship. Subsequently, the brigade's commander,

Brigadier General Alfred W. Ellet, had the entire town of Austin burned, to include a schoolhouse north of town. At least fifty women and children watched as Ellet's soldiers carried out the destructive order, sending their homes up in smoke and flames.[92] In his report on the incident, Ellet claimed that a number of homes exploded, suggesting that they held munitions for bushwhacking. Stating that he searched every home, he wrote, "I burned the town."[93] Later, on 15 June, the brigade continued its retributive binge by burning "everything that was in the shape of a house" outside of one Louisiana town haunted by bushwhackers, according to one Union soldier.[94] Finally, in little Lake Village, Arkansas, the Marine Brigade tore down the majority of the homes in town following a reported "fierce struggle" with local guerrillas.[95]

The extent of the damage caused by the Mississippi Marine Brigade is difficult to ascertain because no exact records were maintained, and much of it was never reported. Historians have generally agreed that it was significant. Mackey claimed that by July 1863, "The entire Mississippi Riverline between Missouri and Louisiana had been devastated" by the Marine Brigade and other angry Union troops. According to another source, the unit became "adept at burning southern villages."[96] Letters and diary entries from Marine Brigade soldiers support these claims of extensive destruction. Union Sergeant Major E. Paul Reichelm recalled "the general burning of nearly all the plantations between Helena and Napoleon [Arkansas—a distance of about 30 miles]," while Captain Frank MacGregor claimed that the troops were "burning and pillaging every place" on their way down the river in January 1863. Even into the spring of 1864, almost daily occurrences of burning could be found along the Mississippi. After witnessing three consecutive days of burnings in March, one Union soldier concluded that the Marine Brigade was setting fire "to the whole surrounding country."[97]

Despite all of this, the guerrillas continued their attacks, apparently unfazed by the Marine Brigade's liberal use of the torch. Even after the Confederate surrender of Vicksburg in July 1863, which guaranteed the Union full control of the Mississippi, Federal vessels still came under frequent attack from the riverbanks. Even as late as July 1864, Colonel George E. Currie reported that the Marine Brigade was involved in daily skirmishes with guerrillas.[98] By the time the special unit was deactivated a month later, it had proven itself a dismal failure. Nothing the brigade did achieved its intended mission of clearing the river of guerrillas, and both Union and Confederate sides lauded its dissolution.[99]

Like Farragut's destruction of Donaldsonville and Sherman's ordered burning of Randolph, the destruction carried out by the Mississippi Marine Brigade was purely punitive in nature. One could argue, as many Union leaders did, that such measures were intended to deny guerrillas subsistence and were therefore a simple act of military necessity. The indiscriminate looting and destruction that the Marine Brigade conducted throughout the Lower Mississippi Valley in 1862 and 1863, however, exceeded what many considered to be the justifiable limits of war. In most cases, no real effort was made to determine if the targeted towns and villages did, in fact, house or supply guerrillas before they were set aflame. For the soldiers of the brigade, their close proximity to guerrilla activity was proof enough.

Even those who endured the constant harassment from guerrillas did not always approve of the brigade's destructive conduct. Such was the case with one senior noncommissioned officer who, after witnessing his comrades respond to guerrilla attacks by burning the town of Napoleon, Arkansas, decried the "wanton destruction of houses and splendid farms" as "deplorable and disgusting" and accused his fellow troops of acting merely out of "a thirst for vengeance, and licentious desire to sack and burn."[100] A soldier from Illinois recalled seeing women and children "standing by the ruins of their burned home" following retaliation to guerrilla attacks. Such images were "scenes I dislike to see," he claimed.[101] Another member of the brigade was so disillusioned by his comrades' conduct that he proclaimed, "This whole institution is more worthy of the name negro thieves than Miss. Marine Brigade, for about all we have done yet that has been worth any notice was stealing negroes."[102] Even one of the brigade's highest-ranking officers considered General Ellet's order to burn Austin, Mississippi, as "an unmilitary act" taken against "innocent victims."[103] These accounts not only suggest that a number of the Mississippi Marine Brigade's soldiers struggled with the moral implications of what they were doing, but more importantly, that the punishment being dealt to communities along the river was so severe that many, despite having already witnessed two years of war, were very much troubled by what they saw.

The more common response among soldiers of the Marine Brigade, however, was to excuse the destruction as a justifiable solution to the guerrilla problem. In village after village, most members of the brigade were more than willing to retaliate against civilian property. Such was the case with Illinois soldier Lucius Barber, who witnessed the retaliation for a guerrilla attack on Union steamers passing by the town of Greenville, Mississippi. In describing how the Union troops "laid everything to waste," Barber acknowledged that such methods might "look barbarous to some," but defended the practice by stating, "It was the only way in which we could check these lawless villains in their murderous schemes."[104] Similar sentiments were displayed by a Union officer in a letter home on 22 December 1862 in which he described the burning of civilian homes as retaliation for the killing of five "Union men" by suspected guerrillas near Friar's Point, Mississippi. Claiming the application of the torch to be "a proper retaliation" for the deaths of the Union men, the officer wrote, "Burning property is certainly a disgraceful way of proceeding even against the enemy, but what can stay the hand of an enraged soldier burning to avenge wrongs inflicted on their brothers in arms? . . . So long as the Southerners act this way, the Northern soldiers will retaliate every opportunity."[105]

Worthy of note was the manner in which the officer, like so many of the Marine Brigade and other Union troops facing the guerrilla problem, chose to view "the Southerners" as the root of the problem, and not some more specific group such as soldiers, guerrillas, or even secessionists. "Southerners" as a whole were seen as the enemy. Even those in the Federal high command viewed the punishment the Marine Brigade exacted on the river towns as a sort of unfortunate military necessity, required to counter the "inhuman practice of firing on unarmed vessels and peaceful citizens" from hidden positions. Such incidents, a Union general admitted, were responsible for "a system of retaliation, when unfortunately, the guilty parties did not always suffer."[106]

In many ways, the campaigns in 1864 that would make Sherman famous were the culmination of eighteen months of frustration with the guerrilla problem, not only for Sherman, but for the Army of the Tennessee as a whole. The wholesale destruction of Grand Gulf, Donaldsonville, Randolph, Hopefield, and the Mississippi Marine Brigade's habitual torching of river towns between Memphis and Vicksburg were all reflections of a changing, embittered attitude within the Union ranks. The retaliation for McCook's killing and the destruction of Greenville in western Tennessee had shown that Union troops could and would resort to punitive war without being ordered to do so, usually with the consent of their officers. Conciliation, as a policy, could not stand the test of daily guerrilla attacks nor could it combat the perceived wealth of support that guerrillas received from the population. Union use of the torch became almost Pavlovian and was more widespread than recent scholarship suggests.[107]

Punitive war was not the only approach taken in the Lower Mississippi. Federal leaders throughout the region adopted other methods to confront the guerrilla problem, such as establishing systems of blockhouses, the extensive use of provost guards and local antiguerrilla militias, and conducting antiguerrilla cavalry operations. Historians Robert Mackey and Andrew Birtle examined these methods in their attempts to demonstrate the versatility of the Union approach to the guerrilla problem.[108] While some of these "direct" measures proved successful, particularly in northern Arkansas during the final month of the war, reports that the region was still "infested with guerrillas" were made until the last weeks of the war. Several decentralized groups of bushwhackers roamed back and forth between Missouri and Arkansas. In Louisiana, guerrilla gangs still prowled the banks of the Mississippi River well into the spring.[109] Neither blockhouses, cavalry patrols, nor homegrown militias were able to provide a durable means to rid the Mississippi Valley of guerrillas. As such, none of these measures were as trusted or commonly used as punitive measures against civilians and their property.

With the exception of Vicksburg, the Mississippi Valley did not see the amount of extensive campaigning that was seen in the East. This did not mean, however, that it did not feel the same effects of the war. The long Union presence and effort to gain and maintain control of the Mississippi River resulted in the region's receiving its fair share of devastation, due in no little part to the guerrilla problem. The real legacy of the Mississippi Valley was the experience it provided for the Union armies that eventually moved to the east. The soldiers that marched through Mississippi, Georgia, and the Carolinas in 1864 and 1865 had suffered the deadly annoyance of bushwhacking for almost two years in the Mississippi Valley. Armed with a growing sense of invincibility and a hardened attitude toward the people of the South, Sherman's men were prepared to follow their general's destructive lead, and follow it they would.

CHAPTER FOUR

War and Individual Ruin: Sherman's Campaigns of 1864

General Sherman does not play at war.
—*Harper's Weekly*, 10 December 1864

Despite its struggles with guerrilla harassment along the river, the Union Army took a giant step toward ultimate victory when, on 4 July 1863, it finally captured the Confederate defenses at Vicksburg, along with 29,491 half-starved rebel soldiers commanded by Major General John C. Pemberton.[1] In doing so, the Union finally gained control of the Mississippi, effectively enveloping the western flank of the Confederacy. Combined with Robert E. Lee's defeat at Gettysburg the day before, Ulysses S. Grant's victory at Vicksburg marked a tremendous upswing in the fortunes of war for the Union. However, the hard-fought battles of Chickamauga and Chattanooga in the latter months of 1863 resulted in over 21,000 Federal casualties, proving that there was much work still to be done. With possession of Chattanooga, the Union secured an open path into the heartland of the Confederacy, and its crown jewel, the industry and rail hub of Atlanta.

William T. Sherman began the year of 1864 still primarily known in the North for his supporting role in the Vicksburg campaign and the lingering questions about his sanity.[2] Ever at odds with the newspapers, his popularity paled in comparison to that of Grant, whose successes at Vicksburg and Chattanooga earned him lavish praise from the Northern press and public. There was even talk of Grant's being nominated for president.[3] In March, Grant was promoted to lieutenant general and placed in command of all the Union armies, replacing Henry Halleck. Within a year, however, Sherman's name was on the lips of every Northerner and in the headlines of every major newspaper. With the departure of Grant, Sherman was elevated to the commander of Union armies in the West. This new level of command and his tight relationship with the new general-in-chief would ultimately allow Sherman to wage the style of war he envisioned. His campaigns in Mississippi and Georgia that year would lead the Union to victory and many to later proclaim him the progenitor of modern warfare.[4] It is impossible to truly examine the relationship between Sherman, the guerrilla problem, and punitive war without considering these particular campaigns and how they were conducted. 1864 proved to be the decisive year of the contest, with Sherman and his rough, ruthless brand of war making taking center stage.

With Vicksburg and Chattanooga secured, and the bruised Confederate Army of Tennessee gathering itself in Georgia, Sherman was free to make a jab at what he believed to be a significant target. For months, he had considered moving against the rail junction at Meridian, Mississippi, where the Mobile & Ohio and Vicksburg & Selma Railroads crossed. The destruction of this junction, Sherman predicted, would "paralyze" all of Mississippi and completely isolate the remaining Confederate force in the state commanded by Major General Leonidas Polk, which lingered in Meridian.[5] It would also enable Sherman to send a force against the intrepid Nathan Bedford Forrest, whose cavalry had long threatened the Union armies in the region and done significant damage to supply lines. Furthermore, the move on Meridian would allow Sherman to direct a measure of punishment against the people that supplied Forrest and the guerrillas operating in the area. Although the specified objective of the expedition was the rail network, Sherman's march to Meridian was also designed as a destructive show of force, or as Charles Royster stated, "a punitive assault of civilians' spirit," the kind for which Sherman would be famous before the year was out.[6]

Sherman returned to Vicksburg in January 1864 and gathered an army of close to 26,000, most of them hardened veterans. To move deep into Mississippi's interior meant abandoning the large Union presence on the river, the control of which was turned over to the Mississippi Marine Brigade and the U.S. Navy. On 30 January, Sherman wrote to Lieutenant Commander E. K. Owen encouraging him to keep the pressure on the "disloyal citizens" that supported guerrilla attacks on Union ships navigating the river. "Impress on the people," he wrote, "that we intend to hold them responsible for all acts of hostility to the river commerce." Furthermore, "They must be active friends or enemies. They cannot be silent or neutral," Sherman urged.[7] By demanding that the people of the South be "active" supporters of the Union, Sherman was making it easier to justify the amount of destruction that he was about to bring to the interior of Mississippi. He knew that he would find very few, if any, citizens willing to openly endorse the Union in one of the most staunchly rebellious states.

The Meridian expedition began on 3 February 1864, with Sherman's Sixteenth and Seventeenth Corps heading east from Vicksburg in two columns toward Jackson. As they marched, most of the Federal soldiers were unsure of their objective. The strategically important port city of Mobile, Alabama, lay some 200 miles to the southeast and its capture had long been a priority of the Union leadership. Another possibility was to drive deep into central Alabama and capture the rail junction at Selma, which would isolate Mobile from the north. Only some of the officers knew where the column was headed, but most of Sherman's troops were happy to be on the move. The weather had warmed considerably over the previous week, and spirits were up.[8]

For the first two days the Union soldiers marched over the same terrain that had witnessed a number of movements during the Vicksburg campaign, to include the raid on Jackson conducted by Grant's forces the previous summer in which Sherman had taken part. The roads, barns, and houses along the way were mostly deserted, although some people had returned since the Yankees' last visit. On 5 February when the lead elements of Sherman's army moved into Jackson they were met by an outmanned rebel cavalry force commanded by Major General Samuel French. After a sharp skirmish that lasted through the afternoon, French retreated to the east leaving the city to the Federals. When Sherman's troops entered the streets of Jackson, they found very little of military usage remaining, with the exception of the rail yard and a number of public buildings that were still operational. These were quickly set upon by Sherman's troops and destroyed. When William B. Westervelt marched into Jackson with his regiment a few hours later, he found "the Depot and many public buildings on fire."[9] As Sherman's men moved about town they were met with apprehensive stares from the women and children and a gleeful welcome from scores of slaves who quickly fell in behind the marching soldiers. The addition of these "contrabands" to Sherman's column was somewhat of a hindrance, since the general had no intention of feeding or housing them. Throughout the rest of the campaign, and later in Georgia and South Carolina, Sherman made it clear that he would not allow his movement to be slowed or weakened by the thousands of contrabands following behind. He was focused on being a subjugator, not a savior. Sherman wrote to his wife, Ellen, on his last day in Jackson, stating, "I am here again and a new burning has been inflicted on this afflicted town."[10] Much of it reached to several private dwellings, which the Union soldiers watched go up in flames as they made their camp for the night. Miles away Albert Quincy Porter, a Confederate infantryman, noted that citizens of Jackson had fled from the city during the day, carrying all they could with them. The Yankees burned the rest.[11] When Sherman's column departed the next day, Jackson smoldered—thoroughly cleaned out and broken.

The next target in the path of Sherman's march was Brandon. After an insignificant skirmish with retreating Confederates, the Seventeenth Corps moved into the city. There, the scene duplicated that seen in Jackson. Sherman's troops quickly ransacked the stores and businesses in town and took to burning both public and private buildings. There was no rail junction to dismantle or factory to disable, so the destruction focused primarily on the

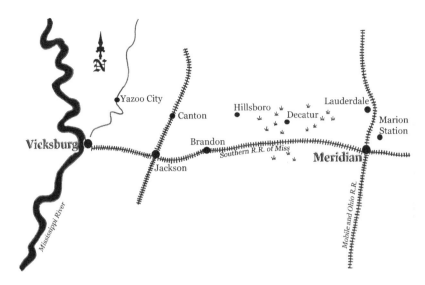

Central Mississippi, 1864

homes of prominent Southern citizens and a recruiting station in town. For-aging soon became pillaging. "Plundered the village of Brandon," one sol-dier noted in his diary, describing how he and other soldiers destroyed "a number of stores and public buildings."[12] Despite orders issued by the corps commander, Major General James McPherson, prohibiting the burning of private homes and property, the Yankees did just that. The officers made no concerted effort to prevent it. The women that had remained in town despite the warnings of Sherman's approach could now only watch as the city's build-ings, and eventually their houses, went up in flames.[13] There was a growing sense among Sherman's men that their destructive behavior would largely go unpunished and was perhaps even welcomed by the officers.

Five days after tearing through Brandon, Sherman's army reached the fo-cal point of the campaign, Meridian, and settled in for what was to be nearly a week's worth of the most detailed and thorough destruction the state had ever seen. The Confederate forces under Polk had pulled out ahead of Sher-man's arrival, much to the surprise of many a Union soldier who believed the rebels would fight until the last man before giving up the important rail hub. But determining that the military supplies and equipment stored in Meridian were more vital than the town itself, Polk ordered the evacuation of the city hours before the first Union elements arrived. When the bluecoats occupied the city on 14 February, they were free to engage in their destructive work. The retreating Confederates had set fires at the rail depot to prevent the use of several cars, and the Union soldiers just continued the work, torching warehouses and public buildings. The most impressive work, however, was done on the railroad. Sherman's men worked tirelessly for four days ripping up the track in all directions. Over a 100 miles of the Mobile & Ohio and Southern Railroads were destroyed along with twenty locomotives and sixty bridges. One Union soldier described how he and his fellows conducted "all manner of damage to public property within sixty miles" of the town. In a letter to his family and friends, another soldier assured them that "the [rail] road and other rebel property suffered."[14] Pleased with his soldiers' performance, Sherman reported to Grant: "We staid [*sic*] at Meridian for a week and made the most complete destruction of the railroads ever beheld," adding a week later that Meridian "no longer exists."[15] Again, Sherman was exaggerating, but not by much. Very little remained in Meridian after Sherman's work was done. In addition to the complete dismantling of the rail junction, Sherman's army had wiped the town clean of any and all subsistence and destroyed all facilities. Reflecting back on the damage, an infantryman noted in his diary, "All the barns, cotton gins, and warehouses filled with cotton, deserted houses and stores all went up as a burnt offering to the demon of treason."[16] Despite some half-hearted attempts on the part of the officers to guard civilian homes from looting or conflagration, many were destroyed.

In less than two weeks, Sherman had covered the entire width of the state, wiped out its most important railroad junction, and sent the remnants of Leonidas Polk's forces fleeing eastward to Alabama. The one failure of the campaign came at the hands of Sherman's cavalry commander, Brigadier General William Sooy Smith, who failed to defeat Nathan Bedford Forrest and ended up retreating into Tennessee. It was a small blot on an otherwise shining achievement, but enough to leave Sherman thoroughly disappointed. In his memoirs, Sherman recalled how Smith "failed utterly" in his mission because he did not "fulfill his orders." Sherman also ignored Smith's many appeals to lighten his criticism of his performance in Mississippi. To do so, Sherman claimed, would "falsify history."[17] Nevertheless, Smith's failure was greatly overshadowed by the successful dismemberment of Meridian. Sherman had effectively knocked Mississippi out of the war. In doing so, he proved that raids, which included living off the enemy's country, were not only possible but relatively easy provided that the Confederate army could not counter the move.

Throughout the length of the Meridian campaign, the only real threat to Sherman's soldiers came from bushwhackers and guerrillas that shadowed the column as it moved, waiting for the most opportune time to ambush stragglers. Small detachments of Confederate cavalry were also present and were able to pounce upon those foraging parties that wandered too far from the column. The Union soldiers attributed all such attacks to the guerrilla problem, with which they were infinitely familiar by that point in the war. Thomas Douglas, an infantryman from Iowa, recalled the danger posed by the lurking, unseen enemy. "All the way through on that march it was dangerous for a man to leave the ranks, for the bushes were full of Rebs on both sides of the road," Douglas wrote. "They would not come out and fight us fair, but they would shoot at us every chance they got."[18] The terrain that Sherman's army crossed on the way to Meridian was perfectly suited for bushwhacking. Thick brush and swampy lowlands hugged the route of march and made the pursuit of any assailant relatively impossible. To make matters worse, guerrillas took to dressing in women's clothing in order to sneak up on unwitting sentinels.[19] All of this combined to produce an atmosphere that kept Sherman's soldiers on edge. They did not dare trust any of the people they marched past, nor did they pity them.

Although the meticulous dismantling of the railroad at Meridian highlighted the campaign, much of the destruction waged by Sherman's soldiers was directed at nonmilitary targets. Not surprisingly, there was little mention of this in official correspondence, but the firsthand accounts of the soldiers that marched through Mississippi describe extensive destruction that extended well beyond railroads and factories. On both the march to Meridian and the return to Vicksburg, Sherman's column was liberal with its use of the torch, often as retribution for guerrilla attacks.

Private John Brobst of the Twenty-Fifth Wisconsin Infantry marveled at the extensive damage done at Jackson, Morton, Brandon, Hillsboro, Meridian, and Marion Station. In a letter home he wrote, "We left every town that we passed through in ashes." Another soldier described how his unit destroyed "everything that would burn." William Westervelt, a member of the Zouaves from the Twenty-Seventh New York Infantry, recalled how his unit was fired upon by bushwhackers as they moved through a swampy area outside of the small town of Decatur. In response, his fellow Zouaves moved into the town and ransacked a number of buildings. "While here some of our Troops amused themselves by setting fire to the few remaining houses of the town," he noted. On approach to Meridian Westervelt wrote, "All along the way we could see the remains of fine large dwellings the ruins of which were still burning."[20] The towns of Clinton, Lauderdale, Canton, New Albany, and Yazoo City, none of which possessed any military significance, shared similar fates. In a formal report, an officer from the Iowa cavalry admitted that many structures in Canton were "wantonly destroyed" by his troops.[21] It is important to note that as Polk's cavalry withdrew before Sherman's advance, it burned cotton, stores, and bridges to prevent them from falling into Union hands. The significant damage done to private property, and particularly houses and barns, however, came at the hands of Sherman's troops.

At the conclusion of the Meridian campaign, a young Union infantry-man named James Hodges questioned the purpose behind all he had just witnessed. "I am not aware of what the object of our expedition was—the Mobile and Ohio R.R. is damaged so that it will take over a year to repair it," he wrote, "but I think the movement meant more than that."[22] He was cor-rect. The entire expedition had been a castigatory stroke aimed at the people of Mississippi, whom Sherman viewed as willing accomplices to the guer-rillas and the Confederate war effort. Particularly along the return route of march, Sherman's troops engaged in destruction for the sake of punishment, nothing more. Anything of use to the Confederate army had been destroyed during the initial approach to Meridian. All burning conducted on the way back to Vicksburg was aimed at hurting the local population, and in particu-lar, those who dared support hostilities against Union troops. One chronicler of the expedition expressed "no regret" that "much public and some private property was destroyed." Like Sherman, he believed that "Mississippians who without compunction have shot the sentinels on their beats . . . and who, in safe company, have boasted of the assassination of soldiers" deserved any punishment they received at the hands of Sherman's incendiaries. The gen-eral himself commented just before departing Vicksburg that the guerrillas harassing his army knew that he would soon "punish the Interior for their rascality." It had mattered little to Sherman that civilians would suffer. "We will take all provisions and God help the starving families," he wrote before starting toward Meridian. "I warned them last year against this last visita-tion, and now it is at hand."[23] Operationally, Sherman's raid into Mississippi served as an effective preparation for his later campaign in Georgia. He had proven to himself and others that his army could penetrate deep into the en-emy's territory, living off the enemy's country. He also learned the amount of damage that his army was capable of producing. It was what historian Charles Royster called "a new extent and severity of ruin," and for Sherman's soldiers, it became their trademark.[24]

The next six months for Sherman and his army of nearly 100,000 involved the methodical advance on Atlanta from Chattanooga. Confederate General Joseph E. Johnston, commanding the Army of Tennessee, was more than willing to trade time for space, as he continued to withdraw and reposition his defenses to counter each of Sherman's maneuvers. A lengthy game of thrust and parry took place with Sherman continually attempting to flank Johnston's defensive position, only to see him withdraw to another one. The two sides fought a frontal engagement at Kennesaw Mountain in late June, which produced nearly 2,000 worthless casualties for Sherman. He there-fore returned to his flanking maneuvers, and within two weeks Johnston's army was pinned against Atlanta's outer works. Alarmed and frustrated with

Johnston's defensive approach, Southern President Jefferson Davis replaced him in favor of the more aggressive Major General John Bell Hood. Hood immediately took the offensive, smashing his army into Sherman's. After three fruitless assaults over ten days, Hood was forced to withdraw into Atlanta's defenses. Sherman settled in for a siege of the city and went to work cutting the railroads leading into Atlanta. When a Confederate attack at Jonesboro on 1 September failed to knock the Union forces back, Hood was faced with the dismal prospect of losing Atlanta or his entire army. The next day, Hood abandoned Atlanta and moved his wounded army to Alabama. The heart of the Deep South was now at the mercy of William T. Sherman.

Of course, the one campaign that made Sherman a giant in the historical sense was his movement from Atlanta to Savannah in November and December 1864, the famous "March to the Sea." Following the operational success of the Meridian campaign, Sherman was anxious to keep the pressure on breaking down the Southern will to continue the war. The momentum gained by the capture of Atlanta needed to be exploited. Just how to achieve that exploitation, however, was uncertain. Sherman believed that a devastating show of force in the form of a move from Atlanta to Savannah would carry the momentum.

The idea to conduct the march across Georgia rather than pursue Hood into Alabama was strictly Sherman's. While Grant would eventually endorse the maneuver, he initially pushed Sherman to go after and finish Hood's wounded army before conducting an extensive march that would stretch supply lines and leave Sherman vulnerable. Frustrated with his own stalled position at Petersburg, Grant was anxious to deliver decisive blows to what remained of the Confederate Army. "Do you not think it advisable," Grant wrote, "to entirely ruin [Hood] before starting on your proposed campaign?" After all, Hood had been badly beaten, but in addition to his aggressive nature he still had approximately 40,000 soldiers capable of a fight. But Sherman, convinced that pursuing Hood played into the Confederates' hands, replied, "If I turn back, the whole effect of my campaign will be lost . . . I am clearly of opinion that the best results will follow my contemplated movement through Georgia." It is unlikely that any other Union leader at the time could have offered such resistance to Grant without being quickly overruled. But this was Sherman, and the partnership that the two had developed, combined with Sherman's decision to dispatch Major General George Thomas with the bulk of Fourth Corps to Nashville to hold off Hood, was enough to win Grant's endorsement. "I do not see that you can withdraw from where you are . . . I say, then, go on as you propose," the general-in-chief ordered on 2 November. Later, Sherman would be very adamant about the fact that he and he alone was responsible for conceiving the idea of the march, something that Grant confirmed in his own memoirs.[25] Despite the reservations held in Washington about the bold move, Sherman received the go-ahead from Grant and spent the next two weeks planning for the campaign that would forever make him the most polarizing figure of the Civil War.

It was to be, as Sherman described, a campaign that would bring about the collapse of the Confederacy. "Until we can repopulate Georgia, it is useless to occupy it," he explained to Grant, "but the utter destruction of its roads, houses, and people will cripple their military resources."[26] By cutting the railroads that connected Georgia's factories, mills, and farms to the rest of the South, Sherman could directly affect Robert E. Lee's Army of Northern Virginia, which was still holding off Grant around Petersburg. As historian Joseph Glatthaar described, Sherman envisioned "a giant raid" that would devastate the state's resources for the war. Sherman explained to the officers of his army that they were facing "a long and difficult march" that would produce "the complete overthrow" of the enemy.[27] Like the Meridian expedition, however, the objective of the march included much more than just the railroads. As Sherman had mentioned to the general-in-chief, the people and their houses needed to be targeted as well, although the targeting would be more psychological than physical. This, he believed, would effectively bring the war to the people's doorstep and demonstrate the hopelessness of the Southern cause. In essence, the march to the sea was just as much a campaign against the population as it was against resources. What Sherman planned to do to Georgia's mills, factories, and railroads, he also hoped to do to the Southern will for war. "By this, I propose to demonstrate the vulnerability of the South and make its inhabitants feel that war & individual Ruin are synonimous [sic] terms," Sherman explained to Major General George Thomas.[28] This intent was clearly understood by Sherman's officers and Soldiers as well. They had fought long and hard over the course of the past year and covered much ground. In doing so, they embraced the ideals and attitude of the man that led them. Reflecting back on the days before the march began, Sherman recalled having been supremely confident that "it would end the war."[29] Nevertheless, with Robert E. Lee still holding the trenches around Petersburg, and John Bell Hood's army still on the move and capable of doing damage, victory was not yet certain.

Before the first steps toward the sea were even made, Sherman's troops proved that the use of punitive war would not stop in Atlanta. They had suffered fewer guerrilla attacks since entering Georgia, and yet the problem still clung tenaciously to their flanks and rear. Alva G. Greist, an infantryman from the Hoosier state, noted in late September that "there are no Rebels here other than Guerrillas, and they are abundant everywhere."[30] As such, Sherman gave his subordinate commanders clearance to burn down towns and villages in which the people displayed "any hostility."[31] The towns of Rome and Acworth went up in flames in the following days, with the destruction primarily aimed at their factories, mills, and foundries. In at least one case, however, the torch was applied in response to civilian hostility. When Union authorities determined in late October that the nearby towns of Canton and Cassville were harboring and supporting rebel guerrillas and cavalry, Sherman ordered a regiment of Ohio Cavalry to immediately move on Canton. "You will permit the citizens to remove what they desire, and burn the town, and after which you will proceed to Cassville and make the same disposition as at Canton."[32] This, Sherman's troops were all too willing to do, especially once it was learned that guerrillas had recently ambushed Yankee troops outside Cassville, killed them, and mutilated the bodies. Cassville was quickly set upon, leaving Illinois soldier Charles Wills to report later, "Our men burned the town." When Cornelius Platter marched through Cassville three weeks later with the Eighty-First Ohio Infantry, he noted that the town was "nothing but a mass of ruins."[33] Unlike the spontaneous destruction carried out by vengeful soldiers that took place on the march back from Meridian, this was a calculated order that came from the top. The directed destruction of Canton and Cassville harkened back to Sherman's iron hand on the Mississippi and served as a harbinger of things to come for other towns that lay in the path of the march. Fully aware of their beloved general's state of mind, some of Sherman's troops expressed pity for what was in store for the people of Georgia. "I don't believe that he has any mercy in his composition," wrote a young cavalry officer as he prepared for the march.[34] Undoubtedly, the people of Cassville shared the same view. When a number of his soldiers were captured by local guerrillas near the town of Kingston, Sherman instructed Brigadier General John E. Smith to arrest those "supposed to be hostile" and to threaten the retaliatory burning of the three closest towns if the Union troops were not returned.[35] It was clear that punitive war would be incorporated in the march to the sea. The extent of its use, however, was still to be determined.

Sherman was fully aware that his intended movement through Georgia required set guidelines to prevent disorder within his ranks. This was not out of any fear for what it meant for the people of Georgia should his army devolve into a gang, but rather, what it meant for his ability to control his force and get it through to Savannah. Sherman's operational instructions for the campaign were published in his Special Field Orders No. 120 on 9 November. Sherman directed that the army would move in two separate wings comprised of two corps in each. The first wing, comprised of the Army of the Tennessee Fifteenth and Seventeenth Corps, was under the command of Major General Oliver O. Howard and would move south from Atlanta toward Jonesboro.

The second wing, made up of the Army of the Cumberland's Fourteenth and Twentieth Corps, was led by Major General Henry W. Slocum. This wing was directed to move to the east, in the direction of Augusta. No exact objective was specified in the order, only that the two columns would proceed on the route of march and "make about fifteen miles per day," unless otherwise directed. In his memoirs, Sherman stated that the purpose for sending out two divergent columns was to prevent any enemy concentration against his force. Their task, he recalled, was to reach the state capital of Milledgeville, approximately 100 miles to the southeast, within seven days.[36] The remainder of Special Field Orders No. 120 addressed the procedures for foraging, the confiscation of property to include livestock, and the handling of freed slaves. Sherman stressed organization and good discipline and disallowed any trespassing or even "abusive or threatening language" to be used toward citizens. As for dealing with the guerrilla problem, however, Sherman stuck to his usual hard line. "Should guerrillas or bushwhackers molest our march, or should the inhabitants burn bridges, obstruct roads, or otherwise manifest local hostility, then army commanders should order and enforce a devastation more or less relentless according to the measure of such hostility."[37]

On this point, Sherman's officers understood his intent clearly. Major Alfred Wilcox of the 105th Ohio Cavalry wrote in a letter as the march began, "If we are molested by bushwackers the country is to be devastated more or less relentlessly as the magnitude of the offense demands," echoing Sherman's order almost word for word.[38] Sherman's subordinates may not have been sure of his strategic and operational goals for the campaign, but they knew exactly what to do should the guerrilla problem present itself. Even so, Sherman intended to damage Georgia significantly but he also wanted to avoid a mob mentality in his men if possible. But the willingness of the officers, soldiers, and even Sherman himself to uphold the limitations set out in the order was yet to be proven. As demonstrated during his time on the Mississippi River, Sherman did not always enforce his own edicts regarding the treatment on Southern property.

When Sherman's army of 62,000 departed Atlanta on 15 November, the city lay smoldering behind. Most of the city's public buildings, warehouses, and mills were no more, and a good number of homes had gone up in flames as well as a result of the extensive bombardment and torching by both retreating Confederates and Union occupiers. Samuel Hurst, an infantryman from Ohio, later wrote about the scene. "We left Atlanta in flames. It was the avowed purpose to burn all those buildings that could render the place valuable in a military point of view," Hurst explained, "In doing this, many other buildings were burned, and more than half of the city was left in ruins." A report filed by Colonel James Robinson of the Eighty-Second Ohio confirmed

Hurst's description. "[Atlanta] was a blazing ruin," he wrote, "abandoned alike by citizens and soldiers to the harsh fortunes of war." Some Union soldiers, like Cornelius Platter, found the widespread burning of Atlanta unsettling. "This wanton destruction would soon demoralize an Army," he wrote in his diary, "I think Sherman intends to [devastate] the whole country as he goes." The majority of Sherman's men, however, met the scene of Atlanta in flames with little to no compunction. Major Henry M. Hitchcock, an officer on Sherman's staff, witnessed the damage being done to Atlanta and knew what the public reaction might be. "[Sherman] will hereafter be charged with indiscriminate burning, which is not true," Hitchcock wrote. "His orders are to destroy only such buildings as are used or useful for war purposes . . . all others are to be spared, and *no dwelling touched*."[39] But touched they were, whether Sherman ordered it or not. The general himself stayed in the city on 15 November to oversee the destruction of the remaining buildings which, in his words, "could be converted to hostile uses."[40] The physical damage done to the city paled in comparison to that done to the Southern hopes for victory. Atlanta, the coveted gem of the lower South, had fallen and fallen hard. The reelection of Lincoln was secured and the sustained Union war effort along with it. All that was left for Sherman to do was conduct his march and demonstrate to the people of the South that he could not be stopped.

There was no significant enemy conventional threat in Sherman's path. John Bell Hood had withdrawn into Alabama and was being held in check by 55,000 troops under Major General George H. Thomas. This, Sherman assured Grant, was "a force sufficient for all probabilities." Sherman wrote to Thomas on the eve of his departure from Atlanta and expressed his confidence that should the enemy attempt to threaten Sherman's rear that Thomas would "whip him out of his boots."[41] A cavalry corps commanded by Major General Joseph Wheeler was the only Confederate force between Atlanta and Savannah. It was too outnumbered and dispersed to offer much damage, although "Fighting Joe" Wheeler would try. Also, by allowing his army to live off the countryside, Sherman was not chained to his supply lines. Therefore, he did not share the concern expressed by those in Washington that he might somehow find himself cut off from the rest of the Union army and stranded deep in enemy territory.

How the Georgians would choose to meet Sherman's advance was unclear. Based on his experiences in the Meridian expedition, Sherman expected some violent resistance, evidenced by his reference to the potential for "guerrillas or bushwhackers" and "local hostility" in his Special Field Order issued before the march.[42] As Union foragers spread out into the countryside, they were often attacked by groups of guerrillas outnumbering them. The further that foraging parties wandered from the safety of the main column,

The burning of Miller Junction (*Harper's Weekly*)

the greater the danger of ambush became. Just after the march began, one Union infantryman noted, "Every tree shields a Confederate bushwacker."[43] For many of Sherman's soldiers, who had grown accustomed to being fired upon by hidden adversaries, it was natural to assume that guerrillas lurked all around. Nevertheless, the problem was largely contained to the flanks and rear of the columns, and was hardly noticeable to those who stuck to the main route of march. Major Henry Hitchcock noted in his diary, "The 'levy en mass' don't take place here, for the men are all gone."[44] Despite appeals from members of the Confederate Congress in Richmond calling on the people of Georgia to "assail the invader in front, flank, and rear," and to "let him have no rest," most citizens chose not to molest Sherman's advancing columns.[45]

The first week of the march saw Sherman's army push methodically to the south and east. Telegraph lines to the North had been cut, leaving the Northern public and Union leadership in Washington in the dark as to the status of the march. Along the way, it passed through a number of small towns in which few of the residents remained. Thousands of citizens fled in advance of the Yankee horde, assuming the worst. The increasingly cold weather spelled trouble for all wooden structures along the route, which were quickly dismantled to provide fuel for campfires. The towns of Sunshine Church, Irwinton,

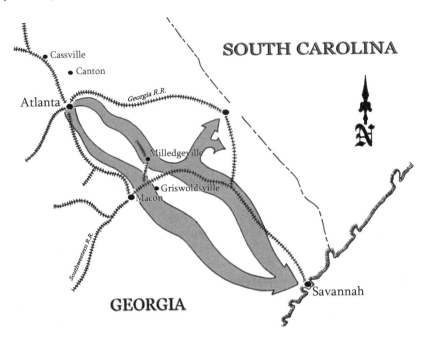

Sherman's march to the sea

Hillsboro, and Clinton were completely cleaned out of food and livestock and a good portion of their buildings were put to the torch.[46] Sherman's men made quick work of the railroads by tearing up the tracks, heating them on piles of burning ties, and wrapping them around trees. This method proved most effective, and the rail lines were damaged beyond repair.

On 22 November, the two columns of Sherman's army converged to within 10 miles of one another near the state capital of Milledgeville. The majority of the town's residents had deserted before the Yankees arrived and the remainder stayed in their homes. Not interested in spending more time than necessary in the town, the Union column moved on after a day spent destroying the arsenal and magazine and relieving the townsfolk of their food, livestock, and finer things. Just past Milledgeville, Sherman's right wing encountered a ragtag force of over 4,000 Georgia militia under the command of Pleasant J. Philips 1 mile outside the town of Griswoldsville. The inexperienced Georgians, made up of both old men and young boys, charged blindly into the Union lines and were promptly mowed down by the battle-hardened troops of the Army of the Tennessee. The Battle of Griswoldsville was more of a massacre, with the Union losing only a dozen men opposed to the nearly 500 dead Confederates. It was one of the few conventional fights that Sherman's men faced as they marched across the state, and its outcome underscored the inability of the South to prevent Sherman from carrying out his destructive plans.

Following the battle, the Union troops marched into Griswoldsville and destroyed most of the town.[47] The numerous factories and mills that had supported the Southern Army up to that point were the first buildings to be burned, followed by many of the houses. For the Union troops watching Griswoldsville burn, the sight had become most familiar. These were the same Ohioans that burned the town of Randolph, Tennessee, more than two years prior. Along the way, they had become hardened and desensitized to applying the torch. In similar examples, the towns of Sandersville and Louisville were partially destroyed by Sherman's left wing. When the soldiers were fired upon from a number of houses in town, they burned them to the ground along with several other buildings. For the remainder of the march, no house located near the site of a guerrilla attack was safe from the torch.

Of all the aspects of Sherman's campaign in Georgia, the greatest historical scrutiny has fallen on the conduct of the Federal "bummers," stragglers who engaged in excessive foraging and looting. They were the true agents of destruction and would forever become the face of the campaign. "No doubt, many acts of pillage, robbery, and violence were committed by these parties of foragers," Sherman admitted after the war, "but these acts were exceptional and incidental." When he did observe such acts, Sherman usually claimed it was beyond his control to prevent and blamed the Confederate government and its supporters for forcing his hand.[48] It was a bit ironic for Sherman, who expected Southern citizens to hold guerrillas in check or suffer the consequences, to claim that he was powerless to control his own soldiers. At no time during or after the march did Sherman suggest that his orders were not followed. In reality, however, Sherman was not overly concerned with the excesses being committed by his bummers and less interested in stopping them. When it came to the destruction of Georgia, Sherman was in earnest. When it came to controlling his bummers, he was not. This was apparent to his staff officers, many of whom began to question the general's commitment to preventing unnecessary destruction. "I am bound to say I think Sherman lacking in enforcing discipline," Henry Hitchcock wrote after seeing the treatment of Milledgeville. "Brilliant and daring, fertile, rapid and terrible, he does not seem to me to carry things out in this respect."[49] A soldier from Illinois confirmed the willingness of many soldiers to violate the rules. "Promiscuous foraging was prohibited," he wrote, but added that "the prohibition was not always obeyed." Accounts such as these led one of Sherman's biographers to describe his attempts to restrain the bummers as "arbitrary" and "almost whimsical."[50] Despite all the legitimate damage done to the military infrastructure in Georgia (which spelled doom for the Confederate Army) it was the depredations committed by Sherman's bummers that would forever serve as the face of the campaign. The bummers gave Sherman's critics all the fodder they needed to depict the general as a merciless conqueror of innocents.

The march to the sea ended with the capture of Savannah in mid-December. It was heralded in the North as an astounding success, a death blow to the fading Confederacy. The impact of the destructive movement was not lost on the people of the South or the soldiers defending Richmond. They knew it spelled impending defeat. Despite all of his talk about the importance of the campaign prior to its execution, Sherman downplayed its significance after the war. "I considered this march a means to an end," he wrote in his memoirs, "not an essential act of war."[51] Nevertheless, Sherman and his soldiers had just completed one of the most noteworthy feats of the war, one that would eventually receive more attention from military theorists, scholars, and strategists than any other campaign of the nineteenth century.

During both the Meridian and Georgia campaigns, the guerrilla problem did not present itself to the same extent that it did during Sherman's time in the Mississippi Valley. The reasoning for this was simple. Both the Meridian expedition and the march to the sea were designed as raids. In both cases, Sherman's army kept on the move and did not linger long enough in any one spot for the frustrating effects of the guerrilla problem to take hold. Had Sherman chosen to occupy Meridian, or had he attempted to guard his extensive supply lines in Georgia, it is quite likely that his troops would have been increasingly beset with guerrillas and bushwhackers just as they were in 1862 and 1863. This was largely a result of the fact that Sherman's army stayed on the move for most of 1864. Guerrillas and bushwhackers could only annoy Sherman's large, destructive machine as it steadily pushed its way across Mississippi and Georgia. It took less than a month for Sherman to march from Atlanta to Savannah, not long enough for the culminating effects of the guerrilla problem to have any real tactical or operational impact.

Nevertheless, without the guerrilla problem, these campaigns would not have been possible. Historian Russell Weigley claimed, "Revenge for the wrongs of rebel guerrillas and prisons, and the destruction not only of Confederate economic resources but of Confederate popular morale through deliberate terrorism—these were what Sherman's march to the sea was all about."[52] Although most of Sherman's troops never personally experienced the horrors of Confederate prisons, the same could not be said about the guerrilla problem. Sherman and his men had absorbed the wrongs of the guerrilla problem on the Mississippi and during the march to Meridian. These experiences were not only important in creating the hardened attitudes that they carried into Georgia and beyond, they were absolutely essential. While it is impossible to know how an army untouched by the menace of the guerrilla problem would have conducted itself on a similar campaign, it seems inconceivable that it would have, or could have, carried out the same extent of destruction as Sherman's army and with the same grim determination of bringing the hardship of war to the people. In essence, the guerrilla problem did not provide Sherman the exact reason to make war against civilians and their property, but it certainly provided the justification.

Without a doubt, Sherman's campaigns in Mississippi and Georgia were classic examples of targeting the enemy's resources, a common and widely accepted practice in the history of warfare. Yet they entailed so much more. Reflecting on Sherman's move across Georgia, Charles Royster wrote, "The main purpose of this campaign was not mayhem, though destruction accompanied Sherman's army everywhere it went."[53] It is true that Sherman's army focused its destructive efforts on the military and economic infrastructure of Georgia. As a campaign to cut railroad lines and deplete the Confederate Army of resources, the march was infinitely successful. It is also true, however, that much of the damage done during the march had nothing to do with military infrastructure. Sherman himself estimated that three-fourths of the damage done to Georgia by his troops was "simple waste and destruction." For this, he was neither apologetic nor disappointed. "This may seem a hard species of warfare," Sherman explained to Grant, "but it brings the sad realities of war home to those who have been directly or indirectly instrumental in involving us in its attendant calamities."[54]

The march to the sea would go down in history as arguably the most famous single campaign of the entire war. It is important to note that the Meridian expedition and the march to the sea were just two sequential steps in a two-year process in which the Union armies in the West became hardened by their experiences. The soldiers and officers of Sherman's army did not become capable of such destruction overnight. As much as they wanted the war to end, and end quickly, they still had to be conditioned by years of hard fighting, anger, and frustration in order to consider the Southern people as the enemy, worthy of losing their property, livestock, and often their homes. They first had to believe that the citizens were guilty and deserving of the cruelties of war. The guerrilla problem made that association possible and gave Sherman's men the justification they needed to view Southern civilians as active participants in the war. Of course, there were other influential elements of the war that contributed to this view, but when Sherman argued, as he so often did, that he was "justified in treating all the inhabitants as combatants," he almost always made directed reference to the guerrillas or bushwhackers.[55] The same was true of his soldiers. On the march, one of Sherman's officers wrote, "We must make war, and it must *be* war, it must bring destruction and desolation, it must make the innocent suffer as well as the guilty, it must involve plundering, burning, and killing. Else it is worse than a sham."[56] It would not have been easy to validate such thinking had it not been for the widely accepted notion that the Union was fighting a hostile and violent population in the South. After enduring almost three years in which guerrilla attacks became almost commonplace, and in some places the norm, it was not difficult for soldiers to reach that conclusion. Once they had, they could rationalize what they had to do, because the war Sherman's army waged in 1864, which Russell Weigley referred to as "campaigns of terror and destruction," did require some rationalization or justification.[57] Despite the fact that the actual damage done to Mississippi and Georgia in 1864 never quite lived up to the bold rhetoric often used by Sherman and his soldiers, what did take place was hardly imaginable three years prior.

Following Christmas in Savannah, Sherman's army pushed north into the Carolinas in early 1865. There Sherman would continue his destructive binge, highlighted by the directed devastation of Columbia, South Carolina. All along their path, Sherman's soldiers put priority in burning as much as they could, torching at least a dozen towns before arriving in the state capital. This "indiscriminate havoc," as Mark Grimsley called it, exceeded previous punitive war measures and showed the worst of what Sherman and his soldiers were capable of doing. According to Joseph Glatthaar, Sherman's "firebugs" practiced their "policy of devastation" in South Carolina with increased severity, eclipsing their work in Georgia.[58] As the army plowed (and burned) its way north, it did so with a sense of vengeful righteousness. The first state to withdraw from the Union was reaping the consequences, and most of Sherman's men were happy to deliver what they saw as a just punishment.[59] They had arrived in the East victorious, carrying their own brand of warfare, born in the Mississippi Valley and hardened from Vicksburg to Savannah, with them as they headed north toward Virginia and eventual victory. They considered themselves harder, more determined, than their contemporaries in the armies of the East which had been embarrassed time and time again by Robert E. Lee.

But the soldiers huddled in the trenches facing Petersburg and marching through the mountain passes of the Blue Ridge were not so different. They were certainly no strangers to the guerrilla threat or the punitive response it evoked. Union troops fighting in the Eastern Theater, and especially in Virginia, suffered the same anger and frustration that Sherman's soldiers had experienced and they reacted in a similar fashion. The tragic dance between the guerrilla problem and punitive war built slowly in the Old Dominion for three years until it reached a violent crescendo at the end of 1864. In one of the South's most picturesque settings, scenes of violence and devastation emerged that rivaled those seen in any other theater of the war.

CHAPTER FIVE

The Valley Aflame: Punitive War in Virginia

There is but one remedy where people have determined upon such diabolism[guerrilla warfare], and that is to smoke them out and drive them with fire and sword until not a vestige of them or their places remains to blot the fair face of the earth.
—*New York Herald*, 8 January 1865

What began in the West ended in the East. As President Abraham Lincoln pulled key leaders from the Western Theater in 1863 and 1864 to remedy the Union's habit of failure in Virginia, he changed the character of the war in the region. Throughout the war, Virginia served as the strategic and political focal point of the Confederacy's fight for independence, and it was there that the conflict was ultimately decided. Considering the great amount of time that Union soldiers spent occupying Virginia, it is not surprising that they quickly became acquainted with the troubles caused by a hostile, and sometimes violent, population. The guerrilla problem presented itself to a limited extent during the Peninsula Campaign of 1862 but sprang up in full force in the mountainous region of western Virginia and eventually infested the Shenandoah Valley. In response, the policies instituted by Generals Ulysses S. Grant and Philip H. Sheridan, all with the approval of Chief of Staff Henry W. Halleck, served as clear evidence of the link between the guerrilla problem and punitive policies adopted by the Union. These veterans of the war in the West, hardened by their experiences with the hostile Southern population, brought a new ruthlessness to the war in the East. Although it took two years for those at the highest levels of Federal command to openly endorse and exercise punitive war in Virginia, the change at ground level began almost immediately.

In many ways, the transition to punitive war in Virginia mirrored that seen in other states, and in previous American wars. First, the guerrilla problem was considered annoying but no real threat to conciliatory policies. Then, Union field commanders began to warn the Southern people against supporting guerrilla activity lest they lose their property. Finally, threats of retributive burning were carried out, often targeting entire towns and counties. The response to guerrilla warfare in Virginia, however, was exceptional because of its sheer magnitude by 1864. Nowhere else did punitive policies receive such attention (and sanction) from the Union leadership, and nowhere else were they such an integral part of the Union war effort. Virginia served as the focal point for the culmination of three years of anger, frustration, and hardened Federal attitudes.

Historians have often made the mistake of overlooking guerrilla activity that took place in Virginia before 1863, the year that famed Confederate partisan leader John Singleton Mosby began his well-documented guerrilla campaign in northern Virginia and the Shenandoah Valley.[1] The state's guerrilla problem, and its debilitating effects on Union soldiers' faith in conciliation, actually began much earlier. In order to fully understand the scope of the Union policies that devastated much of Virginia in the war's final months, one must first consider the long road that led to them, and where it began.

From the beginning of the war, the military and political situation in western Virginia was a mess, even after fifty pro-Union counties in the region broke off to establish the new state of West Virginia in May 1862. A chaotic political and military situation, similar to that seen in Missouri in 1861, gripped the rural Kanawha Valley west of the Allegheny Mountains. Bitter sectional conflict raged between secessionist and pro-Union communities throughout the mountainous region, creating an atmosphere dangerous for soldier and civilian alike. Small gangs of irregular militia and home guards with colorful names, such as "The Black Striped Company" and "Swamp Dragoons," targeted neighboring towns and attacked soldiers and supply trains when they were vulnerable.[2] Federal rail and telegraph lines, always a favorite target of bushwhackers, were damaged almost daily. Predictably, secessionist guerrillas were most active wherever the largest contingent of occupying Union forces were, and in the first year of the war, they plagued the section of western Virginia occupied by the U.S. Army's Mountain Department, which included the Kanawha Valley. According to Major General Jacob D. Cox, the commander of Union forces in the Kanawha District, western Virginia's guerrillas were "in the height of their pernicious activity" during the first two years of the war.[3] Communications between Cox and his counterparts in the spring of 1861 expressed daily frustrations with secessionist bushwhacking. Historian Russell Weigley claimed that the only way the pro-Confederate population of western Virginia could be controlled was "under the bayonets of the Union Army."[4] Although Federal forces under Major General George B. McClellan were able to expel the Confederate Army from the region by the summer of 1861, the problems with local guerrillas were just beginning.

Union officers found it increasingly difficult to maintain troop discipline in the chaotic environment. Brigadier General F. W. Lander alluded to the challenge in early 1862 when he wrote that his command acted "more like an armed mob than an army."[5] Soldiers looking to inflict hardship on local citizens looted and terrorized towns throughout the region. Commenting on the rabid pillaging being conducted by soldiers in the region, one Federal officer claimed, "the evil has grown intolerable," while reminding his men, "The soldiers of the Republic are here to enforce, not violate, the laws."[6] Little could be said or done, however, to assuage the anger Union troops felt whenever one of their own was found dead, shot by opportunistic bushwhackers.

Officers tried to check civil disorder by warning civilians that they would lose their homes and property unless they suppressed guerrilla depredations in their neighborhoods. When Brigadier General Benjamin F. Kelley took command of the Department of Harper's Ferry and the Cumberland in October of 1861, he issued a warning to the local population. "If you attempt to carry on guerrilla warfare against my troops," he cautioned, "you will be considered enemies of your country and treated accordingly."[7] Another commander warned the people of Wardensville that they were to be held "strictly accountable for any future demonstrations of guerrilla warfare," and that "the only way to save their houses from conflagration was for them to defend their territory against incursions of all lawless bands of guerrillas."[8] Although Union field commanders often issued orders to their soldiers prohibiting foraging and the wanton destruction of private property, they were more emphatic in their warnings to Virginians about supporting guerrilla activity. Such was the case with the town of Moorefield, which was told by a Union colonel to expect to feel "the strong arm of the government" should the population become hostile.[9]

For all their talk of conflagration and other severe punishments, Union officers mostly refrained from retaliating against civilians during the summer of 1861. They hoped, instead, that their army would achieve rapid success on the battlefield, leaving the misguided rebels little choice but to accept Union authority. When news of the Partisan Ranger Act surfaced in April 1862, however, Federal officers and soldiers were livid. The Confederate government's authorization of independent guerrilla units was enough to convince many soldiers in blue that they were fighting an enemy who did not abide by the rules of war.

This anger contributed to creating a climate of ruthlessness in the Kanawha Valley in which both sides showed little mercy and took few prisoners. In May 1862, one Union officer reported an attack in which one of his soldiers was beaten to death by bushwhackers at the house of a known secessionist. In response, a Union detachment rode to the scene where they then "shot the owner of the house and burnt the house." Another suspected guerrilla was killed during an attempted escape.[10] In a similar case, some fifty suspected bushwhackers were captured near the small market town of Beverly in Randolph County. According to a member of the Eighty-Seventh Pennsylvania Volunteers, a handful of the prisoners were sent to nearby prisons or paroled, but the remainder was to be shot. "Six of them is centanced [*sic*] all ready to have their Braines Blowed out," he reported the day following their capture.[11] Fresh off his ill-fated command in Missouri, John C. Frémont was reintroduced to the guerrilla problem in the West Virginia mountains, where bushwhackers hounded his soldiers "from right to left." In order to send a message to would-be guerrillas, Frémont "promptly executed by hanging" a number of captured bushwhackers. In his own words, it was "a preventative measure" to warn all guerrillas that they were not to be afforded the rights of regular prisoners of war.[12] These and other similar incidents throughout the western counties demonstrated a growing willingness to forego any arrest or trial procedures, and the belief that summary execution of bushwhackers and their supporters was not only justified, but necessary.

One of those strongly in favor of a no-prisoners policy was Major General George Crook, who wrestled with the guerrilla problem as a brigade commander in the Kanawha Division in 1862. In his memoirs, Crook expressed his disgust with the "cowardly bushwhackers" of western Virginia, who would frequently "waylay the unsuspecting traveler." They were such a threat to Union operations, Crook claimed, that their suppression became "a military necessity." With Union officers and soldiers alike growing increasingly tired of bushwhacking, Crook described the ruthlessness surrounding the handling of captured guerrillas:

> In a short time no more of these [guerrilla] prisoners were brought in. By this time every bushwhacker in the country was known, and when an officer returned from a scout he would report that they had caught so-and-so, but in bringing him in he had slipped off a log while crossing a stream and broke his neck, or that he was killed by an accidental discharge of one of the men's guns, and many like reports. But they never brought back any more prisoners.[13]

On the war's grand stage, however, the killing of a few bushwhackers in the mountains of western Virginia went largely unnoticed, especially during the war's first two years. The Union's largest force in the field, the Army of the Potomac, was preparing for its invasion of the Virginia Peninsula, a campaign they hoped would culminate with the capture of the Confederate capitol of Richmond. All eyes, to include those of the press and Northern public, were on the grand army's preparations. It is not surprising, then, that the rapid demise of conciliation in western Virginia was scarcely mentioned in Federal dispatches. When winter turned to spring in 1862, however, Union commanders from the West began to make their way to Virginia and other parts of the Eastern Theater. They brought with them the seeds of punitive war, borne from their frustrations with guerrillas in Missouri, Mississippi, and Tennessee. With their arrival, the issue of guerrilla warfare in the East gained more attention. It was not until generals such as John Pope, Henry W. Halleck, Ulysses S. Grant, and eventually, Philip H. Sheridan came east that the punitive war that had been escalating in the mountains of West Virginia would receive official sanction and become part of the larger Union war effort.

In June 1862, John Pope was summoned to Washington to assume command of the newly formed Army of Virginia, which consisted of three corps stationed in northern Virginia. President Abraham Lincoln hoped that the aggressive commander could duplicate his success at Island No. 10 and inject some badly needed vigor into the Union campaign in Virginia.[14] Pope immediately issued a series of general orders intended to introduce a new level of severity to the dealings with civilians in the region. Before he took command, Pope had been informed of an escalating guerrilla problem in northern Virginia and the Shenandoah Valley. On 30 June 1862, Pope received word from Major General Franz Sigel that the Shenandoah was "full of small guerrilla bands" requiring a substantial force for guard and patrol duty along the railroads.[15] It appeared that the problem had followed Pope from Missouri, and that he was destined to once again deal with bushwhacking along his railroads and lines of communication. Pope acted quickly by endorsing a system of collective responsibility, just as he had done a year earlier. Pope's General Orders No. 7, issued on 10 July 1862, threatened Virginia's citizens with levies, loss of property, and possible arrest in response to any guerrilla attacks on the railroads or communication lines. Those people "detected in such outrages" against Union troops or property would be shot "without awaiting civil process," Pope ordered. In addition, if Union troops were fired upon from any private house, the structure would be immediately "razed to the ground." All of which was necessary, Pope claimed, to ensure that the citizens of Virginia assumed the responsibility of putting down guerrilla activity.[16] In addition to Orders No. 7, Pope issued Orders 5, 6, and 11, which announced his intention to live off the enemy's countryside and to arrest all "disloyal males" within the Union lines and force them to take the oath of loyalty to the Union. Pope warned that any citizen found to be in violation of the oath after taking it would be shot.[17]

Reactions to Pope's orders were mixed. Confederate authorities predictably decried them as a violation of "the rules of recognized warfare." President Jefferson Davis claimed that Pope was authorizing "savage practices" that could propel the conflict into a war of "indiscriminate robbery and murder."[18] The opponents of conciliation on the Union side applauded the harsh tenor of Pope's directives. Many Union soldiers, frustrated with previous Federal policies that limited retaliation against disloyal civilians, hailed them.[19] And yet, for a number of Union officials, Pope's orders went too far. In Washington, Chief of Staff Halleck expressed disapproval of Pope's directive to force the oath of allegiance upon citizens, claiming the policy to be "injudicious."[20] Given his own rigid policies toward guerrilla sympathizers in Missouri, Halleck's objection was somewhat surprising. Despite his disapproval, he did nothing to stand in the way of the publication of Pope's directives.

Scholars have commonly viewed Pope's orders as a significant milestone in the Union's move toward a more aggressive, more total, war. Daniel Sutherland argued that Lincoln brought Pope east to implement a new "revolutionary policy" of total war. One scholar claimed that Pope's orders "rock[ed] the conservative military establishment and set a new tenor for the conduct of the war in the East."[21] These views and others paint Pope's directives as the opening salvo announcing the Union's decision to make war in earnest (although the definition of "war in earnest" has varied from study to study). With plans for emancipation in the works and efforts made to increase the size of the Union Army in the summer of 1862, Lincoln and his advisors were clearly taking steps to expand the scope of the war.

These events, however important, were not the first triggers that compelled Union soldiers to move past conciliation and fight with a heavier hand. The war at ground level had already become a very "earnest" affair, particularly with the treatment of civilian property. One had only to look to the mountains and valleys in western Virginia during the summer of 1862 to see elements of Union heavy-handedness that would increase as the conflict dragged on. In actuality, Pope's orders in Virginia were just an extension of the policies he had implemented months before in guerrilla-plagued Missouri. They carried the same punitive war message that saw its origins during the first months of the war. Far from a new idea, collective responsibility was officially being introduced to Virginians at about the same time that Grant and Sherman's troops were implementing it in the Mississippi Valley. Indeed, Pope's new orders were, in some cases, more severe than his previous directives. As Daniel Sutherland pointed out, never before had Pope officially mentioned the razing of houses or the exile of citizens in official orders. As such, Sutherland claimed, his previous policies "lacked the ruthless tinge" of his new directives in Virginia.[22] Even so, Pope had previously tolerated, even promoted, the destruction of any property linked to those who threatened or burned the bridges and railroads in guerrilla-infested Missouri.[23] Therefore, the tenor of his previous policies matched that of his orders in Virginia, even if the exact wording did not.

Furthermore, as Mark Grimsley noted, Pope's orders were never truly enforced during his tenure as a commander in Virginia.[24] During his relatively short two-month command, which ended ingloriously in defeat at Second Manassas, little was done to punish Virginians for guerrilla activity. If nothing else, the orders stood as further evidence that the attitudes of the Union military and political leadership were catching up to those of their angry, frustrated soldiers. For Pope, it was the solidification of a course he had set months before and would continue in his dealings with Indians in the Midwest later in the war.[25] It would not take long, however, for the threats mentioned in Pope's orders to be carried out against Virginians.

The most compelling reason to view Pope's orders as a significant development in the East stems from their stark contrast with the policies of his predecessor, Major General George B. McClellan. The "Young Napoleon" was a champion of the conciliatory approach if there ever was one. The extreme caution he employed on the battlefield (his ultimate undoing) extended to his treatment of the Southern people. It had been McClellan who, in the war's first months, promised the people of western Virginia that all of their rights were to be "religiously respected" by the Union Army. "Remember that your only foes are the armed traitors," McClellan reminded his Ohio regiments before they marched into western Virginia, "and show mercy even to them when they are in your power, for many of them are misguided."[26] Even after being battered by General Robert E. Lee's army during the Seven Days Battles in June of 1862 and forced into an embarrassing retreat to the James River, McClellan held firm to his conciliatory convictions. On 7 July, McClellan presented President Lincoln with his famous Harrison's Landing Letter, in which he called for the government to develop a "civil and military policy" that would address the difficulties of dealing with the enemy population. "It should not be a war looking to the subjugation of the people," McClellan argued, "In prosecuting the war, all private property and unarmed persons should still be strictly protected . . . and offensive demeanor by the military toward citizens promptly rebuked."[27] Included in the letter were McClellan's warnings against allowing the war to interfere with slavery and the consequences of living off the enemy's country. Certainly, when compared to McClellan's emphasis on restraint, Pope's orders appeared to be a radical shift toward a more severe method of war making.

Because McClellan was so emphatic about the careful treatment of civilians, some historians have concluded that the entire Army of the Potomac upheld his views. Such was not always the case. Although their commander was steadfast in his support for conciliation, officers and soldiers of McClellan's army were quick to speak up against the policy when they realized that much of Virginia's population was hostile and, at times, violent. Even early on, some expressed interest in seeing disloyal citizens on the Peninsula hanged.[28] Others believed that the ruthless behavior of their rebel enemies, both regular and guerrilla, would eventually make conciliation impossible. After hearing that local rebels had executed a group of captured Union soldiers in early May 1862, Captain Francis A. Donaldson claimed that such events were "taking the poetry off the honorable conduct which I always believed actuated belligerents."[29] McClellan's failure in the Peninsula Campaign may have rankled the Northern politicians and public, making them eager for a more aggressive prosecution of the war, but the soldiers in the Army of the Potomac began to question the utility of conciliation well before they left the Peninsula.

The radical disparity between McClellan's attitude toward the treatment of civilians and Pope's orders was just one indication of the changes in store for the people of Virginia. Perhaps no other state in the occupied South witnessed such an immediate and drastic reversal in official Union policy. But official policies were not all that Virginians had to worry about. One had only to look to the western mountains to see Union troops and field commanders taking matters into their own hands, regardless of the official policy.

When early conciliatory tones failed to prevent guerrilla trouble around secessionist strongholds in the Allegheny Mountains, Union commanders and troops quickly focused their antiguerrilla efforts on the local population. This was done not in response to Pope's authorization orders, because it began even before they were published. To the young officers and soldiers trying in vain to get a handle on the chronic bushwhacking taking place in the Kanawha Valley, it seemed like the next logical step. The citizens were, after all, the eyes and ears of every small community and were expected to know who the guerrillas were and where they could be found. In late May 1862, a number of soldiers from Lieutenant Colonel Stephen Downey's Potomac Infantry Brigade were killed by guerrillas outside the town of Wardensville, located just 4 miles from the border with Virginia. Downey quickly gathered the townspeople together to deliver a stern warning. "The citizens were warned that they would be held strictly accountable for any future demonstrations of guerrilla warfare," he reported, "and plainly informed that the only way in which they could save their houses from conflagration was for them to defend their territory against incursions of all lawless bands of guerrillas."[30] It was a common refrain—the same heard by citizens wherever the guerrilla problem flourished—if they wanted to protect their homes and property they would have to somehow stop the guerrillas from attacking. In most cases, it was an unreasonable expectation. In some places, it was an impossible one. On the rare occasion that a community was able to coerce guerrillas and bushwhack-ers to halt or suspend their operations in their area, there was no guarantee that it would last. Of course, many citizens did actively know and support the guerrillas and chose to feign ignorance in hopes of avoiding Union reprisal, a tactic that worked less and less as the war went on.

Major General George Crook, an Indian-fighter before and after the war, was at the forefront of dealing with the guerrilla problem in West Virginia. After the war, he reflected on the futility of pursuing bushwhackers through the mountain passes. "It was an impossibility for them to be caught," Crook remembered. As a result, he claimed, his troops would "burn out" entire coun-ties "to prevent the people from harboring them [guerrillas]."[31] The practice of burning suspected guerrilla hideouts was adopted by Federal troops in Virginia as early as January 1862, when an Ohio regiment burned the town of Guyandotte.[32] At a time when the Army of the Potomac was preparing for what was expected to be the campaign to capture Richmond, however, the burning of a small town here or there did not make headlines. Nevertheless, it was a sure indicator that the conciliatory policy was rapidly eroding from the ground up. Some might argue that the relative isolation of the western portion of Virginia made the survival of conciliation in that region less than a priority, but its close proximity to the contested border states of Kentucky and Maryland made the situation there all too important.

While retaliatory burnings were conducted sporadically throughout Vir-ginia during the first two years, Union commanders usually resorted to menacing words first. As in other theaters of the war, threats of collective punishment preceded actual deeds. When suspected guerrillas fired upon Colonel J. P. Taylor's cavalry vedettes patrolling near the town of Warrenton in early 1863, the commander was incensed. "The guerrillas around War-renton are very troublesome . . . the citizens do all in their power to help and encourage these people," he wrote. Taylor then proposed that he could end further attacks by placing his artillery just outside of the town "with orders to open upon this place in case we are disturbed."[33] In another example, when civilians from the town of Lewisburg fired upon wounded Union soldiers from their houses, Crook threatened to burn all the homes and to execute the guilty parties in the main street of town "as examples."[34] Further to the east, in the Tidewater region near the cities of Norfolk and Portsmouth, Briga-dier General Henry Naglee reported his own frustrations with guerrillas. "It is impossible to distinguish them from the farmers of the country," he claimed, adding that his troops were "at a great disadvantage" when trying to avoid guerrilla ambush. As a solution, Naglee claimed he would force "the most influential, restless secessionists of the vicinity" to walk in the forefront of his formations, thereby making them potential targets. He also reported arresting "a large number" of citizens suspected of feeding or otherwise "encouraging" the guerrillas.[35]

Tough talk was not enough to keep guerrillas and bushwhackers from their harassment of Union troops, however, and therefore retaliation against civilian property soon became the norm. In April 1862, a Federal cavalry company entered the small town of Addison during its search for guerrillas in southwestern Virginia. The troops burned the town to the ground after determining that it was a base for guerrilla activity. "The bushwhackers have been taught a lesson by their losses of life and property that they will not soon forget," harped a major of the Thirty-Sixth Ohio who reported the incident.[36] In a similar example, an observer in western Virginia wrote how "infernal guerrillas" had detonated an explosive under a railroad, targeting passenger cars loaded with Union troops. "The perpetrator of this outrage, of course, could not be discovered," he wrote, "but a man living nearby seemed to be implicated, and his house and barn were burnt."[37] Such incidents were not easily justified and were therefore often omitted from official correspondence. Historians that rely strictly upon official reports and records to tally the number of destructive engagements and campaigns fail to identify the incalculable amount of damage that was conducted throughout the South but never reported. So much of the punitive war that was waged against civilians and their property was captured only in the personal letters and diaries of those who witnessed it. One can assume that much of it was never documented at all.

Of course, there were plenty of applications of punitive war that were indeed well documented, even if they did not make headlines at the time. Toland's Raid, which took place in the southwestern mining town of Wytheville, was yet another example of an increasingly heavy Federal hand. On 18 July 1863 a Union column of 872 soldiers under the command of Colonel John T. Toland marched into Wytheville with the intent of destroying the town's productive salt works. As the soldiers reached the outskirts of the town, they came under heavy fire from the surrounding houses. Lieutenant Colonel Freeman Franklin of the Thirty-Fourth Ohio Infantry later reported that "Soldiers, citizens and even women" fired at the Federal column from "both public and private" houses. Toland and another popular young officer were killed during the fighting. In response, Franklin reported, "We burned the town to ashes." West Virginia cavalryman James Abraham's regiment entered the town at the height of the fighting, and what he saw made a lasting impression. "Every window and house top seemed to be a living sheet of flame," he wrote, "the frantic shrieks of women and children as they fled the places of safety all conspired to make up a scene which I cannot describe but which will never be erased from memory." Reporting on the incident days later, Brigadier General E. Parker Scammon acknowledged that his soldiers "totally destroyed the town," given the fact that they were fired upon "by the citizens, even by the women."[38] Apparently, women combatants were deemed even less acceptable than their male guerrilla counterparts.

The damage done during Toland's raid was not unprecedented, but it was more extensive than most other incidents in Virginia up to that point. None of the official reports of the incident mentioned any kind of investigation or civil process used to determine the guilty individuals before the town was set aflame. It is certainly possible, if not probable, that a good number of homes that were burned had indeed been used by rebel cavalry or townspeople to attack the Federal column. In this instance, the Federals could well justify their destruction. Since the majority of the buildings in the town were destroyed, however, it is likely that many of the homes were burned unnecessarily. Also, the relative ease with which the Federal troops took to burning Wytheville in retaliation for the loss of three officers and fourteen soldiers, less than 2 percent of their force, was noteworthy. It highlighted a flaw in the existing legal guidelines provided in the Lieber Code and military thinking of the Union high command that insisted on protection for the lives and property of the "innocent." Guilt or innocence was never truly defined, and both Union troops and Southern civilians found that the guerrilla problem made such definitions nearly impossible.

The importance of Toland's Raid was not that it demonstrated Union willingness to wage punitive war in Virginia. Evidence of that could be seen as early as 1861. The destruction of Wytheville, rather, served as a semi–official endorsement of the notion that civilian innocence was subjective, proof of wrongdoing was not necessary, and that an entire town could be destroyed in retaliation for a few deaths. Toland's Raid meant the same for Virginia that Sherman's destruction of Randolph, Tennessee, had meant for the Mississippi Valley. The idea of collective responsibility had taken root in the Old Dominion, albeit a few months later than in the Western Theater. Also, the proportionality of retribution had no strict guideline. In Wytheville's case, the death of a Union officer warranted the destruction of an entire town in the eyes of the frustrated Federals.

The year of 1863 marked a geographic shift in the focal point of guerrilla activity in the state from the mountains of West Virginia to the Shenandoah Valley and northern Virginia. The character of the guerrilla problem changed as well, from a struggle with unruly, decentralized bushwhackers to a ruthless campaign against more organized guerrilla and partisan bands that hindered Union operations to a greater degree. Whereas West Virginia was a relative sideshow in the war in the Eastern Theater, and therefore easily ignored by the Union leadership, once military operations in the strategically important stretches of northern Virginia and the Shenandoah Valley came under guerrilla attack, the issue received much more attention from the Federal military and political leadership. Many of the soldiers who struggled early on with the bushwhacking population in the Mountain Department of western Virginia experienced similar problems when they moved east of the Shenandoah Mountains.

Any discussion of Virginia's guerrilla problem in the latter years of the war must center, to a large extent, on John Singleton Mosby. A former lawyer turned Confederate cavalry commander, Mosby formed his own battalion of independent partisan rangers in late 1862 in order to harass the Union outposts in his native northern Virginia. He quickly became the state's most prominent, and celebrated, guerrilla leader. Over the years, historians have made concerted efforts to establish Mosby and his command as *partisans*, rather than guerrillas or bushwhackers. Such claims have merit, because Mosby's irregulars did, in fact, wear Confederate uniforms (although not always) and maintained a cohesive unit with a specified operational objective. As such, the men in Mosby's command met Francis Lieber's definition of partisans outlined in General Orders 100.[39] When describing the difference between Mosby's partisans and Missouri's guerrillas, historian Michael Fellman claimed that the Virginians "sometimes disciplined their appetites for the destruction of civilian lives and property."[40] Interested in more than just plunder, Mosby's expressed goal was to compel the Federal enemy to detach large numbers of troops to the rear to guard against his attacks, and to thereby "diminish his aggressive strength."[41] To that end, Mosby constantly harassed the supply lines of nearly every Federal force that crossed into northern Virginia or entered the Shenandoah Valley after 1862. Usually operating with no more than 100 men at a time, Mosby's band would strike quickly capturing loaded wagons, horses, and unsuspecting Union troops and would then rapidly disappear into the tricky network of wooded trails and mountain passes. Confederate military and political authorities thought enough of Mosby's operations to keep his partisans in the field, even after the Partisan Ranger Act was repealed in 1864, which prohibited all other guerrilla outfits from operating because of their uncontrollable, disreputable behavior.[42]

As usual, the fact that Mosby's group carried Confederate commissions and reported to Confederate authorities mattered little to their blue-clad enemies. Union soldiers, commanders, and politicians characterized Mosby as a guerrilla chief, and his operations as guerrilla warfare. While many of his men proudly referred to themselves as guerrillas, this characterization somewhat puzzled Mosby, even after the war. The notion that his irregular operations were somehow illegal or unfair seemed to him silly and naïve. "The complaints against us did not recognize the fact that there are two parties of

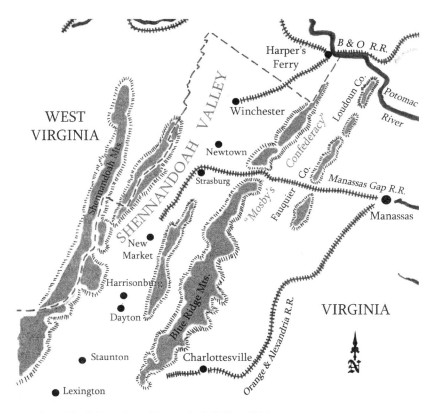

Northern Virginia and the Shenandoah Valley, 1864

equal rights in a war," Mosby penned in his memoirs. "The error men make is in judging conduct in war by the standards of peace." As for the claims that he did not fight fair, the well-educated Mosby replied. "The same complaint was made by the Austrians against Napoleon."[43] Considering his tactics, however, it is not surprising that Mosby's adversaries saw him as a guerrilla. His *modus operandi* on the battlefield mirrored that of other guerrillas and bushwhackers throughout the occupied South. The perturbed Yankees had no reason to assume he was any different.

Brigadier General Henry Lockwood complained about Mosby's "contemptible body of irregulars" operating throughout northern Virginia in the summer of 1863. Lockwood along with several others predicted that the harassing guerrillas could be caught with a simple, coordinated cavalry effort.[44] Within months, Mosby's exploits had become so frequent and well known that a stretch of territory running east from Loudoun County to the Blue Ridge was referred to as "Mosby's Confederacy" by soldiers and reporters

A raid on Union supply wagons by Mosby's men (*Harper's Weekly*)

from both North and South. Mosby himself was given the fanciful moniker "The Gray Ghost." In addition to fear and frustration, Mosby often invoked a warrior's respect from his enemies. "No matter how very much this man is hated by us, and called a guerrilla," a Union captain wrote, "Mosby is a remarkable man, a very active and bold fellow."[45]

Because of Mosby's battlefield celebrity, Union soldiers often made the mistake of assuming that all irregulars operating in northern Virginia and the Shenandoah belonged to his command, an error that scholars have often made as well.[46] In truth, guerrillas in the region came in all sorts. According

Colonel John S. Mosby, Virginia's most accomplished guerrilla leader (Library of Congress)

to historian Bruce Catton, most of them were "about one degree better than plain outlaws, living for loot and excitement."[47] Deserters from the Confederate Army often found their way into guerrilla bands operating in the Shenandoah, as did invalids and local ruffians set on giving the Federal occupiers as much problem as possible. John Q. Winfield, Curtis Lincoln (a cousin of the President), Mudwall Jackson, and Buck Woodson all commanded ragtag groups of what historian John Heatwole termed "pick-up irregulars" and "impromptu guerrilla warriors."[48] Despite their lack of organization or recognition from the Confederate government, these groups were deadly at times, and they significantly heightened the anxiety of Union troops moving through the Valley. There were other partisan bands as well, formed under the Confederate Partisan Ranger Act. Like Mosby's crew, the partisan commands of John Hanson McNeill and Elijah White usually wore uniforms, maintained a semblance of organization, and reported regularly to the Confederate authorities. In all, the complex guerrilla problem in Virginia included both organized partisan operations as well as the random, decentralized attacks from opportunistic bushwhackers like those seen in Missouri, Mississippi, and Tennessee. Since their irregular tactics were similar, however, Union officials and troops were content to classify all of them as guerrillas.

Perhaps this indiscriminate approach to the threat created more difficulty for the Federal occupiers. According to one scholar, it was the Union Army's "confusion over the doctrinal differences between bushwhackers, guerrillas, and partisans" in Virginia that resulted in a failed campaign to combat them.[49] Confusion with doctrine, however, was not the real issue; the inability to achieve tactical success against irregulars was. Being able to differentiate between a guerrilla and a partisan did not matter if you could not kill or capture either one of them. Union forces occupying Virginia found themselves in the difficult position of dealing simultaneously with a hostile population, numerous types of irregulars, and elements of the regular Confederate Army. In response, the Federals tried a number of different methods to pacify the region. Among these was a concerted effort to combat irregulars actively, or head-on, using extensive cavalry patrolling as well as their own guerrilla-type tactics. Within the Mountain Department of western Virginia, where bushwhacking was the principal threat to Yankee occupiers, Union generals John C. Frémont, Jacob D. Cox, and George Crook tried at length to pacify the region with cavalry patrolling. It was generally believed that more men on faster horses with better arms would be sufficient to "break up and destroy" the numerous guerrilla parties.[50] Colonel Henry Lazelle, commander of the Sixteenth New York Cavalry, bemoaned the many failures of Union cavalry against the likes of Mosby and proposed to "fight him after his own manner" by breaking the cavalry up into small groups and having them ambush Mosby's horsemen when possible.[51] Several regiments of Federal cavalry, such as the Second and Seventh New York, were given the sole mission of hunting down the Valley's guerrillas in 1863 and 1864.

Union commanders also increased the number of troops stationed along railroads and supply lines to guard against guerrilla attacks. They deployed thousands of men and built several blockhouses all along the Baltimore & Ohio (B&O) and Manassas Gap Railroads, the two major lines connecting Washington with the Shenandoah, during 1864 alone.[52] Major General Christopher C. Augur, responsible for the operation of the Manassas Gap road, described its vulnerability to Halleck in October of 1864. "Simply patrolling the track and guarding the bridges is not going to be sufficient," Augur wrote, "it must be literally guarded the whole way."[53] The longer the war continued, the greater the number of Union soldiers guarding the roads became, and yet, the attacks kept coming. "The guerrillas are keeping us busy," wrote a Union soldier guarding the B&O line near Point of Rocks.

"They make many raids . . . and are generally successful." Another frustrated soldier guarding the B&O commented, "There is lots of them in and around the vacinity [*sic*] but they never show themselves."[54] Portions of the Manassas Gap Railroad became damaged beyond repair, and use of the road was halted altogether in October 1864.

Eventually, a few of the more innovative Union commanders in the field created special counterguerrilla cavalry units to try to beat the guerrillas at their own game. After arriving in the Mountain Department of Virginia, Frémont created one such unit, named "The Jesse Scouts" after his wife, to operate against bushwhackers in the Shenandoah Valley. Active in gathering intelligence for a short time, this small group's exploits were glorified in the Northern newspapers. When Frémont resigned his command of a corps in the newly formed Army of Virginia in July of 1862, the organization began to unravel. According to one scholar, the Jesse Scout company had little effect on the guerrilla situation and "spent most of its time strutting up and down the streets of West Virginia in outlandish costumes."[55] A more notable example of Union special counterguerrilla units was a small company of Ohio cavalry scouts organized by Crook and commanded by Captain Richard Blazer. Armed with Spencer repeating rifles, the Independent Union Scouts, or "Blazer's Scouts," as they became known, lived and operated as irregulars themselves throughout northern Virginia. In one rare instance, Blazer's Scouts were able to corner and defeat a small group of Mosby's force at a skirmish at Myer's Ford in West Virginia on 4 September 1864.[56]

For the most part, however, Union attempts to actively seek out and capture or kill guerrillas in Virginia failed miserably, just as they had in other parts of the South. The guerrillas' innate ability to hide and avoid decisive battle with Union cavalry stymied attempts to kill or capture them. The guerrillas were smart, elusive, and, as one Union officer put it, "sound on the road system of Old Virginny."[57] Even the specialized counterguerrilla detachments were no match for the Valley's seasoned irregulars. Blazer's Scouts were all but wiped out near Kabletown, West Virginia, when they were pounced upon by a large contingent of Mosby's partisans on the afternoon of 18 November 1864. It was one of few occasions during the war when a guerrilla force and Union cavalry met in open battle.[58] Another similar detachment, commanded by Major Henry Young, was able to gather intelligence about guerrillas but never succeeded in stopping, or even hindering, their operations. Despite some Federal ingenuity, the attempts to deal with Virginia's guerrillas directly never changed the fact that, as one Union general admitted, Union troops could not "catch guerrillas in the mountains any more than a cow can catch fleas."[59] Therefore, Union leaders relied heavily on the collective punishment measures that had been growing in severity since the war began.

They received encouragement from several Northern newspapers, such as *Harper's Weekly*, that applauded use of collective responsibility in dealing with Mosby's group:

> These guerrilla enterprises, while they exert no influence upon the issue of the war, are annoying, and must be prevented. They are only possible through the connivance of the inhabitants of the region where they take place, and these should be held accountable for all the damage done by their friends. If this rule is strictly enforced, the aiders and abettors of these marauding gangs will find that they are carrying on a losing business.[60]

Punitive war never ceased being the preferred, and most widely used, method of dealing with the guerrilla problem in Virginia. While harsh policies toward civilians were no more successful than other attempts at hindering or halting guerrilla operations, they did provide frustrated Union soldiers with a target that was easily reached. It was not as satisfying as capturing or killing guerrillas, but punitive war against supposed guerrilla supporters did allow Union troops to exorcise the vengeful demons within.

Virginia's citizens found themselves caught in the middle of an increasingly nasty struggle by 1863 and were left with few solutions for their situation. Southern women and slaves often felt the greatest impact, as they were the only ones left at home to bear the burden of Union reprisals. The stinging rebukes that Southern women commonly flung at the Yankee invaders often made the punishment more severe.[61] Some civilians were active supporters of guerrillas, others maintained Union sympathies, and there were those in the Shenandoah's numerous Quaker and Dunkard sects that wanted nothing to do with the war at all. They were often totally vulnerable, regardless of their loyalties. John P. Dulany, the patriarch of a Southern family living in the thick of Mosby's area of operations in the spring of 1863, expressed sincere concern about the results of partisans' operations on his own property. "These [guerrilla] attacks generally result in them [Union soldiers] making their reprisals on us," he wrote to his son, "it would be better for us if they [Mosby's men] staid [*sic*] away."[62] But the region's guerrillas did not stay away. In fact, they became more active, and as a result, the people of northern Virginia and the Shenandoah Valley witnessed a devastating final year to the war.

As the summer of 1864 approached, newly designated general-in-chief of the U.S. Army Ulysses S. Grant planned a series of campaigns, or "cooperative movements," aimed at attacking the Confederacy on multiple fronts. To the south, the Military Division of the Mississippi, commanded by William T. Sherman, was ordered to take the fight to Joseph Johnston's Confederate Army of the Tennessee, and to inflict as much damage as possible to the "war resources" in the interior of Tennessee and Georgia.[63] Major General

Nathaniel Banks, in command of the Army of the Gulf in Louisiana, was tasked with occupying Confederate forces in Alabama and capturing Mobile. Grant's remaining strokes were aimed at Virginia, and primarily Robert E. Lee's Army of Northern Virginia. Benjamin Butler was to move his Army of the James up the river from Norfolk and advance on Richmond. Grant himself would move with the Army of the Potomac, commanded by George Meade, on its overland campaign targeting Lee's Army of Northern Virginia. Finally, Major General Franz Sigel was directed to advance up the Shenandoah Valley, capture key railroad junctions, and deny the Confederate army access to that region's resources.[64]

Grant's plan quickly ran into problems. Banks's campaign on the Red River in Louisiana proved ineffective, and Butler's lumbering advance became bogged down in the mosquito-infested trenches at Bermuda Hundred between the Appomattox and James Rivers, just eight miles south of Richmond. In the Shenandoah Valley, Sigel's army was repulsed at the Battle of New Market on 15 May by an outgunned Confederate force under Major General John C. Breckenridge. The loss occurred partly due to the fact that Sigel had dispatched a large portion of his cavalry to pursue partisans who had harassed his supply line the previous week.[65] The humbled Federals withdrew northward, out of the Valley, much to the disgust of Grant, Halleck, and Lincoln.

Following Sigel's failed campaign, Major General David Hunter was given command of the Union's Army of West Virginia and charged with the same task as his hapless predecessor.[66] Hunter's movement down into the Valley in late May 1864 marked the arrival of punitive war in the Shenandoah. The surrounding areas west of the Alleghenies, east of the Blue Ridge, south toward Wytheville, and even "Mosby's Confederacy" to the northeast had seen some damage from the war. The Valley, however, with its rich fields and prosperous farming communities, had remained largely unharmed. That would all change when "Black Dave" Hunter, a veteran of campaigns in Missouri and staunch abolitionist, marched his new command south toward the Valley's rail center at Staunton. Within the column, Private Charles Lynch of the Eighth Connecticut Volunteers made a prophetic entry in his diary. "This is beautiful country . . . quiet and peaceful," he wrote, "but the horrors of war are liable to come at most any time."[67] And come they would.

As guerrillas and partisans quickly fell upon Hunter's supply wagons, his soldiers voiced their outrage. One noncommissioned officer described how Mosby's guerrillas were "constantly perpetrating barbarities of all kinds, and of such violation of the rules of war that they should have been followed by a fell retribution."[68] That was just what Hunter had in mind. When the guerrilla attacks came, Hunter did not react as Sigel had, with cavalry, but instead chose to retaliate by burning. If the local population had forgotten Pope's threats regarding guerrillas and their supporters from two years prior, Hunter reminded them with his own. He distributed a letter warning that his cavalry would burn all houses, barns, and property within a 5-mile radius of any guerrilla attack.[69] Valley residents soon came to see that the threat was not idle. Hunter's forces shot a civilian and burned several private homes in the vicinity of Newtown in retaliation for guerrilla attacks on Hunter's nearby supply train on 25 May. Only an impassioned plea from the towns-people kept a Union detachment from carrying out Hunter's order to raze the entire town.[70] At the rail hub of Staunton, Hunter had his men burn the public buildings and mills. Upon seeing the tear-streaked faces of a group of women as they watched Staunton burn, Private Charles Lynch noted in his diary, "Death and destruction follow the path of war."[71] This hardened approach was somewhat of a reversal for Hunter, who less than a year prior, had strongly defended the "laws and usages of civilized warfare" and the protection of civilian property while commanding Union positions along the South Carolina coast. Even then, however, he predicted a time when Southern "wickedness" might put Union troops in a position where the "immutable laws of self-defense and the stern necessity of retaliation will not only justify but enjoin every conceivable species of injury."[72] It would appear that the guerrilla problem in the Shenandoah provided enough wickedness for Hunter to refine his views on military necessity, retaliation, and the use of punitive war.

Further south, the town of Lexington was introduced to Hunter's new-found severity in the early hours of 12 June. It was home to the state's former governor, John Letcher, and the Virginia Military Institute, whose cadets had participated in the Confederate victory at New Market the month before. Hunter considered Lexington to be one of the most disloyal communities in the Valley, and therefore, in dire need of punishment. In addition to destroying all of the iron-works and mills in town, Hunter ordered the burning of the military school's buildings and Letcher's mansion. The burning was conducted, he reported, in response to "a violent and inflammatory order" that Letcher published previously "inciting the population of the country to rise and wage a guerrilla warfare on my troops." Union soldier William G. Watson confirmed the report in his memoirs, claiming that the institute and Letcher's private buildings were burned because circulars had been discovered calling on the local citizens "to bushwhack Yankee invaders."[73] For many troops in Hunter's ranks, such as Charles Lynch, the destruction of Lexington was the largest display of punitive war they had yet seen. "Hunter is applying the torch to many buildings," Lynch wrote in his diary, "It was a grand and awful sight to see so many buildings burning at the same time."[74]

For many of Hunter's troops the significance of what they were involved in was not lost and as with other practitioners of punitive war before them, they sometimes struggled to justify the destruction. For them, it was a salient point in the war, one that was tinged with uncertainty. After witnessing the burning of Lexington, infantryman John P. Suter wrote:

> The destruction of property and injury done to the rebel government by this raid I think exceeds all others ever yet made, though I am sorry to know that it is interspersed to some extent with vandalism, something which is difficult to prevent on expeditions of that character. When soldiers are turned loose to burn and destroy every graveling passion generally rises to the surface in the general ebullition and predominates.[75]

Suter understood what many of his comrades were rapidly learning—that punitive war, once unleashed, was difficult to contain. For those soldiers who had come from the Western Theater, who had fought in Missouri and the Mississippi Valley, this came as little surprise. For the citizens of the Shenandoah, however, the extent of vandalism and looting now taking place around them was unprecedented. They would see much more of it before the summer was out.

The extensive looting and burning at Lexington served little military purpose other than to make Hunter's point to the people—resistance to Union occupation would be punished. Even if the point was made, it did nothing to hinder guerrilla attacks or bushwhacking. When retreating Confederate forces burned a bridge across the Maury River south of Lexington, an angry Hunter took a retaliatory stroke at the closest target, burning a good portion of the town of Buchanan.[76]

By the time Hunter's army reached Lynchburg in mid-June, it was running dangerously low on ammunition and other supplies. Irregulars constantly harassed Union supply trains attempting to follow Hunter's force, preventing all but one from making it through. "Our commissary train with our rations had been unable to reach us," Watson recalled. Private John Weiser of the Twentieth Pennsylvania noted that "seven hundred" supply wagons had been held up because "things began to look Bilious" with the guerrillas lurking up the Valley.[77] As a consequence, Hunter's weakened army was turned back by a bolstered Confederate force at Lynchburg commanded by Jubal Early.[78] With his haggard soldiers down to their last bullets and in danger of being wiped out, Hunter made the questionable decision to retreat through the Alleghenies into West Virginia, leaving the Shenandoah open for Early's Confederate army to charge northward into Maryland and threaten Washington. What happened next, as described by Hunter's men, was something akin to Napoleon's retreat from Moscow, minus the murderous cold and ruthless

Cossacks. Their diaries and letters described a scene of desperation. "With heavy hearts, empty stomachs, and exhausted haversacks, we turned our faces toward the inhospitable mountains of West Virginia," James Abraham noted in a letter. Hunger seems to have been a major concern on the retreat. "Starvation stares us in the face," wrote Albert Artman of the Fourteenth Pennsylvania Cavalry, "100 of our men have starved to death on this retreat." Charles Lynch, who bemoaned the need to shoot the starving horses that could not keep up with the column, described the hard conditions in his diary. "Many [men] are dropping out by the roadside, too weak and used up . . . clothing and shoes giving out," he wrote. "Our suffering is intense."[79] Of all the accounts of the retreat from Lynchburg, infantryman John Suter's was one of the most descriptive, as he told how "General Starvation took up the pennant and pressed hard on flank and rear." According to Suter, many of the retreating soldiers died on the roadside from starvation and exhaustion. "The desire to get something to eat almost took precedence of discipline," he wrote, noting that in a few cases "men were found roaming the woods raving mad eating roots and bark of trees."[80] Hunter's withering army finally staggered into Charlestown, West Virginia, on 30 June, demoralized and thoroughly defeated. Yet another Union commander had failed to execute Grant's plan for the Valley.

After hearing about Hunter's destruction of Staunton, Lexington, and other locations in the Valley, Chief of Staff Halleck condemned the practice of "uselessly destroying private property" and called such methods "barbarous."[81] Halleck's objections may have been prompted by his disgust with Hunter's defeat at Lynchburg or his choice to retreat through West Virginia, because he did not criticize other more successful Union commanders, such as Grant or Sherman, for their burning ways. Also, in the war's coming months, Halleck's own policies regarding the guerrilla problem would make his condemnation of Hunter's methods smack of hypocrisy.

By summer's end, Halleck's rhetoric made it clear that he believed that the guerrilla problem was responsible for the failure of conciliation. "We have tried three years of conciliation and kindness without any reciprocation," Halleck proclaimed to Sherman in September. "On the contrary, those thus treated have acted as spies and guerrillas in our rear and within our lines." In response, Halleck claimed, the Union Army was required to "apply the severe rules of war" to the "so-called non-combatants and rebels." As always, Halleck stopped short of authorizing unrestrained destruction, but at the same time, he specifically included the Southern people in his references to the Union's "inexorable foes."[82] Even more, Halleck did not view the severe rules of war as some regrettable evil, nor did he express any reluctance in resorting to them. He saw them as a tool, essential to teaching the unruly

Southerners a harsh lesson about resisting Union authority. For two years, Halleck's ambiguous rhetoric demanded that the Union army refrain from violating the rights of innocent citizens, and yet he warned against assuming the innocence of the "so-called non-combatants." As a result, a soldier interpreting Halleck's policies would know to retaliate only against the enemy, but he might also consider all Southerners as his enemies. Like the Lieber Code, the vague nature of Halleck's directives limited their usefulness in controlling Union soldiers' retaliatory behaviors.

One notable consequence of Hunter's circuitous retreat through West Virginia was the subsequent Confederate raid into Maryland and Pennsylvania, which was highlighted by the burning of the town of Chambersburg. If there was any question as to the Confederate willingness to wage punitive war as well, it was sharply answered on the morning of 30 July 1864. A rebel brigade under the command of Brigadier General John McCausland entered the town, gathered the citizens in the town square, and demanded that a $500,000 assessment be paid for damages done to Virginia by Hunter's Army. When the citizens refused to pay, McCausland's men set fire to the town. Nearly all of the buildings, stores, and homes went up in flames.[83] Reports of the destruction of Chambersburg evoked immediate outrage from Union officials and soldiers alike. An infantryman from Pennsylvania wrote, "[The burning of Chambersburg] filled us with apprehension for the safety of our native places, the men were so exasperated that, I think, a war of extermination would have been fully endorsed by nearly every man in the regiment." When Major General Darius Couch, the commander of the Department of the Susquehanna, learned of Chambersburg's fate he called it a "premeditated deed of barbarity" conducted with "inhuman and savage ferocity."[84] It had indeed been an act of retribution, but no more barbaric or inhuman than the numerous conflagrations initiated by Union troops throughout the South. Although the guerrilla problem did not have a direct role in Chambersburg's destruction, it was largely responsible for Hunter's devastation of the Shenandoah, which in turn brought McCausland's arsonists to Chambersburg. Although historians have generally portrayed the Confederate invasions of the North as disciplined and restrained, the example of Chambersburg suggests that the rebels were certainly capable of resorting to retributive burning and punitive war. If they had spent more time in the North, occupying cities and dealing with a hostile population, it is quite possible that their actions would have mirrored those of their enemies in the occupied South.

As jarring as the destruction of Chambersburg was, it was overshadowed by the myriad of other challenges facing the Union leadership at the time. One issue that caused those in Washington, and Halleck in particular, considerable apprehension was the vulnerability of the railroads in northern

Virginia. The B&O and the Manassas Gap Railroads were the primary supply and transport arteries linking central and western Virginia. As such, they
were a source of constant worry for Union officials and a frequent target for
Virginia's partisans and guerrillas. As soon as Union troops arrived in the
Valley in May of 1864, the railroads were attacked almost daily. The most
damaging raid occurred on 5 May, when sixty partisans from western Virginia led by Captain John McNeill crossed the south branch of the Potomac
River and stormed into the B&O station at Piedmont, West Virginia. Within
an hour, they completely destroyed the depot, to include all of its machine
shops, repair facilities, railcars, and locomotives.[85]

Federal officials in Washington, to include Halleck and Secretary of War
Stanton, quickly scrambled to increase troop presence along the B&O line
in an attempt to "prevent further disaster."[86] The thousands of Union soldiers sent to patrol and guard the railroads, however, did not stop McNeill or
Mosby from continuing their attacks during the following months. Damage
from these attacks along the Manassas Gap line became so extensive that
Halleck, with approval from Secretary of War Stanton, ordered the complete depopulation and deforestation of the country bordering the railroad.
All houses within 5 miles that were not needed for Union purposes, or owned
by a known Unionist, were to be destroyed. The people were to be arrested
or sent away; none could remain. The order was justified, Halleck claimed,
because the "inhabitants along the Manassas Gap railroad" were guilty of assisting the guerrillas in their attacks.[87] According to Stephen Ash, Halleck's
order to wipe out the 75-mile stretch along the Manassas Gap line amounted
to "the virtual obliteration of an entire district."[88] Indeed, the scale of Halleck's proposed destruction was more extensive than any he had previously
authorized. In addition, the wording of the order violated his own policy of
using retaliation only "after a careful inquiry into the occurrence and character of the misdeeds that demand retribution."[89] The conclusion that all the
inhabitants along a 75-mile stretch of railroad were guilty of aiding in guerrilla attacks hardly constituted "a careful inquiry" into matters. Halleck's
normally erudite language had become tinged with the vindictiveness found
in that of Pope, Sherman, and Hunter. His plan for burning and depopulating
the district displayed the same measure of vindictiveness exhibited by John
M. Schofield in Missouri.

Yet, the worst was still to come for the people of northern Virginia and the
Shenandoah Valley. In the first week of August, Grant sent Major General
Philip H. Sheridan from central Virginia to the Shenandoah to finish the job
that both Sigel and Hunter had failed to accomplish. An accomplished cavalryman known for his aggressiveness and fiery temper, Sheridan had experienced the guerrilla problem firsthand in Mississippi earlier in the war.[90] The

Major General Philip
H. Sheridan. Sheridan
oversaw the destruction
of the Shenandoah Valley
and ordered the "Burning
Raid" on Loudoun
and Fauquier Counties
in December of 1864.
(Library of Congress)

next four months spent in the Shenandoah Valley solidified Sheridan's place in history as one of the war's most enthusiastic practitioners of hard war.

Just days after Sheridan's arrival in the Shenandoah, Mosby and his partisans provided "Little Phil" with a rude welcome. On 18 August, they attacked a convoy of Union supply wagons headed for Winchester as it lumbered past Berryville, capturing or destroying seventy wagons. The next day, Sheridan downplayed the loss, claiming that Mosby had simply "captured a few wagons." Sheridan did, however, provide a glimpse of the severity that was to come by reporting that his men had "hung one and shot six" of Mosby's men the day before.[91] Over the course of the next four months, Sheridan and the Valley's guerrillas engaged in a ruthless contest that became increasingly painful for the people living in Shenandoah. The price the Valley paid became legendary.

Sheridan's destruction of the Shenandoah in the autumn of 1864 has traditionally been viewed as the implementation of Grant and Lincoln's evolving hard war policy and the complement to Sherman's destruction of Georgia. When Sheridan arrived at his new post, Grant instructed him to destroy the Valley's capability to provide food or supplies to the Confederate Army. Should the Confederate Army have plans for the Valley in the war's final years, Grant wanted it to remain "a barren waste."[92] Sheridan was more than willing to comply, and within a few weeks, he began destroying large swaths of countryside and burning mills and warehouses to the ground. The devastation was described by Pennsylvania cavalryman Henry Keiser in his diary. "Our cavalry are burning all the grain, every mill, and every barn," he noted. "The valley is all ablaze in our rear."[93] Retreating Confederates could do nothing but watch the pillars of smoke as they blackened the sky behind them. In his diary entry for 7 October, a young Virginia cavalryman noted, "Going through Page Valley. The enemy is burning all barns, mills, and grain."[94] Indeed, when Sheridan's work was done, there was very little sustenance left in the valley for any army. The strategic importance of scorching the earth was not lost on Sheridan's men. While they did not all enjoy the grizzly work (although many of them did) they saw the necessity of it. "It seemed hard to burn barns," wrote a soldier from the Nineteenth New York, "but if we don't destroy the grain, the rebels would get it for their Army."[95] Such reasoning was used during and after the war to color Sheridan's burning as a justified act consistent with the laws of war. The practice of denying the enemy food was certainly well within the legal limits of nineteenth-century warfare and had been used throughout American history as a means of attrition. It was also common practice for retreating Confederates to burn crops and stores of grain to prevent them from falling into Union hands.

Much of the damage done to the Shenandoah, however, had less to do with Grant's order and more to do with Sheridan's frustration with the local population, whom he believed harbored the guerrillas that bothered him incessantly. It is important to separate Sheridan's retaliatory strikes from his compliance with Grant's order, because it shows that not only was Sheridan waging hard war, but punitive war as well. In doing so, we can substantiate claims like those made by James McPherson, who argued that Sheridan's soldiers were "bluecoated arsonists" who destroyed much of the Valley because they believed civilians were harboring bushwhackers.[96]

Perhaps no single incident in Virginia provided a better example of this than the ordered destruction of the town of Dayton. Located a few miles off the Valley turnpike just south of Harrisonburg, the small town was a trading center for local Mennonite and Dunkard farmers, both pacifist sects. On the gloomy afternoon of 3 October 1864 a small group of Union soldiers led by Lieutenant John R. Meigs, Sheridan's chief engineer and the son of the U.S. Army's chief quartermaster, encountered three Confederate scouts on a road outside of Dayton. A short firefight ensued, and Meigs fell dead from his horse, shot through the face and chest. Word of Meigs's death quickly made its way to Sheridan's headquarters, where it was reported that guerrillas had surprised the young officer and killed him in cold blood.[97] Sheridan was furious. According to Valley historian John Heatwole, what happened next amounted to "a firestorm of devastating proportions."[98]

Fully enraged by the loss of one of his favorite subordinates, Sheridan ordered the Fifth New York Cavalry to burn every building within a 3-mile radius of the site of the attack, to include the town of Dayton. Despite their frustrations with the guerrilla problem, many Union troops were dismayed with the severity of Sheridan's order. "When I heard the work we had to do, I was heartsick!" wrote one officer. "Such duty, I hope, our regiment will never have to perform again. The influence on the command is very demoralizing."[99] With or without moral objections, Sheridan's cavalry carried out the order, burning farms and houses in the surrounding countryside from Dayton to Harrisonburg. A last-minute plea from one of Sheridan's subordinate commanders saved the town of Dayton proper from the torch but did nothing for the scores of outlying homes and barns that went up in flames. In all, Heatwole concluded that "more than two dozen homes" were destroyed in the enforcement of Sheridan's order.[100] A scene of extensive damage is seen in Union troop accounts of the day. A member of the First New York Dragoons recorded from his position a few miles away at Mount Crawford, "The sky tonight is lit up by the burning of the little town of Dayton in retaliation for the murder of Lt. Meigs." Another observer claimed, "The whole country around is wrapped in flames, the heavens are aglow with the light thereof."[101] After his incendiaries had completed their work, Sheridan proudly reported that "all the houses within an area of five miles were burned" in response to the "atrocious act" committed by Meigs's killers. In his eyes, the order needed little justification given his experiences with the local population. "Since I came into the Valley," he wrote, "every train, every small party, every straggler has been bushwhacked by people."[102]

Many of Sheridan's subordinates, however, were not so sure. "It seems to me that the ultimate result of such burning on our cause must be very doubtful," a Union chaplain wrote after Dayton. "It will exasperate some, inciting them to deeds of greater barbarity."[103] Colonel Charles Russell Lowell, commander of one of Sheridan's cavalry brigades, wrote to his wife about the burning around Dayton and claimed, "I am glad my Brigade had no hand in it." In perhaps one of the great understatements of the war, Lowell remarked, "The war in this part of the country is becoming very unpleasant to an officer's feelings."[104] In a bit of a contrast to the soldier-driven punitive war of the Mississippi Valley, punishment in the Shenandoah usually came from the top. As Grimsley observed, commanders such as Hunter and Sheridan struggled little with the moral implications of punitive war, while their soldiers "still retained a basic morality" and often expressed regret over the burning of private homes.[105] Yet, even though they may have felt poorly about it, they still carried out their orders. Their misgivings were not enough to save the communities torched in response to guerrilla attacks.

This was not an integral part of Grant's directed destruction of the Valley. There was no strategic or operational purpose for the burning of homes and barns in and around Dayton. The small town provided little, if any, substance for the rebel army. Sheridan's intent was purely retaliatory in nature; one might even say vengeful. Just a week earlier, Halleck himself voiced his complaints about Hunter's habit of "burning private houses" in the Shenandoah.[106] Clearly, Sheridan's response to Meigs's death tested the ambiguities surrounding the rules of war. Like Sherman's destruction of Randolph, Tennessee, two years earlier, this was destruction of civilian property for the expressed purpose of punishing the local civilians who, according to Sheridan, shouldered the blame for the death of Lieutenant Meigs. No prior warning was given to the citizens. The fact that many of the people living around Dayton were known pacifists mattered little. Also, Sheridan's order showed a hardened sense of proportionality, where the death of a single Union officer justified the destruction of all property within a broad, 20-mile area. Historians who have sought to downplay the destructiveness of the war often emphasize Sheridan's willingness to spare the homes within the Dayton town limits as symbolic of Union restraint, or they ignore the incident completely.[107] Their arguments rest on the assertion that the incident was just one extreme case.

The burning around Dayton, however, was not an aberration. Unfortunately for the people of the Shenandoah, it was just the next step in a punitive process that began with Pope's caustic orders in 1862, continued with Hunter's retaliatory burnings in the region that summer, and was now being fully realized. Although historian Robert Mackey incorrectly claimed that it was Meigs's death that triggered Sheridan's famed devastation of the Valley from Staunton up to Winchester, his conclusion that "retributive burning reached its apogee during the [1864] Valley Campaign" is accurate.[108] Sheridan would burn again, and not just for the purpose of denying the Confederate Army material or food, but to punish yet another community for damage done to his supply lines. The following month, Sheridan's troops burned the town of Newtown and "all the houses within five miles" of a nearby guerrilla attack, according to a Union surgeon.[109] It is true that Sheridan's burnings were not completely unprovoked, but they certainly were not precise, either. In the words of one scholar, Sheridan's application of the torch in response to guerrilla attacks had an element of "arbitrariness" to it.[110] When two more of Sheridan's staff officers were ambushed and killed by guerrillas, Sheridan was furious. "The refugees from Early's army, cavalry and infantry, are organizing guerrilla parties and are becoming very formidable and annoying me very much," he reported to Grant. "I know of no way to exterminate them except to burn out the whole country and let the people go North or South."[111] People in certain sections of northern Virginia would soon come to find out that he was not bluffing.

Sheridan's subordinate commanders shared their leader's faith in retributive burning and did not hesitate to use it when they received reports of guerrilla activity. When Brigadier General George Armstrong Custer, the brash young commander of Sheridan's Third Division, was informed that guerrillas had attacked and killed a number of his soldiers from the Fifth Michigan Cavalry, he had the homes nearest to the attack set ablaze. In another case, Colonel William H. Powell, commander of Sheridan's Second Division, executed a suspected bushwhacker and instructed his cavalry to destroy the family's "residence, barn, buildings, and forage." Even the cool-tempered Colonel Lowell, who expressed dismay at the partial burnings around Dayton, professed the need for scorched-earth policy in order to combat guerrillas: "If it will help end bushwhacking, I approve it," he wrote, "and I would cheerfully assist in making the whole valley a desert from Staunton northward."[112] Clearly, those who oversaw the execution of Sheridan's destructive orders were themselves frustrated by the persistent threat of guerrilla attack and felt that burning of civilian property was justified.

In late October, Sheridan defeated Jubal Early's nearly starved Confederate army in the Battle of Cedar Creek, ending the Confederate Army's presence in the Shenandoah for the remainder of the war. Despite Grant's numerous directives to move his army east through the Blue Ridge and to capture the Confederate railroad junctions at Gordonsville and Charlottesville, Sheridan turned his attention instead to the guerrilla problem that caused him great annoyance throughout the summer. He offered the vulnerability of his supply lines to guerrilla attack as an excuse for delaying his push on the railroad junctions.[113] His claims of vulnerability were not altogether unfounded. Although no regular Confederate Army remained in the Valley, Mosby, McNeill, and other partisan leaders were still fully active, and Union troops in camp continued to live in fear of being bushwhacked or "gobbled up" by guerrillas. Horace Smith, a private from Vermont encamped with his regiment near Winchester, wrote home in early November to state, "The Guerrillos [sic] are troubling us very much . . . I do not venture to march from camp." Smith reported days later that guerrillas gunned down two of his comrades. At the same time, Private James Mulligan from the Fifteenth New York Cavalry confirmed the problem, stating that guerrillas were making "a good deal of trouble" in the lower Valley, enough to prevent Union troops from leaving camp in small groups.[114]

Rather than attempt a risky movement through guerrilla-infested mountain passes toward Charlottesville, Sheridan decided to address one of Grant's earlier directives. That August, Grant had become so tired of hearing about Mosby's exploits in northern Virginia and the upper Shenandoah that he ordered Sheridan to destroy all the crops, livestock, and forage in Loudoun County. In addition, Grant suggested that Sheridan arrest "all men under fifty years of age capable of bearing arms," and if any guerrillas were caught, to "hang them without trial."[115] Although Grant may have spoken more out of anger and frustration than anything else, the order still stood. What Grant was advocating, summary execution without any legal process, conflicted with the guidance provided in the Lieber Code and with other generally accepted rules of law.[116] Such an instance is noteworthy, but not altogether surprising, given Grant's history with the guerrilla problem and the attitude of the Union Army in 1864. The killing of captured bushwhackers and guerrillas was commonplace by the war's third year. Grant's proposal reflected the predominant attitude of his army at the time.

Predictably, Sheridan voiced no objection to Grant's suggested course. In fact, once he had defeated Early, Sheridan was more than ready to embrace Grant's plan to let the people of "Mosby's Confederacy" feel the strains of war. In his message to Halleck near the end of November, Sheridan made clear his belief in the link between guerrilla warfare and the need for punitive war:

> I will soon commence on Loudoun County, and let them know there is a God in Israel. Mosby has annoyed me considerably, but the people are beginning to see that he does not injure me a great deal, but causes a loss to them of all that they have spent their lives in accumulating. Those people who live in the vicinity of Harper's Ferry are the most villainous in this Valley, and have not yet been hurt much. If the railroad is interfered with I will make some of them poor. Those who live at home, in peace and plenty, want the duello part of this war to go on; but when they have to bear their burden by loss of property and comforts they will cry for peace.[117]

Sheridan sounded overly dramatic, but he was serious. He had a good reason to be, because the problem persisted. Mosby's partisans and other bands attacked Union pickets on a daily basis in the last weeks of November. One frustrated Union officer described the offenders as the most "perfect brigands and highwaymen as ever cursed a country" and noted that "their praise is sung on every southern family."[118] Sheridan had to launch a damaging blow and he had to do it quickly before Mosby's men or another partisan band could interfere with the railroad again. And so, he went to work on making the so-called villainous people in the region poor. The day after he sent his "God in Israel" decree to Halleck, he ordered the commander of his

First Cavalry Division, Major General Wesley Merritt, to ride into the area of Loudoun and Fauquier Counties, the region most commonly known as Mosby's Confederacy, and "clear the country" of guerrillas. Sheridan instructed Merritt to destroy "all forage and subsistence" and to burn "all barns and mills and their contents" in the prosperous region. "This section has been the hot-bed of lawless bands," Sheridan explained, adding that "the ultimate results of the guerrilla system of warfare is [*sic*] the total destruction of all private rights in the country occupied by such parties." And while Sheridan did include instructions against burning private houses and physically injuring civilians, he authorized the destruction or confiscation of everything that the citizens owned in the way of livestock, food, or other property.[119]

One might argue that Sheridan's order to Merritt was just part and parcel of Grant's grand plan to make the Shenandoah Valley untenable for the Confederate Army. Loudoun County, however, was on the opposite side of the Blue Ridge, and Sheridan's orders made it clear that the purpose of the devastation was to "clear out" the guerrillas, not to deny the Confederate regular forces provisions. This action, which became known as the "Burning Raid," was Sheridan's most powerful blow against Virginians for supporting the likes of Mosby and his guerrillas. Like his previous directives, it was further evidence of Sheridan's willingness to back up tough talk with tough action.

Merritt's cavalry division carried out the order, laying waste to Loudoun and Fauquier Counties during the first few days of December. Every barn and mill the Federals encountered was totally destroyed and all the livestock they found was either slaughtered or confiscated. In his report to Sheridan, Merritt admitted that he had not been able to catch or kill any guerrillas, but as to Sheridan's calls for destruction, the orders were "most fully carried out."[120] According to Union cavalryman James H. Stevenson, Merritt's cavalry "laid Mosby's Confederacy in ashes; carrying off every animal of any value that could be found. The property captured and destroyed on that occasion was valued at two millions [*sic*] five hundred thousand dollars!"[121] All citizens in the region, regardless of age, profession, or personal politics, were targeted. In the words of one of Sheridan's biographers, "Not even the fact that many of the victims were nonviolent Quakers or Union sympathizers counted for anything to the blue-shirted arsonists."[122] It was one of the most vastly destructive operations of the Civil War. Not quite on the same scale as Sherman's march across Georgia, it was certainly comparable to the execution of Schofield's Order No. 11 in Missouri the year prior.

Even Union troops were in awe of the devastation. "This was a feature of war which the bushwhacking farmers of that region had not foreseen," John Stevenson wrote afterward, "and they stood appalled at the sight. Rich valleys on both sides of the Blue Ridge had been swept by the besom of destruction,

Major General Wesley
Merritt. Merritt led the
"Burning Raid" through
"Mosby's Confederacy."
(Library of Congress)

and rendered untenable for the enemy."[123] Memories of the raid were sometimes somber. A week afterward, one of Merritt's soldiers wrote in his diary,
"The task was not a pleasant one for me . . . for many innocents were made
to suffer with the guilty." However painful, though, the soldier felt the measure was justified. "Something was necessary to clear the country of those
bands of guerillas that were becoming so formidable."[124] In saying so, the
soldier proved he was, perhaps, more sympathetic to the plight of the people
of Mosby's Confederacy than were his commanders. While Sheridan did not
share the soldier's conscience, he did share his reasoning. Should any citizens
of Loudoun County complain about their loss, he told the commander of the
Union garrison at Harper's Ferry, "Tell them that they have furnished too
many meals to guerrillas to expect much sympathy."[125]

On the surface, Merritt's Burning Raid on Mosby's Confederacy is a fair
comparison to Sherman's march to the sea, which occurred almost simultaneously. Both were blows targeted at the will of the people and intended to
bring about a more rapid conclusion to the war. Strategically, however, the
two operations were different. Sherman primarily targeted railroads, mills,
and other infrastructure that could be used to support Confederate Army

operations. Nor was the march to the sea a strictly retaliatory measure. It was an offensive that, at times, contained incidents of retaliation. With the Burning Raid, however, Sheridan directly targeted guerrillas and their supposed supporters for the express purpose of punishing them. In his own words, the raid was conducted strictly "in retaliation for the assistance and the sympathy given" to guerrillas by the local inhabitants. Like his colleague leading the march across Georgia, Sheridan expressed no remorse for employing such measures. Both campaigns were conducted by soldiers familiar with the guerrilla problem, which was instrumental in making them capable of such destruction.

Historian Mark Neely recently downplayed the significance of the Burning Raid, claiming that Merritt's cavalry did not conduct the mass arrest of the male population in Loudoun County that Grant had suggested in August. As a result, he argued that Sheridan's directive was actually a stroke of military pragmatism and that his orders simply sounded worse than they truly were.[126] The fact that Neely seems to ignore, however, is that Sheridan's troops did, in fact, lay waste to two entire counties. They might not have carried out the extreme measure of wholesale arrests, but they did leave very little for the citizens of Loudoun and Fauquier Counties to subsist upon during the coming winter. The draft-age males in the region may have maintained their freedom, but not their livestock, grain, or other property. Neely seems to consider the widespread burning of barns and the confiscating of livestock as trivial compared to arrests. It is doubtful that the people around Dayton, Newtown, or Loudoun and Fauquier Counties would have shared the same view. And given the fact that Sheridan's troops did, indeed, burn private homes around Dayton and Newtown and then burned out nearly all of "Mosby's Confederacy," Mark Grimsley's claim that Sheridan's destruction "concentrated on crops, livestock, mills, and barns, not entire communities" seems less than convincing.[127] Not only did Sheridan burn communities, he sometimes did so for the sake of punishment, and not military necessity.

As in other parts of the occupied South, punitive war in Virginia did not include the mass execution of noncombatants. Grant, Sheridan, or Sherman never endorsed the systematic killing of civilians. Toward the end of 1864, however, Sheridan went further than previous commanders in threatening the lives of Southerners. In late November, Major General Darius Couch wrote to Sheridan from Chambersburg expressing concern about guerrilla operations along the Hagerstown railroad and the loyalties of the local people. Sheridan's response was striking in its ruthlessness. Striking, but not surprising. "If you have spies hang them," he exclaimed, "if you are in doubt, hang them anyway. The sooner such characters are killed off, the better it will be for the community."[128] Although no evidence of subsequent hangings exists, the very nature of Sheridan's directive was certainly noteworthy and a bit alarming. Here was one of the Union Army's most powerful commanders in the Eastern Theater sanctioning the execution of citizens even if their disloyalty was in doubt. Although such methods were frequently used by guerrillas themselves in Missouri, Eastern Tennessee, or West Virginia, they were rarely openly discussed by Union officials, much less mandated in official correspondence. Even if nothing came of Sheridan's demand to "hang them anyway," his willingness to proceed on such a course casts significant doubt on a number of scholarly claims that Sheridan gave up on summary executions after a series of exchanged hangings with Mosby that took place in November.[129] His order also detracts from arguments that Grant and Sheridan merely "talked tough" when responding to the guerrilla problem.[130] As with the Union soldiers operating in the Kanawha Valley earlier in the war, Sheridan's troops were not averse to killing suspected bushwhackers on the spot. When describing an incident in which a headquarters post was fired upon, resulting in the wounding of a Union soldier, Sergeant Edward Davis of the Ninth West Virginia Infantry noted, "We caught three or four of them and shot them."[131] Davis's matter-of-fact tenor in reference to the killing suggests that it was not an extraordinary thing.

As Lee surrendered his army in April of 1865, triggering the collapse of the Confederacy, the Union leadership in the field and Washington kept a keen eye on Virginia's guerrillas. The irregulars posed a significant threat to establishing peace and security in the war-torn state. Should they be able to entice others to follow them up into the mountains, Grant and others believed, the war might continue indefinitely. Officers in the field were ordered to keep a sharp lookout for the movements of Mosby, McNeill, and other guerrilla leaders and were even offered cash rewards for their capture.[132] But rather than take to the bushes and continue, Virginia's partisans chose to cease fighting. Unlike many other bushwhackers and guerrillas operating throughout the South at the end of the war, Mosby and McNeill viewed their cause as an extension of the Confederate struggle. When that was surrendered, they saw no future in continuing the fight. The prospect of surrender, however, was not agreeable to them. Instead, their partisan commands simply disbanded, returning to their homes. Other guerrilla bands throughout the Shenandoah similarly melted away, back to their farms to begin rebuilding. After the war, Mosby claimed that he chose to stop fighting in order to "save the country from destruction."[133] For many towns such as Wytheville, Lexington, Dayton, and throughout Loudoun and Fauquier Counties, there was little left to save; the damage had already been done.

Virginia bore the burden of war as much as any state in the Confederacy, if not more. The substantial amount of guerrilla activity that plagued the state combined with the frustration felt by Union troops and officers after four long, arduous years of war produced punitive war measures that rivaled any seen in America, before or during the Civil War. Historian Anne J. Bailey's claim that "in Virginia the armies generally waged war within the parameters acceptable to nineteenth-century Americans" is correct, but the incidents in which the war moved beyond said parameters were not nearly as rare as Bailey and others have suggested.[134] Unfortunately for the people of Virginia, and the Shenandoah Valley in particular, they witnessed firsthand Sheridan's stated belief that "war is a punishment."[135] And the punishment was keenly felt, as one resident of the Valley observed days after the Confederate surrender, "guerrilla warfare will only result in general ruin."[136] As in Missouri, Tennessee, Louisiana, Mississippi, and other states throughout the defeated South, the guerrilla problem made an already brutal war even worse for the people of the commonwealth.

Conclusion

Despite four years of trying, the Union Army never found a lasting solution for the guerrilla problem. Of course, its main focus was always defeating the Confederate Army on the battlefield, but the considerable effort it made to wipe out guerrillas and punish their supporters never yielded the desired result. General John Pope admitted as much just weeks before the end of the war when he claimed, "Guerrillas and bushwhackers were never yet and will never be put down by the operation of military force alone."[1] Unfortunately for the Union, military force was the primary method employed against guerrillas, and in many cases it was the only method. Even so, all was not for naught. A few counterguerrilla techniques adopted by Union forces proved somewhat successful at limiting the impact and scope of guerrilla depredations. The development of scattered "post colonies" in northern Arkansas in early 1865 showed promise, but with the war ending just two months after their establishment, the durability of the system was never truly tested.[2] Union cavalry operations resulted in the occasional capture of a noted irregular leader, such as John Hunt Morgan in Kentucky or Harry Gilmor in Virginia, but they proved futile much more often than not. The same was true of increased guard details along strategic railroads; they usually kept the tracks operational, but not always. This was evident particularly in Missouri and Virginia, where the railroads seemed to be under a constant threat.

This failure was made glaringly apparent by the abundance of guerrilla activity that existed throughout the South even as the conventional war was ending. In Virginia and North Carolina, bands of guerrillas, partisans, and Confederate deserters continued to attack Union troops and terrorize Southern citizens willing to accept Union authority. In Tennessee, reports of trains being derailed by guerrillas "infesting the region" were still common weeks after the Confederate surrender, and Union officials still held "rebel citizens" accountable for the "outrages" they committed. Throughout the Mississippi Valley, guerrilla bands in "great numbers" continued to cause problems for Union provost guards, attacked Union vessels on the river, and reportedly controlled large stretches of territory in Louisiana and Mississippi. Not surprisingly, the bushwhacking hotbed of Missouri still suffered from the guerrilla problem well after the Civil War came to a close. The chaos and law-lessness that plagued the state during the war's four years raged on into the summer of 1865, with guerrillas targeting not only scattered Union outposts but freed slaves as well. A number of Confederate bushwhackers began their postbellum careers as outlaws; some of them (Jesse James and Cole Younger) would become the subject of American legend. For those who wanted to see a decisive end to guerrilla warfare, "there was no culminating victory, no clear defeat, no catharsis," in the words of one scholar.[3] The South had been de-feated, but not completely pacified. Most regions that experienced the guer-rilla problem at the war's beginning still endured it in some form at war's end; little had improved. The fact that Robert E. Lee and his defeated army did not take to the mountains to wage a new guerrilla war against the Union vic-tors says more about Lee's aversion to that brand of warfare than it does about the Federals' ability to combat it. Fortunately for the Union, when Lee told his soldiers to return home, rebuild, and abandon the struggle, they did.

A number of scholars have been too complimentary of Union efforts to combat the guerrilla problem. In *The Uncivil War*, Robert Mackey argued that the Union Army's "inventive and original" efforts to combat Southern irregulars enabled the Federals to ultimately defeat the menace of irregu-lars.[4] This conclusion seems to ignore the fact that the Union's most innova-tive counterguerrilla measures, such as the post colony system in northern Arkansas and the creation of special counterguerrilla units such as Blazer's Scouts, were either scarcely used, short-lived, or unsuccessful. Given the ex-istence of pockets of guerrilla resistance at war's end, it is hard to agree with Mackey's assertion that the Union Army successfully thwarted the guerrilla problem. If anything, it endured it. Historian Mark Grimsley made no such claims for Union methods, but he did argue that the restraint and forbear-ance demonstrated by the "politically aware" Union Army far outweighed its "necessary but sometimes draconian" response to guerrilla attacks.[5] Andrew Birtle offered a more plausible assessment when he credited the Union ef-fort with containing the guerrilla threat rather than defeating it outright.[6] Few Union officers or soldiers, however, would have admitted to merely try-ing to contain the guerrilla problem; they tried to end it completely. Those who tackled the problem almost always used the words "stop," "destroy," and "exterminate" to define their counterguerrilla goals. They did not use the terms "limit," "control," or "contain." Considering that few, if any, Union commanders found a way to truly hinder guerrilla attacks, much less stop them altogether, their attempts to solve the guerrilla problem, while at times inventive, should be remembered as largely ineffective.

But arguing the success of Union efforts against guerrillas, or the lack thereof, really misses the true importance of the subject. Successful or not, the principal Union response to the guerrilla problem was punitive war, the impact of which spread well beyond the guerrillas and their opponents. As seen in previous American wars that involved some sort of guerrilla problem, the Union came to rely primarily on policies that targeted civilian communities, rather than the guerrillas themselves. In that sense, the Union response was unoriginal. Rather than discovering new methods to combat irregulars, the U.S. Army primarily reacted as it had when it faced the Seminoles in Florida and guerrillas in Mexico. Ultimately, the Civil War witnessed a rediscovery of punitive war, made unique only by its widespread usage and the fact that it was waged against fellow white Americans.

The legacy of the Civil War's guerrilla problem became evident when the U.S. military faced unconventional, guerrilla-style threats in later wars of the nineteenth century. In their attempt to pacify the Western Frontier, veterans of the Civil War such as William T. Sherman, Philip H. Sheridan, and George Crook employed (to a greater extent) the same punitive measures against Indian communities that they relied upon in Missouri, Mississippi, and Virginia years prior. The tactical challenges of Indian-fighting caused the army to pursue the destruction of noncombatant property and foodstuffs, and U.S. soldiers offered the subjugated South as their precedent.[7] This time, however, most of the damage done to Indian communities was part of a pacification strategy, and not just a retaliatory measure. As an official observer during the Franco-Prussian War, Sheridan advised the Prussians that the "proper strategy" for dealing with French guerrillas included "causing the inhabitants so much suffering that they must long for peace"—nearly the exact wording he used to justify the Burning Raid in northern Virginia six years prior.[8] Later, during the Philippine Insurrection of 1899–1902, U.S. Army officers leading destructive campaigns on the islands of Luzon and Samar harkened back to their counterguerrilla experiences under Sherman and Grant in the Civil War. They also offered their own interpretations of General Orders 100 as justification for the burning of houses and the execution of Filipino prisoners.[9] At the turn of the century, the U.S. Army began to employ new organizational and tactical methods to combat irregulars, but punitive war would never disappear completely from American military consciousness.

As much as the Civil War's guerrilla problem meant for the evolution of American counterguerrilla doctrine, its true historical significance lay in its instrumental role in changing the character of the war. Any discussion of irregular warfare in the Civil War should address how guerrillas, bushwhackers, and partisans redefined the Union's war aims from carefully defeating the Confederate government and its army to subduing the entire South through brute force. The Union's transition to a more vigorous prosecution of the war, one that included the destruction of civilian property, did not originate in the minds of the North's radical Republicans, or even that of its president. It originated in the bushes flanking Missouri's railroads, at sharp bends in the Mississippi River, and in the mountain passes of the Kanawha Valley.

Union soldiers of all ranks determined a new course for the war when they concluded that the people of the South were in arms against them. One scholar recently concluded that the Union leadership, to include Abraham Lincoln, came to view the South as "not only a nation of Confederates, but a nation of guerrillas as well."[10] Lincoln, however, was not the creator of punitive war. The soldiers who burned the towns of Donaldsonville, Randolph, and Wytheville in retaliation for guerrilla attacks were themselves agents of the change. Their actions reflected the grim reality on the ground rather than political hand-wringing in Washington or impatience on the Northern home front. Generals, too, responded to their anger and frustration, and they led their soldiers along the path of increased severity. It was no coincidence that the greatest practitioners of punitive war—Henry W. Halleck, Ulysses S. Grant, William T. Sherman, and Philip H. Sheridan—personally experienced the guerrilla problem early on. By the final year of the war, their hardened attitudes defined the Union Army, and they ultimately led it to victory. The pressure to adopt punitive war came from both the upper echelons of the Federal Army and from deep within its ranks. Its origins were in the field, where the smoldering guerrilla menace made a policy of conciliation seem untenable and tragically naïve.

It was a type of war that many Union soldiers struggled with, unsure of its moral justification. Others embraced it, seeing it as the most effective means to combat an enemy that refused to fight within the acceptable parameters of warfare. Still others viewed punitive war as the regrettable, but unavoidable, consequence of Civil War. No matter how they felt about it, punitive war evoked a certain level of passion within soldiers that few things could. It was this passion, this vehemence, that drove soldiers in many cases to fight the war according to their own terms. That is not to say that the most powerful figures in Union blue did not hold sway over the course of the war. Sherman, Grant, Sheridan, and Halleck, the faces of eventual Union triumph, determined the strategic and operational course of the war over the final two years. Each of them experienced the guerrilla problem firsthand, and they were strongly influenced by it. But agency was found throughout the entire ranks, from the most prominent generals to the most anonymous foot soldiers. If nothing else, the guerrilla problem demonstrated that the Civil War itself was an infinitely human affair. The participants were primarily driven by their emotion and instinct, not by doctrine or policy. Charles Royster was correct when he argued that the "expansion of violence" in the Civil War "came less from the belligerents' rational calculation than from their passion."[11] Nowhere was this more evident than in the Union soldiers' relationship with the hostile, and often violent, Southern people.

In addition, the guerrilla problem shows us that violence in the Civil War was not confined to battlefields, nor was the suffering. For many civilians living in small towns and villages throughout the occupied South, the specter of guerrilla warfare was much more palpable, much more real, than battles being fought hundreds or thousands of miles distant. For the people of Missouri, it *was* the Civil War. The appalling scenes at Shiloh, Antietam, and Gettysburg easily overshadow the struggles that the Union Army endured while occupying the South, but at least the concept of conventional battle was easily understood by troops North and South. Such was not the case with the legal and ethical vagaries surrounding occupation duty and the prospect of pacifying a hostile people. Both officers and soldiers caught in this situation learned that war could be a very complicated enterprise. In his emphatic marginalization of Union destructiveness in the Civil War, historian Mark Neely argued that the guerrilla problem had no impact on "the way the generals chose to fight the conventional Confederate armies."[12] This may be true, but it also misses the point. The guerrilla problem influenced how the Union armies viewed things *outside* the conventional battlefield, not on it. If the Union Army had only had to worry about dealing with the Confederates on the battlefield, the Civil War would have been much easier to prosecute. In reality, Union soldiers spent the majority of the war in the time and spaces between conventional battles, and that is where the guerrilla problem had its greatest impact.

It is important to note that the guerrilla problem was not responsible for all of the destruction or hardship that the South endured during the war. There were several other forces at work. Retreating Confederate armies often burned food, mills, and bridges to prevent their use by the enemy. Foraging took a tremendous toll as well. A hungry army, Union or Confederate, could wipe out an entire town just as quickly as a vengeful one. Historian James McPherson called this "the inevitable destruction of war" and noted that "soldiers have pillaged civilian property since the beginning of time." Another scholar blamed "the tyranny of logistics" for creating a situation that required armies in the Civil War to live off the land.[13] So when Southern farms and mills were cleaned out, sometimes reluctantly, by Union soldiers, it was often the result of simple operational necessity and not punitive war.

The issue of emancipation, which equated to war against the property of Southern slaveholders, was another issue not directly linked to the guerrilla problem. President Abraham Lincoln viewed his 1862 decision to free the slaves more as a military and political necessity rather than another means of punishing the people of the South. Emancipation, which Grimsley labeled "the touchstone of hard war," changed the political and social objectives of the war, but did not immediately change the way that Union troops viewed or treated their Southern enemies.[14] The effect it had on Union soldiers' perceptions of their own participation in the war was perhaps more acute. As James McPherson noted in his landmark examination of soldiers' motivations for fighting the war, *For Cause and Comrades: Why Men Fought in the Civil War*, the issue of emancipation "intensified a morale crisis" that struck the Union ranks in 1862.[15] It is true that freed slaves may have conducted their own form of guerrilla warfare by destroying the property of slaveholders and acting as informants for the advancing Yankees, but this would have been much more of a problem for the Confederate Army than for the Union. Ultimately, the decision to free the slaves does not provide an effective explanation for the Union army's physical destruction of civilian property or execution of prisoners.

A final example, the targeting of the Confederate infrastructure as seen in Sherman's Meridian expedition and Sheridan's destruction of the economic capacity of the Shenandoah Valley, was a strike at the South's military means and the will of its people. The railroads destroyed and mills and farms burned were the result of a Federal strategy of exhaustion, one designed to force the rebel nation into submission. As Grant described in his memoirs, this entailed "taking what might be of use to the enemy" and destroying the rest.[16] Even without any guerrilla threat, the Union might very well have resorted to each of these measures in time to hasten the end of the long, painful conflict.

None of these measures, however, fully explain the willingness of Union officers and soldiers to force civilians out of their homes, burn entire towns to the ground, and at times, execute prisoners on the spot. These were the most ruthless aspects of Union war making, and they became increasingly common when Union troops met with unconventional, violent resistance. There is little about foraging, slavery, or the war-sustaining capability of the South's infrastructure that can illustrate how Union troops chose to see civilians, living at home, as active, dangerous enemies worthy of harsh treatment. As one scholar accurately noted, Union retaliation against civilians for guerrilla attacks "wore a guise of reasonableness . . . but was more clearly a product of rage and the desire for revenge."[17] The hardened resolve needed to shoot a prisoner or to burn a house occupied by women and children did not come easily. It took something as sinister and threatening as guerrilla warfare to co-erce the Union soldier into pulling the trigger or throwing a torch through a window. The fact that General Orders No. 100, the Union's most substantial effort to govern the behavior of its army, originated as a response to the guer-rilla problem and not a different issue (such as slavery or logistical demands) proved the problem's significance.

In 1995, Grimsley concluded that "the Federal rank and file were nei-ther barbarians, brutalized by war, nor 'realists' unleashing indiscriminate violence." More recently, Neely echoed this sentiment, saying that "neither side fought without restraint. Neither unleashed the full fury of unbridled wrath."[18] Such conclusions are true, albeit oversimplified and hardly pro-found. Those who seek to emphasize Union restraint in dealing with non-combatants in the Civil War normally underscore the fact that civilians were not systematically killed, nor were they targeted indiscriminately (a claim that is arguable).[19] After all, Grant, Sherman, and Sheridan targeted civilian property, not civilian lives. Does that mean, however, that they were merci-ful? Does it mean that they were justified? Does it mean that the burning of homes, the slaughtering or confiscation of livestock, and the depopulation of entire counties were retaliations proportional to the offense? As Russell Wei-gley correctly concluded, "For a (nineteenth-century) middle-class property owning family, the loss of life's accumulation of belongings is a punishment not much exceeded by death. When we read about Civil War depredations, and judge their morality, we should not forget that fact."[20] Even without pass-ing moral judgment on Federal retaliatory measures, we can conclude that they were indeed brutal steps with potentially devastating effects for those involved.

In order to downplay Union destructiveness in the Civil War, scholars have usually found it necessary to compare it with that seen in wars from other centuries and continents. Grimsley argued that the French devasta-tion of the Palatinate in 1689 made Sheridan's treatment of the Shenandoah Valley seem pedestrian, and Donald Connelly suggested that the violence in Civil War Missouri was greatly eclipsed by that seen in the Vendée during the French Revolution. In her study of the march to the sea, Anne J. Bailey claimed that Sherman's destruction of Georgia came nowhere near the an-nihilation caused by the Allied firebombing of Germany and Japan in World War II.[21] Such comparisons are naturally true, but they amount to little more than straw men. Indeed, no Union general was a Genghis Khan, and Union soldiers were certainly not the Mongol horde. No Confederate city suffered anywhere near the horrors seen at Magdeburg in 1631. These obvious conclu-sions, however, are intended to counter only the most hyperbolic Lost Cause myths about Sherman and Sheridan that flourished during the early to mid-twentieth century but have lost significant momentum over the past thirty years. Although in his book *The Civil War and the Limits of Destruction* Neely made much ado about what he called the "modern cult of violence" in Civil War writing, works citing Union destructiveness are not nearly as common as he suggested and are thoroughly balanced by defenses of Union restraint such as his own and Grimsley's.[22]

The use of punitive war and the destruction it produced were indeed more prevalent than has been previously portrayed. James McPherson made the recent, correct observation that Union troops "burned far fewer houses in reality than they did in Southern memory."[23] They did, however, burn far more than most histories, and memories, account for. The burning of Randolph, the execution of Order No. 11 in Missouri, and the destruction of Wytheville were not isolated events. The "areas of guerrilla warfare" were not nearly as limited as Neely would like us to believe, and neither were the incidents of Union reprisal.[24] Sherman's troops destroyed more than just railroads, and Sheridan's burned more than just grain. We should not assume that punitive war was responsible for the majority of the destruction imposed on the South, because it was not, but it was responsible for the worst of it. The Union Army *did* knock down certain barriers that existed between combatant and noncombatant, and the Civil War *did* become the "fierce and transforming struggle" that Stephen Ash claimed it to be.[25] Perhaps the Union response to the guerrilla problem does not belong among the most brutal examples of military force in history, but when placed in the context of American military experience in the nineteenth century, it was absolutely unparalleled in its destructiveness.

In retrospect, the guerrilla problem and the Union response of punitive war reveal much about the thoroughly complex struggle that made up the American Civil War. Although guerrilla operations themselves did not threaten to defeat the Union Army, the frustration caused by an unseen, elusive enemy proved to be a powerful force—one that was unforeseen at the outset. The brutalization of the conflict occurred at ground level, not simply in the minds of Northern politicians eager for a rapid victory. The tactical difficulty of combating guerrillas led Union forces to rely primarily on the unoriginal, and usually unproductive, tactic of punishing civilians. The problem forced many Union soldiers to ponder the severity of their actions and the war in general. Their introspective searching revealed the type of passion and emotion reserved for a nation at war with itself. The feelings expressed by Illinois infantryman John A. Boon in early 1863 spoke for all of those who struggled with the moral dilemma inherent to punitive war. Upon witnessing the burning of a Tennessee town in retaliation for guerrilla attacks on a nearby railroad, Boon wrote, "Oh, of all the sights I have seen it looked the most awful . . . but I suppose it was necessary."[26] The guerrilla problem and punitive war were just two of the Civil War's awful necessities, but for the citizens caught in between, they were the most awful of all. If we understand this, we gain a greater understanding of the complexity and the depth of that terrible calamity that befell the nation for four long years.

Notes

List of Abbreviations

DUSC	Duke University, Perkins Library Special Collections
LOC	U.S. Library of Congress, Manuscripts Division
OHS	Ohio Historical Society
OR	*Official Records [The War of the Rebellion: A Compilation of the Official Records of the Union and Confederate Armies]*
PSUSC	Pennsylvania State University, Special Collections Library
PUSG	*The Papers of Ulysses S. Grant*
UGA	University of Georgia, Hargrett Rare Book and Manuscript Library
USAMHI	U.S. Army Military History Institute
UVA	University of Virginia, Small Special Collections Library
VMI	Virginia Military Institute Archives

Introduction

1. William Porter Wilkin Papers, USAMHI. Albert O. Marshall, *Army Life: From a Soldier's Journal, Incidents, Sketches, and Record of a Union Soldier's Army Life in Camp and Field: 1861–1864* (Joliet, IL: n.p., 1884), 157.

2. Albert O. Marshall, *Army Life: From a Soldier's Journal, Incidents, Sketches, and Record of a Union Soldier's Army Life in Camp and Field: 1861–1864* (Joliet, IL: 1884), 157.

3. John Ellis, *From the Barrel of a Gun: A History of Guerrilla, Revolutionary, and Counter-Insurgency Warfare from the Romans to the Present* (Mechanicsburg, PA: Stackpole Books, 1975), 12. Ellis attests to the need to "keep the exact definition of guerrilla warfare as wide as possible" due to the many variant forms it can take.

4. Rosecrans to citizens of Western Virginia, 20 August 1861, *OR*, ser. 1, vol. 5, 576.

5. See Robert R. Mackey, *The Uncivil War: Irregular Warfare in the Upper South, 1861–1865* (Norman: University of Oklahoma Press, 2004); Michael Fellman, Lesley J. Gordon, and Daniel Sutherland, *This Terrible War: The Civil War and Its Aftermath* (New York: Longman Press, 2003), 196–199.

6. Mark Grimsley, *The Hard Hand of War: Union Military Policy toward Southern Civilians, 1861–1865* (New York: Cambridge University Press, 1997), 112.

7. John E. Anderson Papers, LOC, 127.

8. Russell F. Weigley, *Towards an American Army: Military Thought from Washington to Marshall* (New York: Columbia University Press, 1962), 81; Charles

Royster, *The Destructive War: William Tecumseh Sherman, Stonewall Jackson, and the Americans* (New York: Vintage Books, 1991), 325; Stephen V. Ash, *When the Yankees Came: Conflict and Chaos in the Occupied South, 1861–1865* (Chapel Hill: University of North Carolina Press, 1995), x.

9. Grimsley, *Hard Hand of War*, 95. Although doubtful of its overall significance, Grimsley does acknowledge the link between guerrillas and harsher Union policies in numerous passages throughout his book; Mark E. Neely, Jr. *The Civil War and the Limits of Destruction* (Cambridge: Harvard University Press, 2007), 206–207.

10. Andrew J. Birtle, *U.S. Army Counterinsurgency and Contingency Operations and Doctrine 1861–1941* (Washington, DC: Center of Military History, Government Printing Office, 2003), 28.

11. Ash, *When the Yankees Came*, 53.

12. Mackey, *Uncivil War*, 4–5, 203–204.

13. Gerald F. Linderman, *Embattled Courage*: *The Experience of Combat in the American Civil War* (New York: Free Press, 1987), 180.

14. Examples can be seen in David S. Heidler and Jeanne T. Heidler, eds., *Encyclopedia of the American Civil War: A Political, Social, and Military History*, 2 vols. (Santa Barbara, CA: ABC–CLIO, 2000), 2: 900–902; David J. Eicher, *The Longest Night: A Military History of the Civil War* (New York: Simon and Schuster, 2001), 753.

Chapter 1. The American Antebellum Experience with Guerrilla Warfare

1. John David Waghelstein, "Preparing for the Wrong War: The United States Army and Low-Intensity Conflict, 1755–1890" (Ph.D. diss., Temple University, 1990), 17.

2. Weigley, *Towards an American Army*, 78. Weigley stresses that American military leaders in 1861 did not anticipate a total war, or a conflict that would involve "mass armies of citizen soldiers 'pitting' nation against nation."

3. Maurice Matloff, ed. *American Military History* (Washington, DC: Center of Military History, Government Printing Office, 1968), 27; Richard A. Preston, Alex Roland, and Sydney F. Wise, *Men in Arms: A History of Warfare and Its Relationships with Western Society* (New York: Praeger, 1991), 163.

4. John Morgan Dederer, *War in America to 1775: Before Yankee Doodle* (New York: New York University Press, 1990), 128; Patrick Malone, *The Skulking Way of War: Technology and Tactics among the New England Indians* (Baltimore: Johns Hopkins University Press, 1993), 102. Malone claims that in colonial America, "the violence inflicted on Indians [by European settlers] was, in fact, even more terrible and less restrained than the horrors of the Thirty Year War."

5. Bruce Lancaster, *The American Revolution* (New York: Houghton Mifflin, 1987), 278–279.

6. Walter Edgar, *Partisans and Redcoats: The Southern Conflict That Turned the Tide of the American Revolution* (New York: Harper Collins, 2001), xviii.

7. Lancaster, *American Revolution*, 304. Lancaster sees these events as the highlight of the "guerrilla-Continental pattern" that Greene employed in the South,

pointing out that both conventional and unconventional fighters relied on one another for success.

8. Piers Mackesy, *The War for America: 1775–1783* (Lincoln: University of Nebraska Press, 1964), 343.

9. John Morgan Dederer, *Making Bricks without Straw: Nathanael Greene's Southern Campaign and Mao Tse-Tung's Mobile War* (Manhattan, KS: Sunflower University Press, 1983), 57. John S. Pancake, *This Destructive War: The British Campaign in the Carolinas 1780–1782* (Tuscaloosa: University of Alabama Press, 1985), 132. Pancake quotes Greene as comparing partisan warfare to "garnish on the table" and claiming that it would not provide any "substantial national security."

10. Weigley, *Towards an American Army*, 7–9. The author claims that America emerged from the Revolution with two distinct, opposing military traditions. One, to which Washington subscribed, was the belief in the need for a European-style, professional army that would fight conventionally. The other was the 'revolutionary' ideal that militias could provide for the nation's security by waging a people's war when necessary.

11. Russell F. Weigley, *The American Way of War: A History of United States Military Strategy and Policy* (Bloomington: Indiana University Press, 1975), 36. Weigley credits Greene with being the only American leader to "master developing a strategy of unconventional war."

12. William B. Skelton, *An American Profession of Arms: The Army Officer Corps, 1784–1861* (Lawrence: University Press of Kansas, 1992), 132.

13. Waghelstein, "Preparing for the Wrong War," 150.

14. Weigley, *American Way of War*, 68. Weigley points out that the U.S. Army's increase of regular troop strength from 7,000 to 12,500 not only strained logistics but also made the force clumsy and noisy, thereby making it more difficult to surprise Indians.

15. Ibid., 67.

16. Fairfax Downey, *Indian Wars of the U.S. Army: 1776–1865* (Garden City, NY: Doubleday, 1963), 127. The author places the U.S. casualty toll for the battle at 26 killed and 112 wounded. In addition, he places Indian casualties at 12 killed and an unknown number of wounded; Francis P. Prucha, *The Sword of the Republic: The United States Army on the Frontier, 1783–1846* (Lincoln: University of Nebraska Press, 1969), 292.

17. Prucha, *Sword of the Republic*, 293.

18. Robert M. Utley and Wilcomb E. Washburn, *Indian Wars* (New York: Mariner Books, 2002), 134; Prucha, *Sword of the Republic*, 297.

19. Downey, *Indian Wars of the U.S. Army*, 128.

20. Prucha, *Sword of the Republic*, 301.

21. Ibid.

22. Weigley, *American Way of War*, 68.

23. Charles E. Vetter, *Sherman: Merchant of Terror, Advocate of Peace* (Gretna, LA: Pelican Publishing, 1992), 35. In his account of Sherman's service in the Seminole Wars, Vetter claims that it was common and acceptable for U.S. soldiers "to deviate from the accepted techniques of warfare" against the Indians.

24. Waghelstein, "Preparing for the Wrong War," 161–162. The author emphasizes the newfound belief in the "value of disciplined regulars' musketry and the bayonet charge."

25. Antoine Henri Jomini, *The Art of War* (Westport, CT: Greenwood Press, 1971 [1862]), 23.

26. Paul Foos, *A Short, Offhand, Killing Affair: Soldiers and Social Conflict during the Mexican-American War* (Chapel Hill: University of North Carolina Press, 2002), 134.

27. Ralph W. Kirkham, *The Mexican War: Journals and Letters of Ralph W. Kirkham*, ed. Robert Ryal Miller (College Station: Texas A&M University Press, 1991), 13.

28. Quoted in Charles L. Dufour, *The Mexican War: A Compact History* (New York: Hawthorne Books, 1968), 226.

29. Carlos Maria de Bustamante, "The New Bernal Diaz del Castillo," in *The View from Chapultepec: Mexican Writers on the Mexican American War*, trans. and ed. Cecil Robinson (Tucson: University of Arizona Press, 1989), 73–74.

30. Letter of Lieutenant Theodore Laidley, 22 March 1848, in *Surrounded by Dangers of All Kinds: The Mexican War Letters of Lt. Theodore Laidley*, ed. James M. McAffrey (Denton: University of North Texas Press, 1997), 152.

31. K. Jack Bauer, *The Mexican War, 1846–1848* (New York: Macmillan, 1974), 214. Bauer uses Taylor's expedition to Ramos as an example.

32. Justin H. Smith, "American Rule in Mexico," *American Historical Review* 23, no. 2 (January 1918): 294.

33. Bauer, *Mexican War*, 222.

34. Winfield Scott, *Memoirs of Lieutenant-General Scott*, vol. 2 (New York: Sheldon & Company, 1864), 559–560. Scott places most of the blame for undisciplined acts on volunteer units, claiming, "Among all new levies, there are always a few miscreants in every hundred" (557). Scott was most concerned with these miscreants.

35. Bauer, *Mexican War*, 333.

36. Ibid., 225.

37. Birtle, *U.S. Army Counterinsurgency*, 17. Birtle claims that Scott's twin policies of "Reconciliation and Retribution" were successful in keeping the guerrillas "in check" but never "completely subdued" them.

38. Bauer, *Mexican War*, 223.

39. Ibid., 332–333. Bauer suggests that internal disagreements between guerrilla leaders were "more disastrous" to their cause than any counterguerrilla efforts undertaken by the U.S. Army.

40. Waghelstein, "Preparing for the Wrong War," 178. Waghelstein argues that "the brevity of the Mexican War avoided possible guerrilla activity that may have protracted the conflict."

41. Samuel Ryan Curtis, *Under Fire: Being the Diary of Samuel Ryan Curtis, 3rd Ohio Volunteer Regiment, during the American Military Occupation of Northern Mexico, 1846–1847*, ed. Joseph E. Chance (Fort Worth: Texas Christian University Press, 1994), xvi.

42. Foos, *Short, Offhand, Killing Affair*, 136.

43. Dufour, *Mexican War*, 288.

44. James McPherson, *Battle Cry of Freedom: The Civil War Era* (New York: Ballantine, 1988), 328–329. According to the author, the West Point curriculum "slighted strategic studies" and only provided a "smattering of tactics."

45. Ibid., 331.

46. Weigley, *Towards an American Army*, 55, 57. Weigley claims that Jomini was a strong proponent of eighteenth-century limits on warfare and was much more conservative in his views on war, choosing to focus primarily on the "military questions of strategy, logistics, and tactics" rather than the relationship between society and war.

47. Preston, Roland, and Wise, *Men in Arms*, 204–205. The authors accuse Jomini of failing to understand the changes in warfare caused by the Napoleonic age and of simply viewing the study of war as "a geometric exercise."

48. George S. Pappas, *To the Point: The United States Military Academy, 1802–1902* (Westport, CT: Praeger, 1993), 251.

49. Dennis H. Mahan, *An Elementary Treatise on Advanced-Guard, Out-Post, and Detachment Service of Troops* (New York: John Wiley & Sons, 1847), 190–191.

50. James L. Morrison, Jr., *"The Best School in the World": West Point, the Pre–Civil War Years, 1833–1866* (Kent, OH: Kent State University Press, 1986), 97.

51. Ibid., 217–218, 235.

52. Examples include McPherson, *Battle Cry of Freedom*, 332. McPherson claims "the trial and error of experience played a larger role than theory in shaping Civil War strategy"; Stephen E. Ambrose, *Duty, Honor, Country: A History of West Point* (Baltimore: Johns Hopkins University Press, 1966), 136–137. Ambrose points to the limited amount of instruction on strategy and tactics, stating, "The trouble was that Mahan spent so much time on military and civil engineering that he only had a few days left over for strategy"; Morrison, *"Best School in the World,"* 96.

53. Weigley, *American Way of War*, 89.

54. James L. Morrison, Jr., "Educating the Civil War Generals: West Point, 1833–1861," *Military Affairs* 38, no. 3 (October 1974): 109; General Orders 62, 24 July 1862, Headquarters of the Mississippi, *OR*, ser. 1, vol. 17, 119. In his directive to his subordinates, Sherman directed, "All officers of this command must now study their books; ignorance of duty must no longer be pleaded."

55. Sherston Baker, ed. *Halleck's International Law or Rules Regulating the Intercourse of States in Peace and War*, vol. 1, 3rd ed. (London: Kegan Paul, Trench, Trubner, 1893), 560–562. Halleck devotes just two and one-half pages to the discussion of guerrilla and partisan warfare.

56. Royster, *Destructive War*, xi.

57. Vetter, *Sherman*, 30.

58. McPherson, *Battle Cry of Freedom*, 332.

59. Ibid., 333–334. The author quotes Scott as warning against the possibility of a lengthy and costly occupation that would certainly follow a war of conquest.

60. Archer Jones, *Civil War Command and Strategy: The Process of Victory and Defeat* (New York: The Free Press, 1992), 24.

61. Linderman, *Embattled Courage*, 3. Linderman states, "They grew to respect

and even admire the enemy, but they went on killing him—and took satisfaction from it."

Chapter 2. Proving Ground for Punishment: Pope, Halleck, and Schofield in Missouri

1. For an in-depth analysis of the period see Thomas Goodrich, *War to the Knife: Bleeding Kansas, 1861–1865* (Lincoln: University of Nebraska Press, 2004).

2. A detailed account of Brown's attack at Pottawatomie is found in Stephen B. Oates, *To Purge This Land with Blood: A Biography of John Brown* (New York: Harper & Row, 1970), 133–138. According to Oates, Brown claimed to have carried out the attack in response to the murder of six Kansas abolitionists by proslavery militants.

3. Ibid., 146.

4. Joseph A. Mudd, *With Porter in North Missouri: A Chapter in the History of the War between the States* (Washington, DC: National Publishing, 1909), 12. Mudd's description of the struggles between Missouri and Kansas in the 1850s includes the assertion that the intense hatred between Missourians and Kansans was never duplicated, with the possible exception of the mountaineers of East Tennessee, 23.

5. T. J. Stiles, *Jesse James: Last Rebel of the Civil War* (New York: Vintage, 2002), 52.

6. Michael Fellman, *Inside War: The Guerrilla Conflict in Missouri during the American Civil War* (New York: Oxford University Press, 1989), 23, 25. Fellman notes that in the conflict in Missouri, "terror was both a method and a goal" and that guerrillas "sought to create moments when they were in total dominance and could exact what they wanted at the least possible risk to themselves."

7. Don R. Bowen, "Quantrill, James, Younger, et al.: Leadership in a Guerrilla Movement, Missouri, 1861–1865," *Military Affairs* 41, no. 1 (February 1977): 42.

8. William E. Parrish, *Turbulent Partnership: Missouri and the Union: 1861–1865* (Columbia: University of Missouri Press, 1963), 50. McClellan to Army of the West, 25 June 1861, *OR*, ser. 1, vol. 2, 196. Major General George B. McClellan, commander of Union forces in western Virginia in 1861, appealed to his soldiers to "bear in mind that you are in the country of friends, not of enemies; that you are here to protect, not to destroy. Take nothing, destroy nothing, unless you are ordered to do so by your general officers. Remember that I have pledged my word to the people of Western Virginia that their rights in person and property shall be respected." Smith to citizens of Paducah, 10 October 1861, ibid., vol. 4, 302.

9. Wallace J. Schutz and Walter Trenerry, *Abandoned by Lincoln: A Military Biography of General John Pope* (Chicago: University of Illinois Press, 1990), 66. The authors credit Pope's experience in Mexico with enabling him to initiate antiguerrilla policies "on his own" without waiting for guidance.

10. Pope to Frémont, 16 July 1861, *OR*, ser. 1, vol. 3, 396.

11. John Pope, *The Military Memoirs of General John Pope*, ed. Peter Cozzens and Robert I. Girardi (Chapel Hill: University of North Carolina Press, 1998), 12, 17–18.

In his memoirs, Pope clearly views the pro-South population as the guilty party in regard to the political instability of the region in 1861. "The younger and more violent of the Secessionists," Pope stated, "strove in every way to precipitate a collision and to involve the entire population in war against one another."

12. Frémont to Townsend, 18 July 1861; Lyon to Townsend, 17 July 1861, *OR*, ser. 1, vol. 3, 397–398.

13. Pope to the people of northern Missouri, 21 July 1861, *OR*, ser. 1, vol. 3, 403–404.

14. Pope, *Military Memoirs*, 22. Pope believed collective responsibility would force guerrillas into regular military units, where they could then be controlled through organization.

15. See W. Wayne Smith, "An Experiment in Counterinsurgency: The Assessment of Confederate Sympathizers in Missouri," *Journal of Southern History* 35, no. 3 (August 1969): 362–363. Smith gives a complete examination of the assessment process in Missouri during the war, concluding that the exercise became "an instrument of revenge and abuse" that was popular with Union officials, but one that ultimately "proved a distinct failure."

16. Pope, *Military Memoirs*, 19.

17. Lance Janda, "Shutting the Gates of Mercy: The American Origins of Total War, 1860–1880," *Journal of Military History* 59 (January 1995): 8. As Janda describes, "The application of force against an enemy's noncombatants and resources, the central tenet of total war, had been used since the dawn of civilization when it suited political and military ends"; Doris Appel Graber, *The Development of the Law of Belligerent Occupation, 1863–1914* (New York: Columbia University Press, 1949), 13. In her study of the development of occupational law, Graber claims that "harsh practices" aimed at the people of an occupied country were "the general rule" in warfare from the Middle Ages up to the nineteenth century.

18. Fellman, *Inside War*, 158–159. Fellman gives a complete examination of the Union perspective toward Missouri civilians, in which he concludes that many Union soldiers "believed the enemy was everywhere and everyone" and were convinced that the majority of civilians "secretly supported the guerrillas."

19. Report of Major John McDonald, 17 August 1861, *OR*, ser. 1, vol. 3, 132–133.

20. Letter of J. T. K. Hayward to J. W. Brooks, 13 August 1861, ibid., 460. In his letter, Hayward emphasized the need for Union soldiers to avoid indiscriminate damage to civilian property, which he claims to have been common in August 1861, while at the same time urging a more proactive pursuit of secessionist guerrillas who were operating with impunity against the Hannibal and St. Joseph Railroad.

21. Pope to Frémont, 25 August 1861, ibid., 455–456. Pope stressed that it was "impossible" to apprehend the guerrillas themselves and that the threatened punishment of the civilian populace with assessments and seizure of property was the "only method possible" to overcome the problems of insurgency in Missouri.

22. Pope, *Military Memoirs*, 28.

23. Orders No. 3, 2 August 1861, *OR*, ser. 1, vol. 3, 420–421; Pope, *Military Memoirs*, 22. As Pope described his thinking behind the order, "my purpose was thus to

force [guerrillas] to join the organized forces on one side or the other. Once completely taken out of the communities they disturbed, it would be possible to keep the peace without even the presence of military force."

24. See Fellman, *Inside War*, 58–59. Fellman describes an environment in Missouri in which noncombatants were too powerless or fearful to create any order; Richard Brownlee, *Gray Ghosts of the Confederacy: Guerrilla Warfare in the West 1861–1865* (Baton Rouge: Louisiana State University Press, 1958), 50, 52.

25. George C. Burmeister Papers, USAMHI. Burmeister, a soldier from the 1st Iowa Infantry, reported "numerous R.R. disasters," to include bridge burning, in northern Missouri during the late summer of 1861.

26. Pope to Kelton, 17 August 1861, *OR*, ser. 1 vol. 3, 135.

27. Hurlburt to City of Palmyra, 19 August 1861, ibid.

28. Hurlburt to Smith, 12 August 1861, ibid., ser. 2, vol. 1, 206–207.

29. Pope to Frémont, 25 August 1861, ibid., ser. 1, vol. 3, 456–457; Pope, *Military Memoirs*, 24–25. After the war, Pope viewed the mid-August attacks on the Hannibal and St. Joseph line as a guerrilla attempt to test his resolve.

30. Letter of J. T. K. Hayward to J. W. Brooks, 13 August 1861, *OR*, ser. 1, vol. 3, 459. Hayward lists some of the "irregularities of the [Union] soldiery" in Palmyra as taking "everything they want," searching houses for no expressed purpose, "committing rapes on the negroes," and other acts that served to make the Federal troops "inveterate enemies" of Missourians.

31. W. Wayne Smith, "Experiment in Counterinsurgency," 361; Brownlee, *Gray Ghosts of the Confederacy*, 34–35.

32. Pope, *Military Memoirs*, 25.

33. Brownlee, *Gray Ghosts of the Confederacy*, 35.

34. J. T. K. Hayward to J. W. Brooks, 19 August 1861, *OR*, ser. 1, vol. 3, 461; Wyman to Frémont, 29 August 1861, ibid., 466.

35. Frémont proclamation to the people of Missouri, 30 August 1861, ibid., ser. 2, vol. 1, 221.

36. Pope, *Military Memoirs*, 25. Pope makes reference to Frémont's proclamation resulting in the formation of numerous military detachments along with provost marshals, whom Pope refers to as "that necessary evil of martial law."

37. Frémont proclamation to the people of Missouri, 30 August 1861, 221–222.

38. Parrish, *Turbulent Partnership*, 60. Parrish describes how Lincoln, like the rest of the country, first heard of Frémont's proclamation from the newspapers.

39. Mark E. Neely, *The Fate of Liberty: Abraham Lincoln and Civil Liberties* (New York: Oxford University Press, 1991), 35.

40. Brownlee, *Gray Ghosts of the Confederacy*, 37. The author quotes Gamble as having claimed, "No countenance will be afforded to any scheme or to any conduct calculated in any degree to interfere with the institution of slavery existing in the state."

41. Lincoln to Frémont, 2 September 1861, *OR*, ser. 1, vol. 3, 469–470.

42. Frémont to Lincoln, 8 September 1861, ibid., 477–478; Lincoln to Frémont, 11 September 1861, ibid., 485–486; Burrus M. Carnahan, "Lincoln, Lieber, and the

Laws of War: The Origins and Limits of the Principle of Military Necessity," *American Journal of International Law* 92, no. 2 (April 1998): 220. Reflecting later on his decision to overturn the order, Lincoln claimed that Frémont had overextended the range of military necessity and military law with his proclamation.

43. For an example, see Stephen Ambrose, *Halleck: Lincoln's Chief of Staff* (Baton Rouge: Louisiana State University Press, 1962), 11–12. Ambrose claims that the decision to remove Frémont was the result of his having been "a rabid abolitionist."

44. Andrew Rolle, *John Charles Frémont: Character as Destiny* (Norman: University of Oklahoma Press, 1991), 206.

45. Thompson proclamation, 2 September 1861, *OR*, ser. 1, vol. 3, 693. It should be noted that Thompson does also mention Frémont's provision for the confiscation of property, to include the release of Negroes. His threat, however, appears to offer retaliation only for the execution of armed citizens.

46. Neely, *Fate of Liberty*, 34–35. Neely offers the important observation that Lincoln did not, in fact, deny Frémont's authorization to shoot citizens in arms, but rather, requested that such matters would require his consent. In Neely's words, "What Lincoln tacitly permitted Frémont to do was almost as remarkable as what he disallowed."

47. Quoted in Rolle, *John Charles Frémont*, 209; Neely, *Fate of Liberty*, 34. Neely places some of the blame for Frémont's situation on the fact that he received very little in the form of guidance or direction from Washington during his command in Missouri.

48. Frémont would prove tactically inept in campaigns in Virginia in 1862 (Shenandoah) and 1863 (Second Bull Run), at times placing the security of Washington, D.C., in jeopardy.

49. Lincoln to Commander, Department of the West, 24 October 1861, *OR*, ser. 1, vol. 3, 554. Lincoln displayed optimism that Missouri would quiet down by the first months of 1862, making harsh policies unnecessary. "Before spring the people of Missouri will probably be in no favorable mood to renew for next year the troubles which have so much afflicted and impoverished them during this," Lincoln wrote to Frémont's replacement, "Doubtless local uprisings will for a time continue to occur, but these can be met by detachments and local forces of our own, and will ere long tire out of themselves"; George C. Burmeister Papers, USAMHI.

50. Report of D. R. Anthony, *OR*, ser. 1, vol. 8, 46; Thomas Goodrich, *Black Flag: Guerrilla Warfare on the Western Border, 1861–1865* (Bloomington: Indiana University Press, 1995), 24; Brownlee, *Gray Ghosts of the Confederacy*, 46–47. The unit that attacked Dayton, the Seventh Kansas Cavalry, also known as the Jayhawkers, was primarily made up of bitter abolitionists with ties to the conflicts of Bleeding Kansas. Although they were an official Federal cavalry unit, they often conducted independent operations without sanction from Union command. Led by senator-turned-militia leader Colonel Jim Lane, Kansas cavalry units led punitive campaigns along the border throughout the war. Most Union leaders, to include Halleck, opposed the destructive activities of the Jayhawkers in Missouri.

51. Pope, *Military Memoirs*, 29.

52. William Sherman to John Sherman, 9 January 1862, *Sherman's Civil War: Selected Correspondence of William T. Sherman*, ed. Brooks D. Simpson and Jean V. Berlin (Chapel Hill: University of North Carolina Press, 1999), 183.

53. Grant to Paine, 11 January 1862, *OR*, ser. 1, vol. 8, 495–496; Neely, *Fate of Liberty*, 38.

54. Fellman, *Inside War*, 120–127. While he concludes that willingness to carry out executions of prisoners varied from situation to situation, Fellman suggests that the practice became increasingly more accepted and more frequent as the guerrilla problem in Missouri continued.

55. See Grimsley, *Hard Hand of War*, 143. Grimsley's claim that "From the outset of the conflict, both sides regarded the capture or destruction of railroad property as legitimate" is valid only as long as those involved were members of conventional armies. Clearly, as shown with Pope's, Frémont's, and most explicitly, Halleck's willingness to execute guerrillas caught burning railroad bridges, Union officials did not consider guerrilla attacks on the railroads as legitimate or tolerable.

56. Merrill to soldiers, 29 September 1862, *OR*, ser. 1, vol. 13, 689.

57. Marsh to Frémont, ibid., vol. 1, 449. Marsh's report was made in response to a complaint from the former state governor, Thomas C. Reynolds, about the incident.

58. Wiley Britton, *The Civil War on the Border: A Narrative of Military Operations in Missouri, Kansas, Arkansas, and the Indian Territory during the Years 1863–1865: Based on the Official Reports and Observations of the Author* (New York: G. P. Putnam's Sons, 1899), 11–13. Britton gives a detailed account of the execution and its local political and military effect; Robert J. Futrell, "Military Government in the South, 1861–1865," *Military Affairs* 15, no. 4 (Winter 1951): 186.

59. Report of Lieutenant John Boyd, November 1863, *OR*, ser. 1, vol. 22/1, 746–749. Boyd's commanding general, Brigadier Thomas Davies, ultimately found Boyd's revised explanation to be "satisfactory."

60. John F. Marszalek, *Commander of All Lincoln's Armies: A Life of General Henry W. Halleck* (Cambridge, MA: Belknap Press of Harvard University Press, 2004), 108.

61. Ibid., 43–44.

62. Halleck to McClellan, 26 November 1861, 10 December 1861, *OR*, ser. 1, vol. 8, 818–819. Halleck expresses his concern with the conduct of Union troops, such as the Seventh Kansas, and argues that such activity will turn the sentiments of the state against the Union; Neely, *Fate of Liberty*, 39–40.

63. Seward to Halleck, 2 December 1861, *OR*, ser. 1, vol. 8, 401. This is the first instance of a suspension of *habeas corpus* being mentioned in regard to Missouri.

64. Halleck General Order 34, 26 December 1861, ibid., ser. 2, vol. 1, 155.

65. W. Wayne Smith, *Experiment in Counterinsurgency*, 365–366. Halleck's assessment program was relatively short-lived, but a number of his subordinates, such as John M. Schofield and Benjamin Loan, continued very active programs throughout the war.

66. Halleck to Thomas, 18 January 1862, *OR*, ser. 1, vol. 8, 507.

67. Curtis to Asboth, 22 February 1862, ibid., 562–563; Report of Major General Halleck, 27 February 1862, ibid., 68.

68. Report of Captain James D. Thompson, 30 March 1862, ibid., 357–358.

69. Benjamin F. McIntyre, *Federals on the Frontier: The Diary of Benjamin F. McIntyre,* ed. Nannie M. Tilley (Austin: University of Texas Press, 1963), 42–43.

70. Report of Major General Samuel R. Curtis, January 1865, *OR*, ser. 1, vol. 41/1, 514.

71. Report of Brigadier General Thomas M. Jones, 24 May 1862, ibid., ser. 1, vol. 6, 663–664. Jones's report details the evacuation and subsequent burning of government buildings in Pensacola, Florida. The report includes a copy of a dispatch from Secretary of War Staunton that carries a warning from Lincoln to avoid needless destruction of civilian property. Jones asserts in his report that damage done to private dwellings in Pensacola was minimal.

72. Halleck to Curtis, 1 January 1862, ibid., vol. 8, 475; Ewing to Halleck, 30 December 1861, ibid., ser. 2, vol. 1, 241.

73. Halleck to Ewing, ibid.

74. Fellman, *Inside War*, 88. Fellman stresses the contradicting nature of Halleck's order, by which Halleck "wished to treat soldiers separately from noncombatants," but points out that "in guerrilla war there was no such line, and Halleck was asking his subordinates to make theoretical distinctions on lines erased by the facts."

75. Halleck to Whittlesey, 2 January 1862, *OR*, ser. 1, vol. 8, 481.

76. For an example, see Janda, "Shutting the Gates of Mercy," 11. Janda claims that Halleck "shrank from the idea" of making war on the general population and maintained traditional conciliatory views throughout his term in Missouri.

77. Halleck General Order No. 1, 1 January 1862, *OR*, ser. 1, vol. 8, 476–478.

78. The landmark General Orders 100, issued in April 1863, sought to define such persons and is discussed in detail later in this chapter.

79. General Orders No. 48, 26 February 1862, *OR*, ser. 1, vol. 8, 568.

80. Jay Monaghan, *Civil War on the Western Border, 1854–1865* (Boston: Little, Brown, 1955), 251.

81. General Orders No. 2, 13 March 1863, *OR*, ser. 1, vol. 8, 612.

82. Watson to McDowell, 11 May 1862, ibid., vol. 7/3, 169.

83. Fellman, *Inside War*, 87.

84. Loan to Curtis, 29 March 1863, *OR*, ser. 1, vol. 22/2, 183–184.

85. See Fellman, *Inside War*, 124–126. Fellman asserts that the Union acceptance of guerrilla execution was varied, especially if taken prisoner. "Once officially made captives," he claims, "it was difficult to rationalize the immediate execution of guerrillas."

86. Report of Captain J. C. Smith, 28 June 1863, *OR*, ser. 1, vol. 22/1, 374–375.

87. Birtle, *U.S. Army Counterinsurgency*, 28–29. Birtle concludes that the execution of prisoners was increasingly common during the war; Fellman, *Inside War*, 123–125. According to Fellman, "most units" acted in support of the no-prisoners order, and he concludes that, "as the war continued, increasing numbers of [Union] men shot civilians with decreasing compunction"; Goodrich, *Black Flag*, 64–65.

88. Report of Brigadier General Clinton Fisk, 9 January 1865, *OR*, ser. 1, vol. 28/1, 469.

89. Parker to Curtis, 3 May 1862, ibid., ser. 2, vol. 5, 550.

90. Brownlee, *Gray Ghosts of the Confederacy*, 90–91.

91. Grant to Halleck, 11 March 1862, *OR*, ser. 1, vol. 10/2, 29; General Orders No. 30, 28 April 1862, ibid., ser. 4, vol. 1, 1094–1099; Fellman, *Inside War*, 98–99. Fellman points out that the Partisan Ranger Act was intended "to bring already existing guerrilla bands under [Confederate] command and to channel their growth," rather than calling for an unbridled guerrilla war against the Union invaders.

92. Frank Freidel, "General Orders 100 and Military Government," *Mississippi Valley Historical Review* 32, no. 4 (March 1946): 542.

93. Halleck to Lieber, 6 August 1862, *OR*, ser. 3, vol. 2, 301. Based on the tone of Halleck's letter, it seems that Halleck assumed Lieber's thoughts on guerrillas matched his own.

94. Francis Lieber, "Guerrilla Parties Considered in Reference to the Laws and Usages of War," *OR*, ser. 3, vol. 2, 301–309. In the conclusion to his essay, Lieber stressed the importance of harsh measures in response to those he deemed illegal combatants: "So much is certain, that no army, no society engaged in war, any more than a society at peace, can allow unpunished assassination, robbery, and devastation without the deepest injury to itself and disastrous consequences which might change the very issue of the war." In doing so, Lieber reinforced Halleck's views.

95. Ibid.; Richard S. Hartigan, *Lieber's Code and the Law of War* (Chicago: Precedent, 1983), 4.

96. Marszalek, *Commander of All Lincoln's Armies*, 167.

97. Halleck to Wright, 18 November 1862, *OR*, ser. 1, vol. 20/2, 67–68.

98. See Daniel E. Sutherland, *The Emergence of Total War* (Abilene, TX: McWhiney Foundation Press, 1998); and Grimsley, *Hard Hand of War*. Sutherland views the punitive "Pope-Lincoln Policy" of the summer of 1862 (the result of Lincoln's frustration with the lack of Union success in the East) as the hallmark of the war's transition to a total war; Grimsley argues that McClellan's failed Peninsula Campaign in the summer of 1862 doomed conciliation and convinced Lincoln to pursue a "hard war."

99. Marszalek, *Commander of All Lincoln's Armies*, 168.

100. Freidel, "General Orders 100 and Military Government," 541; Carnahan, "Lincoln, Lieber, and the Laws of War," 231; Hartigan, *Lieber's Code and the Law of War*, 1.

101. General Orders 100, *Instructions for the Government of the Armies of the United States in the Field*, 24 April 1863, *OR*, ser. 2, vol. 5, 677. The other sections of the Lieber Code were devoted to Military Necessity, Personal Property, Deserters and Prisoners, Spies, Prisoner Exchange, Parole, Assassination, and Rebellion.

102. See Fellman, *Inside War*, 165. It was common practice for guerrillas in Missouri and other occupied states to don the Union blue to aid in achieving surprise and to move through guard lines undetected.

103. General Orders 100, 681–682. Section X of the code assigned the authority

to determine which citizens were loyal and which were disloyal to the "military commander of the legitimate government." Missouri was considered a Union state throughout the war.

104. Birtle, *U.S. Army Counterinsurgency*, 34.

105. Hartigan, *Lieber's Code and the Law of War*, 15.

106. General Orders 100, 672.

107. Neely, *Civil War and the Limits of Destruction*, 206; Halleck to Lieber, 6 August 1862. Neely claims that Halleck initially approached Lieber in order to produce a "code of laws that would govern the novel situations that Halleck had encountered in Missouri." Four months removed from Missouri, however, and still hearing reports of the guerrilla problem from field commanders in different parts of the South, it is unlikely that Halleck viewed the issue of guerrilla warfare as "novel" when he solicited Lieber's aid.

108. Harry S. Stout, *Upon the Altar of the Nation: A Moral History of the Civil War* (New York: Penguin Group, 2006), 193.

109. Report of Major General Edward Canby, *OR*, ser. 1, vol. 39/1, 405; Freidel, "General Orders 100 and Military Government," 553; Birtle, *U.S. Army Counterinsurgency*, 35; Hartigan, *Lieber's Code and the Law of War*, 21. These authors all agree that the Lieber Code's influence on the law of war was much more profound following the Civil War rather than during it.

110. John M. Schofield, *Forty-Six Years in the Army* (New York: Century, 1897), 66.

111. Fellman, *Inside War*, 95; Albert Castel, "Order No. 11 and the Civil War on the Border," in *Winning and Losing in the Civil War: Essays and Stories* (Columbia: University of South Carolina Press, 1996), 51. In considering the harsh treatment of civilians in American history, Castel ranks Order No. 11 second only to the internment of Japanese Americans during World War II.

112. Schofield, *Forty-Six Years in the Army*, 358.

113. Brownlee, *Gray Ghosts of the Confederacy*, 108. The author suggests, "Had it not been for the guerrilla war, these troops and the money required to support them would have been potentially available for use elsewhere where the Union was desperately pressed."

114. Fellman, *Inside War*, 94. Schofield's use of assessments was just an extension of the same policy established by Halleck, but on a larger scale.

115. Curtis to Loan, 13 May 1863, *OR*, ser. 1, vol. 22/2, 278.

116. Report of Brigadier General Thomas Ewing, 30 June 1863, *OR*, ser. 1, vol. 22/1, 375–376.

117. Curtis to Loan, 13 May 1863 *OR*, ser. 1, vol. 22/2, 278–279; Schofield to Halleck, 25 August 1863, ibid., 471–472.

118. Historians agree that the women's deaths were accidental, caused when the old warehouse in Kansas City in which they were held collapsed unexpectedly. See Duane Schultz, *Quantrill's War: The Life and Times of William Clarke Quantrill* (New York: St. Martin's Griffin, 1997), 142.

119. Goodrich, *Black Flag*, 77–95; Brownlee, *Gray Ghosts of the Confederacy*, 124.

For a most detailed account of Quantrill's raid, see Duane Schultz, *Quantrill's War*, 147–213; McPherson, *Battle Cry of Freedom*, 786; Charles Mink, "General Orders, No. 11: The Forced Evacuation of Civilians during the Civil War," *Military Affairs* 34 (December 1970): 132; Castel, "Order No. 11 and the Civil War on the Border," 53.

120. Lincoln to Halleck, 31 August 1863, *OR*, ser. 1, vol. 22/2, 488; quoted in Goodrich, *Black Flag*, 96; Brownlee, *Gray Ghosts of the Confederacy*, 125.

121. Schofield to Ewing, 25 August 1863, *OR*, ser. 1, vol. 22/2, 471–472. Schofield later claimed that he authorized the order in an attempt to quell the angry population in Kansas and to prevent an all-out vengeful raid into Missouri to be led by Senator Jim Lane. See Schofield, *Forty-Six Years in the Army*, 81–83.

122. Mink, "General Orders, No. 11," 132; Castel, "Order No. 11 and the Civil War on the Border," 60.

123. Report of Major General John M. Schofield, 24 September 1863, *OR*, ser. 1, vol. 22/1, 575.

124. Goodrich, *Black Flag*, 100.

125. Report of Lieutenant Colonel B. F. Lazear, 27 August 1863, *OR*, ser. 1, vol. 22/1, 587–588.

126. Goodrich, *Black Flag*, 100–101; Fellman, *Inside War*, 95–96; Mink, "General Orders, No. 11," 132; Brownlee, *Gray Ghosts of the Confederacy*, 125–126; Russell F. Weigley, *A Great Civil War: A Military and Political History, 1861–1865* (Bloomington: University of Indiana Press, 2000), 45; Stiles, *Jesse James*, 96; McPherson, *Battle Cry of Freedom*, 786. The exact number of civilians forced out of the four counties has never been determined, but most historians agree on a number of approximately 20,000.

127. McPherson, *Battle Cry of Freedom*, 786. General William T. Sherman's burning of Atlanta and General Phillip Sheridan's "Burning Raid" in Loudoun and Fauquier Counties in Virginia in 1864, both of which are discussed in following chapters, were similar to Schofield's Order No. 11 in their destructiveness. Neither, however, shared the massive displacement of civilians that took place in Missouri, although they came close.

128. Report of General Henry W. Halleck, 25 November 1863, *OR*, ser. 1, vol. 22/1, 11.

129. Mink, "General Orders, No. 11," 135. Mink concluded that the order simply "curtailed" guerrilla activity but did not stop it.

130. Fisk to Rosecrans, 28 September 1864, *OR*, ser. 1, vol. 41/3, 454. Brigadier General Fisk's report covers the attack on the town of Centralia, Missouri, in which a large band of guerrillas under the command of William "Bloody Bill" Anderson robbed a train and executed twenty-three unarmed Union soldiers who were passengers on the train.

131. Goodrich, *Black Flag*, 158–164. A number of Missouri's guerrillas, most famously Jesse James and Cole Younger, continued their bushwhacking ways as outlaws throughout the West. For a detailed account, see Stiles, *Jesse James*.

132. Pope, *Military Memoirs*, 25.

133. Neely, *Fate of Liberty*, 50.

134. Grimsley, *Hard Hand of War*, 119; Neely, *Civil War and the Limits of Destruction*, 207. Grimsley goes on to note that although Union policies in Missouri were atypical, they were influential. "By accustoming Union soldiers to regard Southern civilians as enemies, and by making the destruction of private property a normal practice, the antiguerrilla campaign helped lay the groundwork for the greater hard war measures still to come."

135. James McPherson, "From Limited War to Total War in America" in *On the Road to Total War: The American Civil War and the German Wars of Unification, 1861–1871*, ed. Stig Forster and Jorg Nagler (London: Cambridge University Press, 1997), 302; Sutherland, *Emergence of Total War*, 17.

136. McPherson, "From Limited War to Total War in America," 300.

Chapter 3. A Remedy for All Evils: Retaliatory Destruction on the Mississippi

1. Curtis to Halleck, 6 April 1862, *OR*, ser. 1, vol. 8, 541.

2. Franklin B. Cooling, *Fort Donelson's Legacy: War and Society in Kentucky and Tennessee, 1862–1863* (Knoxville: University of Tennessee Press, 1997), 111.

3. George E. Currie, *Warfare along the Mississippi: The Letters of Lieutenant Colonel George E. Currie*, ed. Norman E. Clarke (Mount Pleasant: Central Michigan University Press, 1961), 57; Johnston to Seddon, 2 September 1863, *OR*, ser. 1, vol. 22/2, 988–989. Johnston refers to Seddon's directive to "harass" the Union traffic on the Mississippi but assumes that Seddon intended for regular detachments of cavalry to be used for it, causing Johnston to request more cavalry for the mission.

4. Moore proclamation, 24 May 1862, *OR*, ser. 1, vol. 15, 744; a copy of another Thomas proclamation is included in *The Private and Official Correspondence of General Benjamin F. Butler* [hereafter referred to as *POCB*], vol. 2 (Norwood, MA: Plimpton Press, 1917), 22; The Confederate Trans-Mississippi District, under the direction of General Thomas C. Hindman, issued General Orders No. 17, which called for the people of Arkansas to form independent bands in order to wage guerrilla warfare throughout the state. For a complete discussion on the "Bands of Ten" Order, see Mackey, *Uncivil War*, 29–31.

5. Michael B. Ballard, *Vicksburg: The Campaign That Opened the Mississippi* (Chapel Hill: University of North Carolina Press, 2004), 37. Ballard notes that the "so-called guerrillas" that constantly harassed Union operations on the Mississippi included such groups as "local militia, private citizens, and occasionally Confederate regulars."

6. Grimsley, *Hard Hand of War*, 119.

7. Mackey, *Uncivil War*, 53.

8. John Bennett Walters, *Merchant of Terror: General Sherman and Total War* (New York: Bobs-Merrill, 1973), xii, 63. Walters emphasizes Sherman's willingness to punish civilians whom he suspected were not directly involved with guerrilla attacks. Yet, it should be noted that Sherman did indeed punish local secessionists at times, to include expelling them from Memphis.

9. Cooling, *Fort Donelson's Legacy*, 110.

10. For the best example, see Philip S. Paludan, *Victims: A True Story of the Civil War* (Knoxville: University of Tennessee Press, 1981). Paludan tells the story of the Confederate execution of Unionists in Shelton Laurel, North Carolina. Noel C. Fisher, *War at Every Door: Partisan Politics and Guerrilla Violence in East Tennessee, 1860–1869* (Chapel Hill: University of North Carolina Press, 1997), 117–118, provides accounts of widespread Confederate destruction of Unionist property in East Tennessee in addition to torture, rape, and murder. Daniel E. Sutherland, ed., *Guerrillas, Unionists, and Violence on the Confederate Homefront* (Fayetteville: University of Arkansas Press, 1999).

11. Grimsley, *Hard Hand of War*, 151–153; James McPherson, "From Limited War to Total War in America," 306. Grimsley sees Grant and Sherman as the original practitioners of what he calls hard war, while McPherson primarily views Sherman as the true pioneer of total war measures in the Civil War. Abraham Lincoln is also often mentioned as a progenitor of hard war in America.

12. McPherson, *Battle Cry of Freedom*, 414. Casualty numbers from Margaret Wagner, Gary W. Gallagher, and Paul Finkelman, eds., *The Library of Congress Civil War Desk Reference* (New York: Simon and Schuster, 2002), 252. The editors place the exact number of total casualties for the battle at 23,746.

13. Ulysses S. Grant, *Personal Memoirs of U.S. Grant* (New York: Da Capo Press, 1982), 191. Immediately after this sentence, Grant discussed his decision to live off the land of the enemy but does not mention taking punitive action against civilians such as burning or forced depopulation.

14. Grimsley, *Hard Hand of War*, 93. Grimsley cites a number of conciliatory-sounding statements that Grant made in the months after Shiloh. It should be noted, however, that Grimsley also relies heavily on postwar writings to support his argument.

15. Brooks D. Simpson, *Let Us Have Peace: Ulysses S. Grant and the Politics of War and Reconstruction, 1861–1868* (Chapel Hill: University of North Carolina Press, 1991), 24–25. Simpson claims that it was "the feisty behavior of hostile citizens" and "the restive populace and the guerrillas, not Shiloh, that toughened Grant to the notion of hard war"; see also Cooling, *Fort Donelson's Legacy*, 90–91. Cooling attributes Grant's acceptance of collective punishment to the persistent guerrilla threat in western Tennessee in the summer of 1862.

16. Russell F. Weigley, "The American Military and the Principle of Civilian Control from McClellan to Powell," *Journal of Military History* 57, no. 5 (October 1993): 34. Weigley specifically addresses Lincoln's attitude toward the war, but he references the summer of 1862 when referring to the "fierceness of Southern warmaking."

17. Simpson, *Let Us Have Peace*, 24.

18. McPherson, *Battle Cry of Freedom*, 513–514. McPherson credits Forrest and Morgan with immobilizing a Union Army of 40,000 with only 2,500 men.

19. Mackey, *Uncivil War*, 124. Mackey describes the commands of Forrest and Morgan as "not part-time guerrillas, but full-time soldiers." He also addresses

Buell's refusal to apply the term "guerrilla" to the raiders, choosing instead to view them as regular cavalry; Cooling, *Fort Donelson's Legacy*, 88. According to the author, Forrest and Morgan were "neither guerrillas nor partisans but regular cavalry." Historians usually agree that their operations were better defined as irregular cavalry raids rather than guerrilla operations. Nevertheless, their hit-and-run tactics were similar to those practiced by small guerrilla bands in the region. As a result, Union troops and officers often referred to the raiders, either mistakenly or not, as guerrillas. For example, one Union brigadier general claimed in May 1862 that his men were "entirely powerless" against the Confederate raiders, and added, "Morgan's guerrillas must be caught before they can be shot." Morgan to Watson, 11 May 1862, *OR*, ser. 1, vol. 2, 182.

20. Letter dated 18 September 1862, John Brandon Papers, USAMHI.

21. Grant to Halleck, 30 June 1862, *PUSG*, vol. 5 (Carbondale: Southern Illinois University Press, 1973), 175.

22. General Orders No. 60, 3 July 1862, ibid., 190.

23. 28 July 1862, ibid., 243; Grant to Halleck, 9 August 1862, *OR*, ser. 1, vol. 17/2, 160.

24. Halleck to Grant, 2 August 1862, *OR*, ser. 1, vol. 17/2, 150. Halleck's guidance was reflected in subsequent orders to Grant's subordinates. Four days later, Brigadier General William Elliot issued the following order for units under his command in the Army of the Mississippi: "Notify the inhabitants within reach of your lines that any words or actions hostile to the Government will oblige you to treat the parties as enemies, who can receive only the rights of belligerents, whose property belongs to the United States. The women and children will be ordered beyond our lines, their property seized for the benefit of the United States, and their houses burned." Elliot to Morgan, 6 August 1862, ibid., 154.

25. Grant to Halleck, 8 July 1862, *PUSG*, vol. 5, 204.

26. Report of Brigadier General Gordon Granger, 28 August 1862, *OR*, ser. 1, vol. 27/1, 40.

27. Grant to Hurlburt, 3 January 1863, ibid., vol. 27/2, 525.

28. Royster, *Destructive War*, 107; Vetter, *Sherman*, 134; Edward Hagerman, *The American Civil War and the Origins of Modern Warfare: Ideas, Organization and Field Command* (Bloomington: Indiana University Press, 1988), 208; Buck T. Foster, *Sherman's Mississippi Campaign* (Tuscaloosa: University of Alabama Press, 2006), 13. All of these studies focus primarily on Sherman's mentality, and not that of his soldiers.

29. Mark E. Neely, "Was the Civil War a Total War?," in Forster and Nagler, *On the Road to Total War*, 38, 43.

30. Quoted in Cooling, *Fort Donelson's Legacy*, 111; McPherson, "From Limited War to Total War in America," 297. McPherson states that the rhetoric of Sherman and others "was far more ferocious than anything that actually happened."

31. Royster, *Destructive War*, 358.

32. Grimsley, *Hard Hand of War*, 118.

33. Charles W. Wills, *Army Life of an Illinois Soldier, Including a Day-by-Day*

Record of Sherman's March to the Sea (Carbondale: Southern Illinois University Press, 1996) 122–121. Wills makes repeated mention of the guerrillas that "infest" the local area.

34. Steven E. Woodworth, *Nothing but Victory: The Army of the Tennessee, 1861–1865* (New York: Alfred A. Knopf, 2005), 212.

35. Grimsley, *Hard Hand of War*, 81. Throughout the book, Grimsley uses the Ninth Ohio as an example of Union soldiers that eschewed conciliation in favor of hard war.

36. F. W. Keil, *The Thirty-Fifth Ohio Regiment: A Narrative of Service from August 1861 to 1864* (Fort Wayne, IN: Archer, Housh, 1894), 85; *Harper's Weekly*, 30 August 1862, 551. The Thirty-Fifth Ohio marched with the Ninth on the day of the attack.

37. Thomas to Buell, 7 August 1862, *OR*, ser. 1, vol. 16/1, 839.

38. John Beatty, *The Citizen-Soldier; or, Memoirs of a Volunteer* (Cincinnati: Wilstach, Baldwin, 1879), 169.

39. Keil, *Thirty-Fifth Ohio Regiment*, 83–85; Constantin Grebner, *We Were the Ninth: A History of the Ninth Regiment, Ohio Volunteer Infantry, April 17, 1861 to June 7, 1864* (Kent, OH: Kent State University Press, 1987), 107–108; George Crook, *General George Crook: His Autobiography*, ed. Martin F. Schmidtt (Norman: University of Oklahoma Press, 1947), 112–113; entry for 7 January 1863, Alva G. Griest Papers, USAMHI. The exact details of the killing of McCook are still uncertain. There are a number of different locations given for the attack. While Griest names the town of Lavergn as the setting of the incident, Schmitt claims that McCook's brigade was headed for Dercherd, Tennessee, and official Union reports refer to the town as New Market (in northern Alabama); Amos Fleagle Papers, USAMHI; see also, Cooling, *Fort Donelson's Legacy*, 76. Cooling claims that the Ninth Ohio "wreaked vengeance up and down that part of the Tennessee River Valley for miles" in retaliation for the killing of McCook. Cooling points out that Gurley was "apparently" a member of the Fourth Alabama Cavalry. All Union accounts of the incident, however, label Gurley's group as guerrillas; *Harper's Weekly*, 30 August 1862, 551. The reporter names Charles Wood as the guerrilla who shot McCook.

40. Keil, *The Thirty-Fifth Ohio Regiment*, 85; Jabez Banbury Papers, USAMHI. Banbury, a colonel in the Fifth Iowa Infantry, agreed with Keil's assessment of the local people, claiming that the town seemed like a natural habitat for murderers.

41. General Orders 100, *OR*, ser. 2, vol. 5, 673. Article 28 of Section 1 of the order stated the following in regard to military retaliation: "Retaliation will therefore never be resorted to as a measure of mere revenge but only as a means of protective retribution and moreover cautiously and unavoidably; that is to say retaliation shall only be resorted to after careful inquiry into the real occurrence and the character of the misdeeds that may demand retribution. Unjust or inconsiderate retaliation removes the belligerents farther and farther from the mitigating rules of a regular war and by rapid steps leads them nearer to the internecine wars of savages"; Henry W. Halleck, "Retaliation in War," *American Journal of International Law* 6, no. 1 (January 1912): 109. In addressing the issue of "reciprocity" Halleck wrote the following: "If he

[enemy] becomes barbarous and cruel in his conduct, we cannot, as a general thing, follow and resort upon his subjects, by treating them in a like manner."

42. General Orders No. 8, 7 August 1862, *OR*, ser. 1, vol. 16/1, 839.

43. Fry to Thomas, 8 August 1862, ibid., vol. 16/2, 290; Buell to Thomas, ibid.

44. Negley to Fry, 9 August 1863, ibid., 300.

45. Linderman, *Embattled Courage*, 198.

46. Hamlin Alexander Coe, *Mine Eyes Have Seen the Glory: Combat Diaries of Union Sergeant Hamlin Alexander Coe* (Cranbury, NJ: Associated University Presses, 1975), 98.

47. Beatty, *Citizen Soldier*, 138–139.

48. Ibid., 139.

49. Butler to Williams, 1 June 1862, *OR*, ser. 1, vol. 15, 25; Butler to Stanton, 28 June and 3 July 1862, ibid., 502, 504. Butler's message makes it clear that he saw no difference between partisans and guerrillas and considered each to be illegitimate combatants.

50. Report of Brigadier General Thomas Williams, 29 May 1862, ibid., 24.

51. Charles O'Neil Diaries, LOC.

52. McIntyre, *Federals on the Frontier*, 195.

53. Robert J. Schneller, Jr., *Farragut: America's First Admiral* (Washington, DC: Brassey's, 2002), 64–65.

54. George Gilbert Smith, *Leaves from a Soldier's Diary: The Personal Record of Lieutenant George G. Smith, Co. C, 1st Louisiana Regiment Infantry Volunteers (White) during the War of the Rebellion* (Putnam, CT: G. G. Smith, 1906), 31. Smith notes in his diary that his ship "burned the village of Donaldsonville" on 9 August. It is uncertain how many, if any, citizens were killed or wounded from Farragut's attack on the town.

55. Schneller, *Farragut*, 64; James P. Duffey, *Lincoln's Admiral: The Civil War Campaigns of David Farragut* (New York: Wiley, 1997), 156.

56. William C. Holton, "Diary of William C. Holton," in *Cruise of the U.S. Flagship Hartford* (Tarrytown, NY: William Abbatt, 1922), 34; Smith, *Leaves from a Soldier's Diary*, 31.

57. Butler to Santa Maria Clara, 2 September 1862, *OR*, ser. 1, vol. 15, 563.

58. Quoted in Schneller, *Farragut*, 65.

59. Roe to Morris, 11 September 1862, *OR*, ser. 1, vol. 15, 569; Butler endorsement, 13 September 1862, ibid.

60. No mention of Donaldsonville is found in any of the following: Grimsley, *Hard Hand of War*; Royster, *Destructive War*; Neely, *Fate of Liberty*; or Birtle, *U.S. Army Counterinsurgency*.

61. Sherman to Hindman, 28 September 1862, Simpson and Berlin, *Sherman's Civil War*, 308; Sherman to Maria Boyle Ewing Sherman, 6 August 1862, ibid., 262. The order of these letters had been arranged for clarity.

62. On 17 June 1862, Hindman issued Order No. 17, which called for the formation of independent guerrilla bands in the Trans-Mississippi District for "the more effectual annoyance of the enemy on our rivers and in our mountains and woods."

General Orders No. 17, 17 June 1862, *OR*, ser. 1, vol. 13, 835; Sherman to Hindman, 28 September 1862, ibid., vol. 13, 683; Sherman to Chase, quoted in Sherman, *Memoirs*, 245.

63. Orders No. 49, 7 July 1862, *OR*, vol. 17/2, 81.

64. Sherman to Hurlburt, ibid., 88–89.

65. For every example of Sherman attempting to limit the destruction caused by his soldiers, there is an opposing example of his tolerating, or even initiating, such behavior; see Joseph T. Glatthaar, *The March to the Sea and Beyond: Sherman's Troops in the Savannah and Carolinas Campaign* (New York: New York University Press, 1985), 151–153. Glatthaar points out that Sherman's men were not given free rein to loot and pillage, but when guerrillas or bushwhackers killed a Union soldier, Sherman "had his men burn all the buildings within a certain distance of the body."

66. Letter dated 20 July 1862, Schuyler P. Coe Papers, USAMHI; entry dated 18 July 1862, Thomas K. Mitchell Diary, Kansas Collection, Kenneth Spencer Research Library, University of Kansas.

67. Coe Papers, USAMHI; William W. McCarty Papers, ibid.

68. Letter to editors of the *Memphis Bulletin* and the *Memphis Appeal*, 21 August 1862, Simpson and Berlin, *Sherman's Civil War*, 283–285.

69. Sherman to Walcutt, 24 September 1862, *OR*, ser. 1, vol. 17/2, 235–236. In his order Sherman admitted to Walcutt that the guerrillas guilty of the attack would no longer be in Randolph when the regiment arrived, and yet he wanted the town destroyed.

70. Sherman to Grant, 26 September 1862, ibid., vol. 17/1, 144–145.

71. Walters, *Merchant of Terror*, 62, 64; Grimsley, *Hard Hand of War*, 115.

72. Grimsley, *Hard Hand of War*, 116; Sherman to Rawlins, 26 September 1862, *OR*, ser. 1, vol. 17/1, 145.

73. Special Orders No. 238, 18 October 1862, *OR*, ser. 1, vol. 17/ 2, 280–281; Sherman to Rawlins, 21 October 1862, ibid., 285.

74. Sherman to Grant, ibid.

75. Sherman to Carr, ibid., vol. 18, 748.

76. *New York Herald*, 27 October 1862. The *Herald* correspondent projected that a total of forty families would be forced to leave Memphis following the attacks.

77. Sherman to Hurlburt, 7 November 1862, *OR*, ser. 1, vol. 17/2, 860.

78. Walters, *Merchant of Terror*, passim.

79. Caleb Carr, *The Lessons of Terror: A History of Warfare against Civilians* (New York: Random House, 2003), 6.

80. Sherman to Grant, 26 August 1863, *OR*, ser. 1, vol. 17/1, 145.

81. Henry A. Kircher, *A German in the Yankee Fatherland: The Civil War Letters of Henry A. Kircher*, ed. Earl J. Hess (Kent, OH: Kent State University Press, 1983), 41.

82. Report of Brigadier General James Veatch, 21 February 1863, *OR*, ser. 1, vol. 22/1, 231.

83. Samuel Calvin Jones, *Reminiscences of the Twenty-Second Iowa Volunteer Infantry . . . As Taken from the Diary of Lieutenant S. C. Jones of Company A* (Iowa City, IA: n.p., 1907), 164.

84. Charles Holbrook Prentiss Papers; Charles Weiser Papers, USAMHI.

85. Mackey, *Uncivil War*, 55; Birtle, *U.S. Army Counterinsurgency*, 47; Chester G. Hearn, *Ellet's Brigade: The Strangest Outfit of All* (Baton Rouge: Louisiana State University Press, 2000), xii, 1.

86. Currie, *Warfare along the Mississippi*, 56–57.

87. Letter dated 27 February 1863, Frank MacGregor Papers, USAMHI.

88. Mackey, *Uncivil War*, 13–14. Mackey divides operations against irregulars into three separate categories: antiguerrilla operations, counterguerrilla operations, and counterinsurgency operations. According to the author, antiguerrilla operations are "direct combat operations aimed at destroying irregular units," while counter-guerrilla operations are more "passive" in nature, designed to defend against attacks from irregulars. Mackey describes counterinsurgency operations as efforts to reduce the support for guerrilla activity in a certain area and gives "rebuilding the legiti-macy of the Federal authority" as an example. Mackey's definition of antiguerrilla operations is somewhat confusing in that he describes them as aimed at the sole pur-pose of killing guerrillas, and yet he includes the "punitive burning of a village" as an example of this approach. The burning of villages in retaliation for guerrilla attacks constitutes an indirect approach to combating guerrillas and falls more in the realm of denying them a base of support, or simply punishing their sympathizers, rather than trying to deal with guerrillas directly.

89. *New York Herald*, 25 July 1863.

90. Entry dated 15 June 1863, Josiah H. Goodwin Papers, USAMHI.

91. Entry dated 19 April 1863, ibid.

92. See Hearn, *Ellet's Brigade*, 158–163; Currie, *Warfare along the Mississippi*, 80–84; entry for 24 May 1863, Goodwin Papers. Goodwin's entry does not mention the town by name, but the date of his entry suggests that the small village that he observed "all a blaze [*sic*]—all burnt but one frame dwelling" was Austin.

93. Report of Brigadier General Alfred W. Ellet, 25 May 1863, *OR*, ser. 1, vol. 24/2, 431.

94. Entry dated 15 June 1863, Josiah H. Goodwin Papers, USAMHI.

95. Currie, *Warfare along the Mississippi*, 108.

96. Mackey, *Uncivil War*, 56; Hearn, *Ellet's Brigade*, 164.

97. E. Paul Reichelm Papers, LOC; Letter dated 24 January 1863, Frank MacGregor Papers, USAMHI; entry for 16 March 1864, Josiah H. Goodwin Pa-pers, USAMHI.

98. Currie, *Warfare along the Mississippi*, 113.

99. See Mackey, *Uncivil War*, 58; Birtle, *U.S. Army Counterinsurgency*, 47; Hearn, *Ellet's Brigade*, 266. While Mackey claims that the Mississippi Marine Bri-gade "never truly did the job it was designed to do," Birtle suggests that the brigade was somewhat effective.

100. E. Paul Reichelm Papers, LOC. Reichelm states specifically that the Union troops' burning of the town was not, in fact, "a military necessity" in his view, but rather an act of revenge both "horrible and disgusting."

101. Joseph Stockton Papers, USAMHI.

102. Entry for 11 July 1863, Josiah Goodwin Papers, USAMHI.

103. Currie, *Warfare along the Mississippi*, 78, 84. The burning of Austin was one of many factors that caused Currie to think poorly of Ellet. In lamenting the action at Austin, Currie criticizes what he sees as Ellet's inability to "judge dispassionately and without motives of revenge," claiming that such officers "should never be a commander of men."

104. Lucius W. Barber, *Army Memoirs* (Chicago: J. M. W. Jones Stationery and Printing, 1894), 107.

105. Entry for 22 December 1862, Frank MacGregor Papers, USAMHI.

106. Porter to Stevenson, 2 March 1863, *OR*, ser. 1, vol. 24/3, 78.

107. See Neely, "Was the Civil War a Total War?" 46–48. Neely asserts that Grant and other Union leaders advocated punitive policies "only in bitterly disloyal areas infested with guerrillas." The problem is, such a description fits much of the territory occupied by the Union Army during the war; see also Grimsley, *Hard Hand of War*, 204. Grimsley, too, seeks to emphasize the restraint practiced by Union soldiers in the war, concluding that they "stayed their hands as often as they impelled retribution."

108. See Mackey's *Uncivil War*, 58–71. Mackey describes the Union Army's establishment of fortified Unionist farm colonies and Union cavalry operations that were successful in combating the guerrilla threat in northern Arkansas in 1865; Birtle, *U.S. Army Counterinsurgency*, 40–47. Birtle describes a number of tactical "counterguerrilla methods" adopted by the U.S. Army to include special cavalry units and passive defense measures. While Birtle claims that these methods were somewhat successful, he also concludes that punitive measures against civilians were widespread.

109. Report of First Lieutenant John F. Parker, 24 March 1865, *OR*, ser. 1, vol. 48/1, 1250–1251; Cameron to Maloney, 14 April 1865, ibid., vol. 48/2, 94; Report of Brigadier General Cyrus Bussey, 6 April 1865, ibid., vol. 48/1, 165.

Chapter 4. War and Individual Ruin: Sherman's Campaigns of 1864

1. Ballard, *Vicksburg*, 398.

2. William T. Sherman, *Memoirs of General W. T. Sherman* (New York: Penguin Books, 2000), 192–198. In November 1861, Sherman was relieved of command and placed on furlough for suggesting that a force of 200,000 would be necessary to defeat the Confederate forces in the West. Most of his contemporaries found this estimate ridiculous and concluded that Sherman had lost his senses. He was sent to St. Louis, but his career was revived by his performance at the Battle of Shiloh in April 1862.

3. Charles Bracelen Flood, *Grant and Sherman: The Friendship That Won the Civil War* (New York: Harper Perennial, 2006), 224–225.

4. For examples, see Royster, *Destructive War*; Hagerman, *American Civil War and the Origins of Modern Warfare*, xiii–xiv.

5. Sherman, *Memoirs*, 364.

6. Royster, *Destructive War*, 325.

7. Sherman to Owen, 30 January 1864, *OR*, ser. 1, vol. 32/1, 185.

8. Foster, *Sherman's Mississippi Campaign*, 41–42.

9. William B. Westervelt Papers, USAMHI.

10. Sherman to Ellen Sherman, 7 February 1864, Simpson and Berlin, *Sherman's Civil War*, 602.

11. Albert Quincy Porter Papers, LOC; Foster, *Sherman's Mississippi Campaign*, 65–66.

12. Stephen H. Smith Papers, USAMHI.

13. Foster, *Sherman's Mississippi Campaign*, 58–69; Woodworth, *Nothing but Victory*, 483.

14. John A. Logan, ed., *History of the 31st Illinois Infantry Volunteers* (Evansville, IN: Keller Printing and Publishing, 1902), 84; Matthew B. Schofield Papers, USAMHI.

15. Report of Major General Sherman, 27 February 1864, *OR*, ser. 1, vol. 32/1, 173; Sherman to Grant, 7 March 1864, ibid., 176.

16. Stephen H. Smith Papers, USAMHI.

17. Sherman, *Memoirs*, 364–365. While blasting Smith's conduct during the campaign, Sherman claimed that "General Smith never regained my confidence as a soldier, though I still regard him as a most accomplished gentleman and skillful engineer."

18. Thomas D. Douglas Papers, USAMHI.

19. Foster, *Sherman's Mississippi Campaign*, 130–131.

20. Margaret Brobst Roth, ed., *Well, Mary: Civil War Letters of a Wisconsin Volunteer* (Madison: University of Wisconsin Press, 1960), 37; James Hodges Papers, LOC; William Westervelt Papers, USAMHI.

21. R. L. Howard, *The History of the 124th Regiment: Illinois Infantry Volunteers* (Springfield, IL: H. W. Rokker, 1880), 188. Howard, a regimental chaplain, described the burning of Hillsboro in response to shots fired from houses in town; Stanley P. Hirshon, *The White Tecumseh: A Biography of William T. Sherman* (New York: Wiley, 1997), 183; Foster, *Sherman's Mississippi Campaign*, 131; William Westervelt Papers, USAMHI. Westervelt commented on finding Clinton "where most of the houses were in ruins"; Report of Colonel Edward F. Winslow, 29 February 1864, *OR*, ser. 1, vol. 32/1, 251.

22. James Hodges Papers, USAMHI.

23. Howard, *History of the 124th Regiment*, 123. The order of the quotations was rearranged for clarity; Sherman to Logan, 20 January 1864, Simpson and Berlin, *Sherman's Civil War*, 588; Sherman to Ellen Sherman, 28 January 1864, ibid., 594.

24. Royster, *Destructive War*, 325.

25. Sherman, *Memoirs*, 530–533; Grant, *Personal Memoirs*, 500. Grant mentioned that Lincoln had reservations about the march, while Halleck was strongly against it; Weigley, *Great Civil War*, 388–389.

26. Sherman to Grant, 9 October 1864, *OR*, ser. 1, vol. 39/3, 162. This dispatch included Sherman's infamous promise to "Make Georgia Howl."

27. Glatthaar, *March to the Sea and Beyond*, 6; Special Field Orders No. 119, 8 November 1864, *OR*, ser. 1, vol. 39/2, 701.

28. Sherman to Thomas, 20 October 1864, *OR*, ser. 1, vol. 39/3, 377–378.

29. Sherman, *Memoirs*, 535.

30. Alva G. Griest Papers, USAMHI.

31. Sherman to Vandever, 15 August 1864, *OR*, ser. 1, vol. 38/5, 517; Sherman to Smith, 16 August 1864, ibid., 540.

32. Budlong to Heath, 30 October 1864, ibid., vol. 39/3, 513; Sherman to Webster, 23 December 1864, ibid., vol. 44, 788; Anne J. Bailey, *War and Ruin: William T. Sherman and the Savannah Campaign* (Wilmington, DE: Scholarly Resources, 2003), 31–32. Bailey labels the burning of Cassville as the "only incident of deliberate total destruction" but fails to consider Canton. She also acknowledges that other towns in Georgia were destroyed to some extent.

33. Wills, *Army Life of an Illinois Soldier*, 310. Wills offered no further explanation or justification of the burning of Cassville, suggesting that such practices were accepted and common by this point in the war; Cornelius C. Platter Papers, UGA.

34. Alfred G. Wilcox Papers, USAMHI.

35. Sherman to Smith, 8 November 1864, *OR*, ser. 1, vol. 34/2, 703.

36. Sherman, *Memoirs*, 542–543.

37. Special Field Orders No. 120, 9 November 1864, *OR*, ser. 1, vol. 39/2, 713.

38. Alfred G. Wilcox Papers, USAMHI.

39. Samuel Hurst, *Journal-History of the Seventy-Third Ohio Volunteer Infantry* (Chillicothe, OH: n.p., 1866), 154; Report of Colonel James S. Robinson, 28 December 1864, *OR*, ser. 1, vol. 44, 252–253; Cornelius Platter Papers, UGA; Henry M. Hitchcock, *Marching with Sherman: Passages from the Letters and Campaign Diaries of Henry Hitchcock, Major and Assistant Adjutant General of Volunteers, November 1864–May 1865* (Lincoln: University of Nebraska Press, 1995), 57–58.

40. Sherman, *Memoirs*, 543.

41. Sherman to Grant, 11 November 1864, *OR*, ser. 1, vol. 39/3, 740; Sherman to Thomas, 11 November 1864, ibid., 746.

42. Special Field Orders No. 120, 9 November 1864, *OR*, ser. 1, vol. 39/2, 713–714.

43. Hurst, *Journal-History of the Seventy-Third Ohio Volunteer Infantry*, 159.

44. Hitchcock, *Marching with Sherman*, 89.

45. Sherman, *Memoirs*, 552–553. Upon arriving in the town of Milledgeville, Sherman came across a number of these calls to arms printed in Southern newspapers. He claims to have found them humorous, considering the "feeble resistance" that his army had faced up to that point.

46. Bailey, *War and Ruin*, 72.

47. Ibid., 72–74; Woodworth, *Nothing but Victory*, 596–597.

48. Sherman, *Memoirs*, 547; Hitchcock, *Marching with Sherman*, 77.

49. Hitchcock, *Marching with Sherman*, 86–87.

50. Logan, *History of the 31st Regiment Illinois Volunteers*; Mark Coburn, *Terrible Innocence: General Sherman at War* (New York: Hippocrene Books, 1993), 164–165.

51. Sherman, *Memoirs*, 581. Sherman argued that the overall importance of the march to the sea paled in comparison to that of his subsequent campaign in the Carolinas.

52. Weigley, *Great Civil War*, 393.

53. Royster, *Destructive War*, 328.

54. Sherman to Grant, 1 January 1865, *OR*, ser. 1, vol. 44, 13.

55. Sherman to Hill, 7 September 1863, ibid., vol. 30/3, 401–402.

56. Hitchcock, *Marching with Sherman*, 77.

57. Weigley, *American Way of War*, 149. Weigley argues that Sherman practiced a "deliberate strategy of terror against the enemy people's minds" and that he treated depredations conducted by his men leniently.

58. Grimsley, *Hard Hand of War*, 200; Glatthaar, *March to the Sea and Beyond*, 140, 142–145.

59. Woodworth, *Nothing but Victory*, 607, 624.

Chapter 5. The Valley Aflame: Punitive War in Virginia

1. See Anthony James Joes, *America and Guerrilla Warfare* (Lexington: University Press of Kentucky, 2000), 52–55; Mackey, *Uncivil War*, 72–94; Neely, *Fate of Liberty*, 79. All three authors limit their discussions of guerrilla warfare in Virginia to Mosby's operations.

2. Report of Col. E. Siber, 23 January 1862, *OR*, ser. 1, vol. 5, 501; Report of Brigadier General John D. Imboden, ibid., vol. 29/1, 107. The Black Striped Company, reported to be some sixty or seventy pro-Southern guerrillas, skirmished with Union troops near the Coal and Guyandotte Rivers in the winter of 1861–1862. The Swamp Dragoons were a Unionist cavalry detachment that clashed periodically with Confederate irregulars and cavalry in western Virginia.

3. Jacob D. Cox, *Military Reminiscences of the Civil War*, vol. 1 (New York: Scribner's, 1900), 424.

4. Weigley, *Great Civil War*, 55.

5. Lander to McClellan, 16 January 1862, *OR*, ser. 1, vol. 5, 703.

6. General Orders No. 36, 7 April 1862, ibid., vol. 12/3, 54.

7. Proclamation to the people of Hampshire County and the Upper Potomac, ibid., vol. 5, 638.

8. Report of Lieutenant Colonel Stephen W. Downey, 20 May 1862, ibid., vol. 15, 457.

9. Joseph Warren Keifer, General Order No. 2, General Order Book 1862–1863, DUSC.

10. Report of Brigadier General Robert C. Schenck, 10 May 1862, *OR*, ser. 1, vol. 15, 496.

11. Thomas O. Crowl Letters, PSUSC.

12. Report of Major General John C. Frémont, 30 December 1865, *OR*, ser. 1, vol. 12, 5.

13. Crook, *Autobiography*, 87.

14. Daniel E. Sutherland, "Abraham Lincoln, John Pope, and the Origins of Total War," *Military History* 56, no. 4 (October 1992): 569.

15. Sigel to Pope, 30 June 1862, *OR*, ser. 1, vol. 12/3, 447.

16. General Orders No. 7, 10 July 1862, ibid., pt. 2, 51. As in Missouri, the main

purpose behind Pope's directive was to provoke local communities into pacifying their neighborhoods and preventing guerrillas from operating against Union military assets or Unionist families.

17. General Orders No. 56, 18 July 1862; General Orders No. 11, 23 July 1862; General Orders No. 18, 6 August 1862, ibid., 50, 52, 53.

18. Davis to Lee, 31 July 1862, ibid., ser. 2, vol. 4, 830–831.

19. Grimsley, *Hard Hand of War*, 88.

20. Halleck to McClellan, 7 August 1862, *OR*, ser. 1, vol. 11, 359.

21. Sutherland, "Abraham Lincoln, John Pope, and the Origins of Total War," 567–568; Peter Cozzens, *General John Pope: A Life for the Nation* (Urbana: University of Illinois Press, 2000), 86.

22. Sutherland, "Abraham Lincoln, John Pope, and the Origins of Total War," 579.

23. Halleck to McClellan, 24 December 1861, *OR*, ser. 1, vol. 8, 42–43. It was reported that Pope's cavalry destroyed property in and around Lexington in its search for bridge-burners.

24. Grimsley, *Hard Hand of War*, 90–91. Grimsley contends, "One of the most striking things about Pope's orders is their lack of real impact."

25. See Richard N. Ellis, *General Pope and U.S. Indian Policy* (Albuquerque: University of New Mexico Press, 1970), 8. Ellis notes how Pope began his tenure as the commander of the Department of the Northwest by looking to punish the Indian population by destroying "crops and property."

26. Proclamation to the People of Western Virginia, *OR*, ser. 1, vol. 2, 48–49; Address to the Soldiers of the Expedition, ibid., 49.

27. McClellan to Lincoln, 7 July 1862, *OR*, ser. 1, vol. 11/1, 73–74.

28. See Reid Mitchell, *Civil War Soldiers* (New York: Viking Penguin, 1988), 138.

29. Francis Adams Donaldson, *Inside the Army of the Potomac: The Civil War Experience of Captain Francis Adams Donaldson*, ed. J. Gregory Acken (Mechanicsburg, PA: Stackpole Books, 1998), 73.

30. Report of Lieutenant Colonel Stephen W. Downey, 20 May 1862, *OR*, ser. 1, vol. 12/1, 457.

31. Crook, *Autobiography*, 88.

32. Report of Colonel E. Siber, 23 January 1862, *OR*, ser. 1, vol. 5, 501–503.

33. Taylor to Wier, 16 November 1863, *OR*, ser. 1, vol. 29/2, 467–468.

34. Report of General George Crook, 23 May 1862, ibid., vol. 12, 806.

35. Naglee to Hoffman, 28 September 1863, ibid., vol. 27/3, 846. It should be noted that Naglee also voiced concern over the difficulty of enforcing both civil and martial law within the community, claiming that martial law could result in "utter destitution" of the population.

36. Report of Major Ebenezer Andrews, 22 April 1862, ibid., vol. 12, 440.

37. Charles Fessenden Morse, *Letters Written during the Civil War*, 1861–1865 (privately published, 1898), 224.

38. Report of Lieutenant Colonel Freeman E. Franklin, 23 July 1863, *OR*, ser. 1,

vol. 27/2, 942–943; James Abraham Papers, USAMHI; Report of Brigadier General E. Parker Scammon, 24 July 1863, *OR*, ser. 1, vol. 27/2, 941–942.

39. General Orders 100, *OR*, ser. 2, vol. 5, 676. The order defines partisans as "soldiers armed and wearing the uniform of their army but belonging to a corps which acts detached from the main body for the purpose of making inroads into the territory occupied by the enemy. If captured they are entitled to all the privileges of the prisoner of war." The men in Mosby's command, however, did not always wear uniforms, and sometimes disguised themselves in Union blue.

40. Fellman, *Inside War*, 82.

41. Report of Major John S. Mosby, 30 September 1863, *OR*, ser. 1, vol. 29/1, 80–81; John Singleton Mosby, *The Memoirs of Colonel John S. Mosby* (Nashville: J. S. Sanders, 1995), 148–150.

42. General Orders No. 29, Confederate Congress, 5 March 1864, *OR*, ser. 4, vol. 3, 194. As a result of numerous complaints from Confederate field officers about the unreliability and dishonorable practices of most guerrilla bands, the Partisan Ranger Act was repealed by the Confederate Congress on 17 February 1864. At the recommendation of General J. E. B. Stuart, only Mosby and John Hanson McNeill were officially authorized to maintain their commands.

43. Mosby, *Memoirs*, 157.

44. Lockwood to Couch, 1 August 1863, *OR*, ser. 1, vol. 27/3, 826–827.

45. Donaldson, *Inside the Army of the Potomac*, 288.

46. An example is seen in Joes, *America and Guerrilla Warfare*, 52–55.

47. Bruce Catton, *A Stillness at Appomattox* (Garden City, NY: Doubleday, 1954), 283.

48. John Heatwole, *The Burning: Sheridan's Destruction of the Shenandoah Valley* (Charlottesville, VA: Rockbridge Publishing, 1998), 123–129. Heatwole gives a thorough account of many of the lesser-known guerrilla outfits that operated in the Shenandoah; Crowninshield to Forsyth, 1 October 1864, *OR*, ser. 1, vol. 43/1, 250.

49. Mackey, *Uncivil War*, 121. Mackey's conclusion about the Union's failure to understand the threat they faced in Virginia is, perhaps, the least compelling of his arguments. While stating that the Federals mistook their partisan enemies as guerrillas, Mackey seems to ignore the numerous nonpartisan irregulars operating in the Valley. He also claims that this misunderstanding resulted in the Federals' implementing the wrong methods to combat the threat, but he never really explains *how* Union counterguerrilla operations would have been more successful had they viewed the enemy as partisans.

50. Frémont to Stanton, 7 April 1862, *OR*, ser. 1, vol. 12/3, 55. Frémont appealed to Secretary of War Stanton to arm him with enough cavalry and repeating rifles to handle the significant guerrilla threat.

51. Lazelle to Taylor, 19 July 1864, *OR*, ser. 1, vol. 37/2, 387–390.

52. Kennedy to Crook, 3 December 1864, ibid., vol. 43/1, 736; Birtle, *U.S. Army Counterinsurgency*, 41.

53. Augur to Halleck, 10 October 1864, *OR*, ser. 1, vol. 43/1, 335.

54. Entry for 23 December 1863, Charles H. Lynch, *The Civil War Diary,*

1862–1865, of Charles H. Lynch, 18th Connecticut Volunteers (Hartford, CT: Case, Lockwood & Brannard, 1915); James W. Mulligan Papers, USAMHI.

55. Birtle, *U.S. Army Counterinsurgency*, 45.

56. Darl L. Stephenson, *Headquarters in the Brush: Blazer's Independent Union Scouts* (Athens: Ohio University Press, 2001), 124–125.

57. Donaldson, *Inside the Army of the Potomac*, 286.

58. Stevenson to Forsythe, 19 November 1864, *OR*, ser. 1, vol. 43/1, 648; Stephenson, *Headquarters in the Brush*, 166–170; Mackey, *Uncivil War*, 109.

59. Quoted in McPherson, *Battle Cry of Freedom*, 303.

60. 5 September 1863, *Harper's Weekly*, 567.

61. See Laura F. Edwards, *Scarlett Doesn't Live Here Anymore: Southern Women in the Civil War Era* (Chicago: University of Illinois Press, 2000), 80–81. Edwards points out that women of the planter class were the most vocal in their resistance of Union occupation, primarily during the first year of the war. After several years of hardship brought on by Federal occupation, most women gave up their "militant pride" and focused on protecting their families and property from destruction.

62. John P. Dulany to Richard Dulany in Margaret A. Vogtsberger, *The Dulanys of Welbourne: A Family in Mosby's Confederacy* (Berryville, VA: Rockbridge Publishing, 1995), 79. The Dulany family was, at times, supportive of Mosby's partisan band, providing them food and other supplies.

63. Grant, *Personal Memoirs*, 364–366, 377; Grant to Sherman, 4 April 1864, *OR*, ser. 1, vol. 32/3, 246. This was the directive that ultimately led to Sherman's march across Georgia.

64. McPherson, *Battle Cry of Freedom*, 722. It should be noted that the topography of the Shenandoah Valley increases in altitude as one moves from north to south. Therefore, in the traditional Virginian colloquialism to move "up" the Valley means to move southward. Conversely, to move "down" the Valley is to head north.

65. See John C. Mountcastle, "A Stain upon Civilization: Guerrilla Warfare in Civil War Virginia, 1862–1865" (M.A. thesis, Duke University, 2003), 25–27.

66. Grant to Hunter, 6 June 1864, *OR*, ser. 1, vol. 37/1, 598. Grant directed Hunter to move south to Lynchburg, turn east, and then strike at the Virginia Central Railroad, "destroying it completely and thoroughly."

67. Entry for 31 May, 1864, Lynch, *Civil War Diary*.

68. John Chester White Papers, LOC.

69. Clifton M. Nicholas, *A Summer Campaign in the Shenandoah Valley in 1864* (Springfield, OH: New Era, 1899), 67.

70. Memoir entry of Robert T. Barton in Margaretta Barton Colt, *Defend the Valley: A Shenandoah Family in the Civil War* (New York: Orion Books, 1994), 318; Nicholas, *Summer Campaign*, 67.

71. Albert Artman Papers, USAMHI; Lynch, *Civil War Diary*, 72.

72. Hunter to Montgomery, 9 June 1863, *OR*, ser. 1, vol. 14, 466–467.

73. Report of Major General David Hunter, 8 August 1864, ibid., vol. 37/1, 97; William G. Watson Papers, Preston Library Archives, VMI; James A. Thompson, "The Lynchburg Campaign," in *G.A.R. War Papers*, vol. 1 (Cincinnati: Fred C.

Jones, post no. 401), 130. Watson and Thompson confirmed Hunter's connection of the burning with the circular.

74. Lynch, *Civil War Diary*, 75.

75. John P. Suter Papers, USAMHI.

76. Albert Artman Papers, USAMHI.

77. William G. Watson Papers, VMI Archives; John S. Weiser Papers, USAMHI.

78. See Mountcastle, "A Stain upon Civilization," 28–29. A number of historical accounts support the conclusion that guerrilla attacks were largely responsible for the weakened condition of Hunter's army at Lynchburg.

79. James Abraham Papers, USAMHI; Albert Artman Papers, ibid.; Lynch, *Civil War Diary*, 83.

80. John P. Suter Papers, USAMHI.

81. Halleck to Sherman, 28 September 1864, *OR*, ser. 1, vol. 39/2, 503.

82. Ibid.

83. McPherson, *Battle Cry of Freedom*, 757.

84. Edgar A. Walters Papers, USAMHI; Report of Major General Darius N. Couch, 8 August 1864, *OR*, ser. 1, vol. 37/1, 333.

85. Roger U. Delauter, Jr., *McNeill's Rangers* (Lynchburg, VA: H. E. Howard, 1986), 66; Garrett to Stanton, 5 May 1864, *OR*, ser. 1, vol. 37/1, 382.

86. Halleck to Heintzelman, 5 May 1864, *OR*, ser. 1, vol. 37/1, 391; Stanton to Brough, ibid.

87. Halleck to MacCullum, 12 October 1864, ibid., vol. 43/1, 348.

88. Stephen V. Ash, *When the Yankees Came*, 67.

89. Halleck, "Retaliation in War," 108. Halleck quotes the Lieber Code, using it to explain his own position on retaliation.

90. Report of Brigadier General Gordon Granger, 26 August 1862, *OR*, ser. 1, vol. 17/1, 39.

91. Virgil Carrington Jones, *Gray Ghosts and Rebel Raiders: The Daring Exploits of the Confederate Guerillas* (New York: Holt Publishers, 1956), 276–277; Sheridan to Grant, 17 August 1864, *OR*, ser. 1, vol. 43/1, 822.

92. Grant to Sheridan, 26 August 1864, *OR*, ser. 1, vol. 43/1, 971; Heatwole, *Burning*, 42, 50.

93. Henry Keiser Papers, USAMHI.

94. Isaac N. Baker Papers, VMI.

95. Moran L. Lindsey Papers, USAMHI.

96. McPherson, *Battle Cry of Freedom*, 779. McPherson was paraphrased to fit the context of this sentence. The exact quote from the book states, "Enraged by these incidents [guerrilla attacks on Sheridan's staff] bluecoated arsonists took it out on civilians whom they believed to be sheltering these 'bushwhackers.'"

97. Heatwole, *Burning*, 89–92. Heatwole provides the most thorough discussion of the killing of Lieutenant Meigs to date. Heatwole concludes that the men that Meigs encountered were not guerrillas, but rather, regular Confederate cavalry scouts from a brigade camped nearby.

98. Ibid., 89.

99. Louis N. Beaudry, *War Journal of Louis N. Beaudry, Fifth New York Cavalry; The Diary of a Union Chaplain, Commencing February 16, 1863* (Jefferson, NC: McFarland, 1996), 175.

100. Heatwole, *Burning*, 114; A. D. Slade, *A. T. A. Torbert: Southern Gentleman in Union Blue* (Dayton, OH: Morningside House, 1992), 171. Slade places the number of homes burned around Dayton at seventeen.

101. Howard Malcolm Smith Papers, LOC, 147; entry for 4 October 1864, William T. Peterson Diary, OHS.

102. Report of Major General Philip H. Sheridan, 7 October 1864, *OR*, ser. 1, vol. 43/1, 30.

103. Beaudry, *War Journal*, 175.

104. Edward Waldo Emerson, *The Life and Letters of Charles Russell Lowell* (Boston: Houghton Mifflin, 1907), 353.

105. Grimsley, *Hard Hand of War*, 185; Carol Bundy, *The Nature of Sacrifice: The Biography of Charles Russell Lowell, Jr., 1835–1864* (New York: Farrar, Straus, and Giroux, 2005), 446. Bundy claims that Union troops involved in the burning of the Shenandoah often felt "horror and self-disgust."

106. Halleck to Sherman, 28 September 1864, *OR*, ser. 1, vol. 39/2, 503.

107. See Grimsley, *Hard Hand of War*, 184–185; Neely, *Fate of Liberty*, 79–80. Grimsley emphasizes the remorse many Union soldiers felt with the order to burn Dayton, while Neely conveniently fails to mention the incident at all in his discussion of Sheridan's response to Meigs's death.

108. Mackey, *Uncivil War*, 114. The author seems to misinterpret historian John Heatwole's explanation of "The Burning" by suggesting that Meigs's death served as Sheridan's reason to conduct his devastation of the Valley. Given Grant's prior order to deplete the Valley of its agricultural resources, something he had instructed Hunter to do earlier that summer, it would seem that "The Burning" would have occurred with or without the death of Lieutenant Meigs and Sheridan's subsequent order to burn Dayton.

109. Richard R. Duncan, ed., *Alexander Neil and the Last Shenandoah Valley Campaign* (Shippensburg, PA: White Mane Publishing, 1996), 70.

110. Mackey, *Uncivil War*, 114.

111. Sheridan to Grant, 11 October 1864, *OR*, ser. 1, vol. 43/1, 32. Lieutenant Colonel Tolles, Sheridan's Chief Quartermaster, and Dr. Emil Ohlenschlager, an assistant surgeon, were attacked outside of Winchester.

112. Jones, *Gray Ghosts and Rebel Raiders*, 281; Report of Colonel William H. Powell, 27 October 1864, *OR*, ser. 1, vol. 43/1, 509; Emerson, *Life and Letters of Charles Russell Lowell*, 353.

113. Roy Morris, Jr., *Sheridan: The Life and Wars of General Phil Sheridan* (New York: Crown Publishers, 1992), 226.

114. Horace Smith Papers, DUSC; James W. Mulligan Papers, USAMHI.

115. Grant to Sheridan, 16 August 1864, *OR*, ser. 1, vol. 43/1, 811.

116. See General Orders 100, 24 April 1864, *OR*, ser. 2, vol. 5, 671–672. The first

section of the Lieber Code addressed military law and retaliation. The order cites that "military offenses," within or without a statute law, must be tried by military court before death sentences could be carried out.

117. Sheridan to Halleck, 26 November 1864, ibid., ser. 1, vol. 43/1, 671–672.

118. John P. Suter Papers, USAMHI.

119. Sheridan to Merritt, 28 November 1864, *OR*, ser. 1, vol. 43/1, 679. It appears from the wording of Sheridan's order that his primary intention of the raid was to destroy all food and forage in the region, thereby making it difficult for guerrillas to operate there. In other words, Sheridan wanted to conduct an indirect attack on the guerrillas by attacking their supply base.

120. Merritt to Sheridan, 3 December 1864, ibid., 761. In his report, Merritt claimed that "all attempts to run them [guerrillas] down or capture them by stratagem" failed.

121. John H. Stevenson, *Boots and Saddles: A History of the First Volunteer Cavalry of the War. Known as the First New York (Lincoln) Cavalry, and also as The Sabre Regiment. Its Organization, Campaigns, and Battles* (Harrisburg, PA: Patriot Publishing Company, 1879), 324; Howard Malcolm Smith Papers, LOC, 157. According to Smith, a major in Merritt's Division, the raid resulted in the confiscation of 2,240 head of cattle, 1,000 sheep, 400 hogs, between 300 and 400 horses, and the destruction of millions of dollars of property. In all, Smith claimed, Loudoun County "was completely laid waste."

122. Morris, *Sheridan*, 230.

123. Stevenson, *Boots and Saddles*, 324.

124. Howard Malcolm Smith Papers, LOC, 158.

125. Sheridan to Stevenson, 28 November 1864, *OR*, ser. 1, vol. 43/1, 687.

126. Neely, *Fate of Liberty*, 80; Neely, *Civil War and the Limits of Destruction*, 134.

127. Grimsley, *Hard Hand of War*, 186. Grimsley is correct in his assertion that Sheridan's destruction did not compare to that conducted by the French against the Palatinate in 1689, but his claim that Sheridan did not target private homes or communities is not supported by the details surrounding Dayton, Newtown, and the Burning Raid.

128. Sheridan to Halleck, 26 November 1864, *OR*, ser. 1, vol. 43/2, 671; Sheridan to Couch, 27 November 1864, ibid., 682.

129. See Morris, *Sheridan*, 228.

130. Neely, *Fate of Liberty*, 81. Central to Neely's argument is the contention that Grant and Sheridan thought and spoke about severe treatments toward civilians but rarely carried out such deeds. Such an argument does not stand up to Sheridan's record of punitive actions in the Valley very well.

131. Entry for 21 May 1864, Edward Davis Papers, USAMHI.

132. Stanton to Hancock, 16 April 1865, *OR*, ser. 1, vol. 46/3, 799; Hancock to Stanton, 22 April 1865, ibid., 897; Sherman to Grant, 25 April 1865, ibid., vol. 47/3, 303. At the end of the war, Sherman predicted, "we will have to deal with numerous bands of desperadoes headed by such men as Mosby, Forrest, Red Jackson, and others."

133. John S. Russell Papers, DUSC.

134. Bailey, *War and Ruin*, 133.

135. Report of Major General Philip H. Sheridan, 4 August 1864, *OR*, ser. 1, vol. 36/1, 801.

136. Entry for 20 April 1865, Joseph A. Waddell Diary, UVA.

Conclusion

1. Pope to Fletcher, 3 March 1865, *OR*, ser. 1, vol. 48/1, 1075. In Pope's message to Governor Fletcher, he called for the people of Missouri to take responsibility for security of the state and claimed that the Army could not end the bushwhacking without the full participation of the population.

2. See Ash, *When the Yankees Came*, 210. Ash identifies the system in northern Arkansas as a "fortunate exception," while in the rest of the South, "the forces of chaos held the upper hand as long as the war continued."

3. Bertollette to Gamble, 12 June 1865, *OR*, ser. 1, vol. 47/3, 502; Cooper to Kilpatrick, 15 May 1865, ibid.; Stanley to Thomas, 20 April 1865, ibid., vol. 49/2, 414; Special Orders No. 64, vol. 49/1, 892; Ramsey to Johnson, 22 January 1865, ibid., vol. 45/2, 626; Cameron to Speed, 8 January 1865, ibid., vol. 48/1, 775; Dodge to Harding, 13 May 1865, ibid., vol. 48/2, 430; Leeper to Dodge, March 1865, ibid., vol. 48/1, 1054; Fisk to Saunders, 3 March 1865, ibid., 1078. All of these official reports address widespread guerrilla activity soon before or soon after the Confederate surrender in April 1865; Fellman, *Inside War*, 232. The author addresses the fate of Missourians specifically.

4. Mackey, *Uncivil War*, 202–204, 197. The greatest problem with Mackey's assessment is his classification of the guerrilla problem as a distinct Confederate strategy, one which they intentionally employed in order to gain victory. By virtue of winning the Civil War, Mackey claims, the Union was able to defeat the Confederate guerrilla strategy in the process. His suggestion that the Confederate government and its military leadership made a concerted effort to wage a guerrilla war in conjunction with the conventional war is misleading. The most persistent irregular threat had very little to do with Confederate authorization or sanction. Mackey offers almost no explanation for the continuation of guerrilla violence up to war's end, especially the decentralized, bushwhacking resistance that Union troops faced throughout the occupied South.

5. Grimsley, *Hard Hand of War*, 185, 210. In fairness, Grimsley makes the comparison to debunk previous claims that the Union Army was as destructive as those seen in European wars of the seventeenth and twentieth centuries.

6. Birtle, *U.S. Army Counterinsurgency*, 47.

7. See ibid., 81–82, 91; Janda, "Shutting the Gates of Mercy," 21–26.

8. Quoted in Paul Andrew Hutton, "Paladin of the Republic: Philip H. Sheridan," in *With My Face to the Enemy: Perspectives on the Civil War*, ed. Robert Cowley (New York: Berkley Books, 2001), 357.

9. Brian M. Linn, *The Philippine War, 1899–1902* (Lawrence: University Press of

Kansas, 2000), 94–95, 211–212. Linn gives the examples of brigadier generals Lloyd Wheaton and Jacob Smith, who oversaw destructive pacification campaigns on the islands of Luzon and Samar. Wheaton served under Sherman in the Civil War.

10. Stout, *Upon the Altar of the Nation*, 381.

11. Royster, *Destructive War*, 359.

12. Neely, *Civil War and the Limits of Destruction*, 65. Neely makes his reference in relation to the war in Missouri but applies it to conclusions that historians such as James McPherson and Charles Royster have made about the Civil War in general.

13. McPherson, *Battle Cry of Freedom*, 501; Grimsley, *Hard Hand of War*, 213.

14. Grimsley, *Hard Hand of War*, 120.

15. James McPherson, *For Cause and Comrades: Why Men Fought in the Civil War* (New York: Oxford University Press, 1997), 123.

16. Grant, *Personal Memoirs*, 476.

17. Mitchell, *Civil War Soldiers*, 135.

18. Grimsley, *Hard Hand of War*, 225; Neely, *Civil War and the Limits of Destruction*, 59.

19. Neely, "Was the Civil War a Total War?" 50–51; Mark Grimsley, "'Rebels' and 'Redskins': U.S. Military Conduct toward White Southerners and Native Americans in Comparative Perspective," in *Civilians in the Path of War*, ed. Mark Grimsley and Clifford Rogers (Lincoln: University of Nebraska Press, 2002), 146–148.

20. Weigley, *Great Civil War*, 373.

21. Grimsley, *Hard Hand of War*, 222; Donald B. Connelly, "The Politics of War in the Department of Missouri, 1861–1864," in *Armed Diplomacy: Two Centuries of American Campaigning* (Fort Leavenworth, KS: Combat Studies Institute Press, 2003), 30; Bailey, *War and Ruin*, 135.

22. Neely, *Civil War and the Limits of Destruction*, 219.

23. James McPherson, *This Mighty Scourge: Perspectives on the Civil War* (New York: Oxford University Press, 2007), 128.

24. Neely, *Civil War and the Limits of Destruction*, 71. It should be noted that in his argument for Union restraint, Neely's references to incidents of Union reprisal throughout the South are extremely limited. He does not account for the destruction of Randolph, Wytheville, or most other towns that were destroyed in retaliation for guerrilla attacks. Despite devoting an entire chapter to Missouri, he makes no mention of Order No. 11 or its execution.

25. Ash, *When the Yankees Came*, 67.

26. Letter dated 10 January 1863, John A. Boon Papers, USAMHI.

Bibliography

Unpublished Primary Sources

Duke University, Perkins Library Special Collections
Durham, North Carolina

Joseph Warren Kiefer Order Book, 1862–1863
Lieber, Francis. "Guerilla Parties: Considered with Reference to the Laws and
  Usages of War. Written at the Request of Major-General Henry W. Halleck."
  Washington: U.S. Army Printing Office, August 1862.
John S. Mosby Papers
John Hassett Pierce Papers
John S. Russell Papers
Horace Smith Papers
John C. Van Duzer Papers

Ohio Historical Society, Columbus, Ohio

William T. Peterson Diary

Pennsylvania State University Special Collections Library
State College, Pennsylvania

Thomas O. Crowl Papers

U.S. Army Military History Institute, Carlisle, Pennsylvania, Miscellaneous Civil War
Collection and Harrisburg Civil War Roundtable Collection

James Abraham Papers
Jared L. Ainsworth Papers
Albert Artman Papers
Benjamin Ashenfelter Papers
Jabez Banbury Papers
Jacob Behm Papers
John A. Boon Papers
John V. Boucher Papers
David C. Bradley Papers
John. Brandon Papers
George C. Burmeister Papers
Hugh T. Carlisle Papers
Schuyler P. Coe Papers

Edward Davis Papers
Robert M. Dihel Papers
Thomas B. Douglas Papers
Amos Fleagle Papers
Josiah H. Goodwin Papers
Alva G. Griest Papers
Jacob Haas Papers
Henry Keiser Papers
Morgan W. Lindsley Papers
Frank MacGregor Papers
William W. McCarty Papers
James W. Mulligan Papers
Mungo P. Murray Papers
Clement D. Potts Papers
Charles Holbrook Prentiss Papers
Francis A. Reges Papers
Matthew B. Schofield Papers
Edward E. Schweitzer Papers
George Shuman Papers
Stephen H. Smith Papers
William A. Smith Papers
Joseph Stockton Papers
John P. Suter Papers
William A. Tall Papers
Thomas Thompkins Papers
James A. Thompson Papers
Edgar A. Walters Papers
Charles Weiser Papers
John S. Weiser Papers
William B. Westervelt Papers
Alfred G. Wilcox Papers
William Porter Wilkin Papers

U.S. Library of Congress, Manuscripts Division, Washington, DC

John E. Anderson Papers
Charles Buford Papers
Balzar Grebe Papers
William G. Hills Diary
James Hodges Papers
Low-Mills Family Papers
Charles O'Neil Diaries
Albert Quincy Porter Papers
E. Paul Reichelm Papers
Howard Malcolm Smith Papers

Oscar Smith Papers
Thomas W. Taylor Papers
John Chester White Papers

University of Georgia, Hargrett Rare Book and Manuscript Library, Athens, Georgia

Cornelius C. Platter Papers

University of Kansas, Kenneth Spencer Research Library, Lawrence, Kansas

Thomas Carney Papers
Henry C. Fike Papers
James W. Jessee Papers
Thomas K. Mitchell Diary
Samuel F. Tappan Papers

University of Virginia, Small Special Collections Library, Charlottesville, Virginia

Joseph A. Waddell Diary, 1855–1865

Virginia Historical Society Research Library, Richmond, Virginia

Amanda Virginia Edmunds Papers
John S. Mosby Papers

Virginia Military Institute Archives, Lexington, Virginia

Isaac N. Baker Papers, 1862–1865
Sidney Martin Papers, 1864
William G. Watson Papers, 1863–1864

Published Primary Sources

Barber, Lucius W. *Army Memoirs*. Chicago: J. M. W. Jones Stationery and Printing, 1894.

Beatty, John. *The Citizen-Soldier; or, Memoirs of a Volunteer*. Cincinnati: Wilstach, Baldwin, 1879.

Beaudry, Louis N. *War Journal of Louis N. Beaudry, Fifth New York Cavalry; The Diary of a Union Chaplain, Commencing February 16, 1863*. Jefferson, NC: McFarland, 1996.

Boyd, Cyrus F. *The Civil War Diary of C.F. Boyd*. Millwood, NY: Kraus Reprint, 1977.

Britton, Wiley. *The Civil War on the Border: A Narrative of Military Operations in Missouri, Kansas, Arkansas, and the Indian Territory during the Years 1863–1865: Based on the Official Reports and Observations of the Author*. New York: G. P. Putnam's Sons, 1899.

Bustamante, Carlos Maria. "The New Bernal Diaz del Castillo," in *The View from Chapultepec: Mexican Writers on the Mexican American War*. Translated and edited by Cecil Robinson. Tucson: University of Arizona Press, 1989.

Butler, Benjamin F. *The Private and Official Correspondence of General Benjamin F. Butler*, vol. 2. Norwood, MA: Plimpton Press, 1917.

Byers, Samuel Hawkins. *With Fire and Sword*. New York: Neale, 1911.

Coe, Hamlin Alexander. *Mine Eyes Have Seen the Glory: Combat Diaries of Union Sergeant Hamlin Alexander Coe*. Cranbury, NJ: Associated University Presses, 1975.

Cox, Jacob D. *Military Reminiscences of the Civil War*, vol. 1. New York: Scribner's, 1900.

Crook, George. *General George Crook: His Autobiography*. Edited by Martin F. Schmidtt. Norman: University of Oklahoma Press, 1946.

Currie, George E. *Warfare along the Mississippi: The Letters of Lieutenant Colonel George E. Currie*. Edited by Norman E. Clarke. Mount Pleasant: Central Michigan University Press, 1961.

Curtis, Samuel Ryan. *Mexico under Fire: Being the Diary of Samuel Ryan Curtis, 3rd Ohio Volunteer Regiment, during the American Military Occupation of Northern Mexico, 1846–1847*. Edited by Joseph E. Chance. Fort Worth: Texas Christian University Press, 1994.

Donaldson, Francis Adams. *Inside the Army of the Potomac: The Civil War Experience of Captain Francis Adams Donaldson*. Edited by J. Gregory Acken. Mechanicsburg, PA: Stackpole Books, 1998.

Duncan, Richard R., ed. *Alexander Neil and the Last Shenandoah Valley Campaign*. Shippensburg, PA: White Mane Publishing, 1996.

Du Pont, H. A. *The Campaign of 1864 in the Valley of Virginia and the Expedition to Lynchburg*. New York: National Americana, 1925.

Emerson, Edward Waldo, ed. *Life and Letters of Charles Russell Lowell*. Boston: Houghton Mifflin, 1907.

Grant, Ulysses S. *Personal Memoirs of U.S. Grant*. New York: Da Capo Press, 1982.

———. *The Papers of Ulysses S. Grant*. Edited by John Y. Simon. Vol. 5. Carbondale: Southern Illinois University Press, 1973.

Grebner, Constantin. *We Were the Ninth: A History of the Ninth Regiment, Ohio Volunteer Infantry, April 17, 1861 to June 7, 1864*. Kent, OH: Kent State University Press, 1987.

Hitchcock, Henry M. *Marching with Sherman: Passages from the Letters and Campaign Diaries of Henry Hitchcock, Major and Assistant Adjutant General of Volunteers, November 1864–May 1865*. Lincoln: University of Nebraska Press, 1995.

Holton, William C. *Cruise of the Flagship Hartford*. Tarrytown, NY: William Abbatt, 1922.

Howard, R. L. *The History of the 124th Regiment: Illinois Infantry Volunteers*. Springfield, IL: H. W. Rokker, 1880.

Howe, M. A. DeWolfe, ed. *Home Letters of General Sherman*. New York: Charles Scribner, 1909.

Hurst, Samuel. *Journal-History of the Seventy-Third Ohio Volunteer Infantry*. Chillicothe, OH: n.p., 1866.

Husby, Karla J., and Eric J. Wittenburg, eds. *Under Custer's Command: The Civil War Journal of James Henry Avery.* Washington, DC: Brassey's, 2000.

Jones, Samuel Calvin. *Reminiscences of the Twenty-Second Iowa Volunteer Infantry . . . As Taken from the Diary of Lieutenant S. C. Jones of Company A.* Iowa City, IA: n.p., 1907.

Keil, F. W. *The Thirty-Fifth Ohio Regiment: A Narrative of Service from August 1861 to 1864.* Fort Wayne, IN: Archer, Housh, 1894.

Kircher, Henry A. *A German in the Yankee Fatherland: The Civil War Letters of Henry A. Kircher.* Edited by Earl J. Hess. Kent, OH: Kent State University Press, 1983.

Kirkham, Ralph W. *The Mexican War: Journals and Letters of Ralph W. Kirkham.* Edited by Robert Ryal Miller. College Station: Texas A&M University Press, 1991.

Laidley, Theodore. *Surrounded by Dangers of All Kinds: The Mexican War Letters of Lt. Theodore Laidley.* Edited by James M. McAffrey. Denton: University of North Texas Press, 1997.

Logan, John A., ed. *History of the 31st Illinois Infantry Volunteers.* Evansville, IN: Keller Printing and Publishing, 1902.

Lynch, Charles H. *The Civil War Diary, 1862–1865, of Charles H. Lynch, 18th Connecticut Volunteers.* Hartford, CT: Case, Lockwood & Brannard, 1915.

Marshall, Albert O. *Army Life: From a Soldier's Journal, Incidents, Sketches, and Record of a Union Soldier's Army Life in Camp and Field: 1861–1864.* Joliet, IL: n.p., 1884.

McIntyre, Benjamin F. *Federals on the Frontier: The Diary of Benjamin F. McIntyre.* Edited by Nannie M. Tilley. Austin: University of Texas Press, 1963.

Morse, Charles Fessenden. *Letters Written during the Civil War, 1861–1865.* Privately published, 1898.

Mosby, John Singleton. *The Memoirs of Colonel John S. Mosby.* Nashville: J. S. Sanders, 1995.

Mudd, Joseph A. *With Porter in North Missouri: A Chapter in the History of the War between the States.* Washington, DC: National Publishing, 1909.

Nicholas, Clifton M. *A Summer Campaign in the Shenandoah Valley in 1864.* Springfield, OH: New Era, 1899.

Pope, John. *The Military Memoirs of General John Pope.* Edited by Peter Cozzens and Robert I. Girardi. Chapel Hill: University of North Carolina Press, 1998.

Roth, Margaret Brobst, ed. *Well, Mary: Civil War Letters of a Wisconsin Volunteer.* Madison: University of Wisconsin Press, 1960.

Schofield, John M. *Forty-Six Years in the Army.* New York: Century, 1897.

Scott, Winfield. *Memoirs of Lieutenant-General Scott*, vol. 2. New York: Sheldon & Company Publishers, 1864.

Sheridan, Philip H. *Personal Memoirs of P.H. Sheridan.* New York: De Capo Press, 1992.

Sherman, William T. *Memoirs of General W. T. Sherman.* New York: Penguin Books, 2000.

Simpson, Brooks D., and Jean V. Berlin, eds. *Sherman's Civil War: Selected Correspondence of William T. Sherman, 1860–1865.* Chapel Hill: University of North Carolina Press, 1999.

Smith, George Gilbert. *Leaves from a Soldier's Diary: The Personal Record of Lieutenant George G. Smith, Co. C, 1st Louisiana Regiment Infantry Volunteers (White) during the War of the Rebellion.* Putnam, CT: G. G. Smith, 1906.

Stevenson, John H. *Boots and Saddles: A History of the First Volunteer Cavalry of the War. Known as the First New York (Lincoln) Cavalry, and also as The Sabre Regiment. Its Organization, Campaigns, and Battles.* Harrisburg, PA: Patriot Publishing Company, 1879.

Thompson, James A. "The Lynchburg Campaign," in *G.A.R. War Papers*, vol. 1. Cincinnati: Fred C. Jones, post no. 401: 121–147.

United States War Department. *The War of the Rebellion: A Compilation of the Official Records of the Union and Confederate Armies.* 128 vols. Washington: Government Printing Office, 1880–1901.

Wills, Charles W. *Army Life of an Illinois Soldier, Including a Day-by-Day Record of Sherman's March to the Sea.* Carbondale: Southern Illinois University Press, 1996.

Wright, Charles. *A Corporal's Story: Experiences in the Ranks of Company C, 81st Ohio Volunteer Infantry, during the War for the Maintenance of the Union, 1861–1864.* Philadelphia, 1882.

Periodicals

Harper's Weekly, 1861–1865
New York Herald, 1862–1865
Richmond Examiner, 1860–1865
Washington Daily National Intelligencer, 1863–1865

Secondary Sources

Adams, Michael C. C. *Our Masters the Rebels: A Speculation on Union Military Failure in the East, 1861–1865.* Cambridge, Mass.: Harvard University Press, 1978.

Ambrose, Stephen E. *Duty, Honor, Country: A History of West Point.* Baltimore: Johns Hopkins University Press, 1966.

———. *Halleck: Lincoln's Chief of Staff.* Baton Rouge: Louisiana State University Press, 1962.

Ash, Stephen V. *When the Yankees Came: Conflict and Chaos in the Occupied South, 1861–1865.* Chapel Hill: University of North Carolina Press, 1995.

Bailey, Anne J. *War and Ruin: William T. Sherman and the Savannah Campaign.* Wilmington, DE: Scholarly Resources, 2003.

Baker, Sherston, ed. *Halleck's International Law or Rules Regulating the Intercourse of States in Peace and War*, vol. 1, 3rd ed. London: Kegan Paul, Trench, Trubner, 1893.

Ballard, Michael B. *Vicksburg: The Campaign That Opened the Mississippi.* Chapel Hill: University of North Carolina Press, 2004.

Bauer, K. Jack. *The Mexican War, 1846–1848.* New York: MacMillan Publishing, 1974.

Beckett, Ian F. W. *Encyclopedia of Guerrilla Warfare.* New York: Checkmark, 2001.

———. *Modern Insurgencies and Counter-Insurgencies: Guerrillas and Their Opponents since 1750.* London: Routledge, 2001.

Birtle, Andrew J. *U.S. Army Counterinsurgency and Contingency Operations and Doctrine 1861–1941.* Washington, DC: Center of Military History, Government Printing Office, 2003.

Bowen, Don R. "Quantrill, James, Younger, et al.: Leadership in a Guerrilla Movement, Missouri, 1861–1865." *Military Affairs* 41, no. 1 (February 1977): 42–48.

Brownlee, Richard. *Gray Ghosts of the Confederacy: Guerrilla Warfare in the West 1861–1865.* Baton Rouge: Louisiana State University Press, 1958.

Bundy, Carol. *The Nature of Sacrifice: The Biography of Charles Russell Lowell, Jr., 1835–1864.* New York: Farrar, Straus, and Giroux, 2005.

Burne, Alfred H. *Grant, Lee and Sherman: A Study in Leadership in the 1864–1865 Campaign.* New York: Charles Scribner's Sons, 1939.

Carnahan, Burrus M. "Lincoln, Lieber, and the Laws of War: The Origins and Limits of the Principle of Military Necessity." *American Journal of International Law* 92, no. 2 (April 1998): 213–231.

Carr, Caleb. *The Lessons of Terror: A History of Warfare against Civilians.* New York: Random House, 2003.

Castel, Albert. *Winning and Losing in the Civil War: Essays and Stories.* Columbia: University of South Carolina Press, 1996.

Catton, Bruce. *A Stillness at Appomattox.* Garden City, NY: Doubleday, 1954.

Coburn, Mark. *Terrible Innocence: General Sherman at War.* New York: Hippocrene Books, 1993.

Colt, Margaretta Barton. *Defend the Valley: A Shenandoah Family in the Civil War.* New York: Orion Books, 1994.

Connelly, Donald B. "The Politics of War in the Department of Missouri, 1861–1864," in *Armed Diplomacy: Two Centuries of American Campaigning.* Fort Leavenworth, KS: Combat Studies Institute Press, 2003, 17–38.

Cooling, Franklin B. *Fort Donelson's Legacy: War and Society in Kentucky and Tennessee, 1862–1863.* Knoxville: University of Tennessee Press, 1997.

Cozzens, Peter. *General John Pope: A Life for the Nation.* Urbana: University of Illinois Press, 2000.

Davis, William C. *An Honorable Defeat: The Last Days of the Confederate Government.* New York: Harcourt, 2001.

Dederer, John Morgan. *Making Bricks without Straw: Nathanael Greene's Southern Campaign and Mao Tse-Tung's Mobile War.* Manhattan, KS: Sunflower University Press, 1983.

———. *War in America to 1775: Before Yankee Doodle.* New York: New York University Press, 1990.

Delauter, Roger U., Jr. *McNeill's Rangers*. Lynchburg, VA: H. E. Howard, 1986.

Downey, Fairfax. *Indian Wars of the U.S. Army: 1776–1865*. Garden City, NY: Doubleday, 1963.

Duffey, James P. *Lincoln's Admiral: The Civil War Campaigns of David Farragut*. New York: Wiley, 1997.

Dufour, Charles L. *The Mexican War: A Compact History*. New York: Hawthorne Books, 1968.

Duncan, Richard. "The Raid on Piedmont and the Crippling of Franz Sigel in the Shenandoah Valley." *West Virginia History* 55 (1996): 25–40.

Edgar, Walter. *Partisans and Redcoats: The Southern Conflict That Turned the Tide of the American Revolution*. New York: Harper Collins, 2001.

Edwards, Laura F. *Scarlett Doesn't Live Here Anymore: Southern Women in the Civil War Era*. Chicago: University of Illinois Press, 2000.

Eicher, David J. *The Longest Night: A Military History of the Civil War*. New York: Simon and Schuster, 2001.

Ellis, John. *From the Barrel of a Gun: A History of Guerrilla, Revolutionary, and Counter-Insurgency Warfare from the Romans to the Present*. Mechanicsburg, PA: Stackpole Books, 1975.

Ellis, Richard N. *General Pope and U.S. Indian Policy*. Albuquerque: University of New Mexico Press, 1970.

Fellman, Michael. *Inside War: The Guerilla Conflict in Missouri during the American Civil War*. New York: Oxford University Press, 1989.

Fellman, Michael, Lesley J. Gordon, and Daniel Sutherland. *This Terrible War: The Civil War and Its Aftermath*. New York: Longman Press, 2003.

Fisher, Noel C. *War at Every Door: Partisan Politics and Guerrilla Violence in East Tennessee, 1860–1869*. Chapel Hill: University of North Carolina Press, 1997.

Flood, Charles Bracelen. *Grant and Sherman: The Friendship That Won the Civil War*. New York: Harper Perennial, 2006.

Foos, Paul. *A Short, Offhand, Killing Affair: Soldiers and Social Conflict during the Mexican-American War*. Chapel Hill: University of North Carolina Press, 2002.

Forster, Stig, and Jorg Nagler, eds. *On the Road to Total War: The American Civil War and the German Wars of Unification, 1861–1871*. London: Cambridge University Press, 1997.

Foster, Buck T. *Sherman's Mississippi Campaign*. Tuscaloosa: University of Alabama Press, 2006.

Freidel, Frank. "General Orders 100 and Military Government." *Mississippi Valley Historical Review* 32, no. 4 (March 1946): 541–556.

Futrell, Robert J. "Military Government in the South, 1861–1865." *Military Affairs* 15, no. 4 (Winter 1951): 181–191.

Glatthaar, Joseph T. *The March to the Sea and Beyond: Sherman's Troops in the Savannah and Carolinas Campaign*. New York: New York University Press, 1985.

Goodrich, Thomas. *Black Flag: Guerrilla Warfare on the Western Border, 1861–1865*. Bloomington: Indiana University Press, 1995.

————. *War to the Knife*: *Bleeding Kansas, 1861–1865*. Lincoln: University of Nebraska Press, 2004.

Graber, Doris Appel. *The Development of the Law of Belligerent Occupation, 1863–1914*. New York: Columbia University Press, 1949.

Grimsley, Mark. *The Hard Hand of War: Union Military Policy toward Southern Civilians, 1861–1865*. New York: Cambridge University Press, 1995.

————. "'Rebels' and 'Redskins': U.S. Military Conduct toward White Southerners and Native Americans in Comparative Perspective," in *Civilians in the Path of War*. Edited by Mark Grimsley and Clifford Rogers. Lincoln: University of Nebraska Press, 2002.

Hagerman, Edward. *The American Civil War and the Origins of Modern Warfare: Ideas, Organization and Field Command*. Bloomington: Indiana University Press, 1992.

Halleck, Henry W. "Retaliation in War." *American Journal of International Law* 6, no. 1 (January 1912): 107–118.

Hartigan, Richard S. *Lieber's Code and the Law of War*. Chicago: Precedent, 1983.

Hearn, Chester G. *Ellet's Brigade: The Strangest Outfit of All*. Baton Rouge: Louisiana State University Press, 2000.

Heatwole, John. *The Burning: Sheridan's Devastation of the Shenandoah Valley*. Charlottesville, VA: Rockbridge Publishing, 1998.

Heidler, David S., and Jeanne T. Heidler, eds. *Encyclopedia of the American Civil War: A Political, Social, and Military History*, vol. 2. Santa Barbara, CA: ABC-CLIO, 2000.

Hirshon, Stanley P. *The White Tecumseh: A Biography of William T. Sherman*. New York: Wiley, 1997.

Hutton, Paul Andrew. "Paladin of the Republic: Philip H. Sheridan," in *With My Face to the Enemy: Perspectives on the Civil War*. Edited by Robert Cowley. New York: Berkley Books, 2001. 348–363.

Janda, Lance. "Shutting the Gates of Mercy: The American Origins of Total War." *Journal of Military History* 59 (January 1995): 7–26.

Joes, Anthony James. *America and Guerrilla Warfare*. Lexington: University Press of Kentucky, 2000.

Jomini, Antoine Henri. *The Art of War*. Westport, CT: Greenwood Press, 1971 [1862].

Jones, Archer. *Civil War Command and Strategy: The Process of Victory and Defeat*. New York: The Free Press, 1992.

Jones, Archer, and Herman Hattaway. *How the North Won: A Military History of the Civil War*. Chicago: University of Illinois Press, 1983.

Jones, Virgil Carrington. *Gray Ghosts and Rebel Raiders: The Daring Exploits of the Confederate Guerillas*. New York: Holt Publishers, 1956.

Koblas, John J. *J.J. Dickinson: Swamp Fox of the Confederacy*. St. Cloud, MN: North Star Press, 2000.

Kutger, Joseph P. "Irregular Warfare in Transition." *Military Affairs* 24, no. 3 (Autumn 1960): 113–123.

Lancaster, Bruce. *The American Revolution.* New York: Houghton Mifflin, 1987.

Laqueur, Walter. "The Origins of Guerrilla Doctrine." *Journal of Contemporary History* 10 (July 1975): 341–382.

Liddel-Hart, B. H. *Sherman: The Genius of the Civil War.* London: Eyre and Spottswoodie, 1933.

Linderman, Gerald F. *Embattled Courage: The Experience of Combat in the American Civil War.* New York: Free Press, 1987.

Linn, Brian M. *The Philippine War: 1899–1902.* Lawrence: University Press of Kansas, 2000.

Mackesy, Piers. *The War for America: 1775–1783.* Lincoln: University of Nebraska Press, 1964.

Mackey, Robert R. *The Uncivil War: Irregular Warfare in the Upper South, 1861–1865.* Norman: University of Oklahoma Press, 2004.

Mahan, Dennis H. *An Elementary Treatise on Advanced-Guard, Out-Post, and Detachment Service of Troops.* New York: John Wiley & Sons Publishers, 1847.

Malone, Patrick. *The Skulking Way of War: Technology and Tactics among the New England Indians.* Baltimore: Johns Hopkins University Press, 1993.

Marszalek, John F. *Commander of All Lincoln's Armies: A Life of General Henry W. Halleck.* Cambridge, MA: Belknap Press of Harvard University Press, 2004.

Matloff, Maurice, ed. *American Military History.* Washington, DC: Center of Military History, Government Printing Office, 1968.

McPherson, James. *Battle Cry of Freedom: The Civil War Era.* New York: Ballantine, 1988.

———. "From Limited War to Total War in America," in *On the Road to Total War: The American Civil War and the German Wars of Unification, 1861–1871.* Edited by Stig Forster and Jorg Nagler. London: Cambridge University Press, 1997.

———. *For Cause and Comrades: Why Men Fought in the Civil War.* New York: Oxford University Press, 1997.

———. *This Mighty Scourge: Perspectives on the American Civil War.* New York: Oxford University Press, 2007.

Mink, Charles. "General Orders, No. 11: The Forced Evacuation of Civilians during the Civil War." *Military Affairs* 34 (December 1970): 132–136.

Mitchell, Reid. *Civil War Soldiers.* New York: Viking Penguin, 1988.

Monaghan, Jay. *Civil War on the Western Border, 1854–1865.* Boston: Little, Brown, 1955.

Morris, Roy, Jr. *Sheridan: The Life and Wars of General Phil Sheridan.* New York: Crown Books, 1992.

Morrison, James L., Jr. *"The Best School in the World": West Point, the Pre–Civil War Years, 1833–1866.* Kent, OH: Kent State University Press, 1986.

———. "Educating the Civil War Generals: West Point, 1833–1861." *Military Affairs* 38, no. 3 (October 1974): 108–111.

Mountcastle, John C. "A Stain upon Civilization: Guerrilla Warfare in Civil War Virginia, 1862–1865." M.A. thesis, Duke University, 2003.

Neely, Mark E., Jr. *The Civil War and the Limits of Destruction.* Cambridge: Harvard University Press, 2007.

————. *The Fate of Liberty: Abraham Lincoln and Civil Liberties*. New York: Oxford University Press, 1991.

————. "Was the Civil War a Total War?," in *On the Road to Total War: The American Civil War and the German Wars of Unification, 1861–1871*. Edited by Stig Forster and Jorg Nagler. London: Cambridge University Press, 1997.

Oates, Stephen B. *To Purge This Land with Blood: A Biography of John Brown*. New York: Harper & Row, 1970.

O'Brien, Sean Michael. *Mountain Partisans: Guerrilla Warfare in the Southern Appalachians*. Westport, CT: Praeger, 1999.

Paludan, Philip S. *Victims: A True Story of the Civil War*. Knoxville: University of Tennessee Press, 1981.

Pancake, John S. *This Destructive War: The British Campaign in the Carolinas 1780–1782*. Tuscaloosa: University of Alabama Press, 1985.

Pappas, George S. *To the Point: The United States Military Academy, 1802–1902*. Westport, CT: Praeger, 1993.

Parrish, William E. *Turbulent Partnership: Missouri and the Union: 1861–1865*. Columbia: University of Missouri Press, 1963.

Preston, Richard A., Alex Roland, and Sydney F. Wise. *Men in Arms: A History of Warfare and Its Relationships with Western Society*. New York: Praeger, 1991.

Prucha, Francis P. *The Sword of the Republic: The United States Army on the Frontier, 1783–1846*. Lincoln: University of Nebraska Press, 1969.

Ramage, James A. *Gray Ghost: The Life of Colonel John Singleton Mosby*. Lexington: University of Kentucky Press, 1999.

Rolle, Andrew. *John Charles Frémont: Character as Destiny*. Norman: University of Oklahoma Press, 1991.

Royster, Charles. *The Destructive War: William Tecumseh Sherman, Stonewall Jackson, and the Americans*. New York: Vintage Books, 1991.

Schneller, Robert J., Jr. *Farragut: America's First Admiral*. Washington, DC: Brassey's, 2002.

Schultz, Duane. *Quantrill's War: The Life and Times of William Clarke Quantrill*. New York: St. Martin's Griffin, 1997.

Schutz, Wallace J., and Walter Trenerry. *Abandoned by Lincoln: A Military Biography of General John Pope*. Chicago: University of Illinois Press, 1990.

Simpson, Brooks D. *Let Us Have Peace: Ulysses S. Grant and the Politics of War and Reconstruction 1861–1868*. Chapel Hill: University of North Carolina Press, 1991.

Skelton, William B. *An American Profession of Arms: The Army Officer Corps, 1784–1861*. Lawrence: University Press of Kansas, 1992.

Slade, A. D. *A. T. A. Torbert: Southern Gentleman in Union Blue*. Dayton, OH: Morningside House, 1992.

Smith, Justin H. "American Rule in Mexico." *American Historical Review* 23, no. 2 (January 1918): 287–302.

Smith, W. Wayne. "An Experiment in Counterinsurgency: The Assessment of Confederate Sympathizers in Missouri." *Journal of Southern History* 35, no. 3 (August 1969): 361–380.

Stephenson, Darl L. *Headquarters in the Brush: Blazer's Independent Union Scouts.* Athens: Ohio University Press, 2001.

Stiles, T. J. *Jesse James: Last Rebel of the Civil War.* New York: Vintage Books, 2002.

Stout, Harry S. *Upon the Altar of the Nation: A Moral History of the Civil War.* New York: Penguin Group, 2006.

Sutherland, Daniel E. "Abraham Lincoln, John Pope, and the Origins of Total War." *Journal of Military History* 56, no. 4 (October 1992): 567–586.

———. *The Emergence of Total War.* Abilene, TX: McWhiney Foundation Press, 1998.

———, ed. *Guerrillas, Unionists, and Violence on the Confederate Homefront.* Fayetteville: University of Arkansas Press, 1999.

———. "Sideshow No Longer: A Historiographical Review of the Guerilla War." *Civil War History* 46, no. 1 (March 2000): 5–23.

Utley, Robert M., and Wilcomb E. Washburn. *Indian Wars.* New York: Mariner Books, 2002.

Vetter, Charles E. *Sherman: Merchant of Terror, Advocate of Peace.* Gretna, LA: Pelican Publishing, 1992.

Vogtsberger, Margaret Ann. *The Dulanys of Welbourne: A Family in Mosby's Confederacy.* Berryville, VA: Rockbridge Publishing, 1995.

Waghelstein, John David. "Preparing for the Wrong War: The United States Army and Low-Intensity Conflict, 1755–1890." Ph.D. diss., Temple University, 1990.

Wagner, Margaret, Gary W. Gallagher, and Paul Finkelman, eds. *The Library of Congress Civil War Desk Reference.* New York: Simon and Schuster, 2002.

Walters, John Bennett. *Merchant of Terror: General Sherman and Total War.* Indianapolis: Bobbs-Merrill, 1973.

Weigley, Russell F. *A Great Civil War: A Military and Political History, 1861–1865.* Bloomington: University of Indiana Press, 2000.

———. "The American Military and the Principle of Civilian Control from McClellan to Powell." *Journal of Military History* 57, no. 5 (October 1993): 27–58.

———. *The American Way of War: A History of United States Military Strategy and Policy.* Bloomington: Indiana University Press, 1975.

———. *Towards an American Army: Military Thought from Washington to Marshall.* New York: Columbia University Press, 1962.

Wert, Jeffry D. *Mosby's Rangers.* New York: Simon and Schuster, 1990.

Woodworth, Steven E. *Nothing but Victory: The Army of the Tennessee, 1861–1865.* New York: Alfred A. Knopf, 2005.

Index

Abraham, James, 112, 124
Ambrose, Stephen, 151n52, 155n43
American Revolution, 17
 guerrilla warfare in, 8, 9–10, 20, 148–
 149n7
 military traditions emerging from, 149n10
Anderson, John E., 4
Anderson, William "Bloody Bill," 160n130
Antietam, 6, 67, 142
Arkansas
 and the Battle of Pea Ridge, 37
 counterguerrilla measures in, 83–84, 138,
 139, 168n108, 178n2
 guerrilla warfare in, 41, 56–57, 59, 63–64,
 161n4
 and punitive war along the Mississippi, 76,
 79, 81, 82
 See also Lower Mississippi Valley;
 Mississippi Marine Brigade
Army of the Cumberland, 66, 95
Army of the Gulf, 121
Army of the James, 121
Army of the Mississippi, 62
Army of Northern Virginia, 93, 121
Army of the Potomac, 106–107, 109–110, 111,
 121, 126
Army of the Tennessee, 56, 62, 64, 83, 91–92,
 94–95, 98–99, 120, 161n3
Army of West Virginia, 121. See also Hunter,
 David
Artman, Albert, 124
Ash, Stephen V., 4, 5, 126, 145, 178n2
assessments
 levied by Halleck, 34–35, 54, 60, 156n65
 levied by Pope, 25–26, 27–29, 32, 60,
 153n21

levied by Schofield, 47, 156n65, 159n114
 See also "collective responsibility," system of
Atlanta (GA), 1–2, 98 (map), 100
 Sherman's burning of, 95–96, 97 (image),
 160n127
 Sherman's capture of, 91–92, 93, 170n45
 strategic importance of, 85
Augur, Christopher C., 118
Austin (MS), 80–81, 82

B & O (Baltimore & Ohio) Railroad, 115 (map),
 118, 126
Bailey, Anne J., 137, 144, 170n32
Banks, Nathaniel, 120–121
Barber, Lucius, 82
Bauer, Jack, 15, 150n39
Beatty, John, 65
Birtle, Andrew J.
 on the Lieber Code, 44, 159n109
 and the Mississippi Marine Brigade,
 167n99
 and punitive measures against civilians,
 157n87, 168n108
 and Union approach to guerrilla threat, 5,
 83, 139
 on Winfield Scott's handling of Mexican
 War guerrillas, 16, 150n37
Black Striped Company, 104, 171n2
Blazer, Richard, 119
Blazer's Independent Union Scouts, 119, 139
"Bleeding Kansas," 21–22, 155n50. See also
 Jayhawkers; Kansas-Missouri border war;
 Quantrill's raid
Bowen, Don R., 22
Boyd, John, 33, 156n59
Brandon (MS), 87–88, 88 (map), 90

Breckenridge, John C., 121

Brobst, John, 90

Brown, John, 21, 152n2

Buell, Don Carlos, 60–61, 66–67, 161–163n19

"bummers," 99–100

Bundy, Carol, 176n105

Burmeister, George C., 31, 154n25

"Burning Raid," Merritt's. *See* Merritt, Wesley

Bustamante, Carlos Maria de, 14

Butler, Benjamin F., 57, 68–69, 71, 121, 165n49

Byers, Samuel H., 21

Canton (GA), 94, *98* (map), 170n32

Canton (MS), *88* (map), 90

Carr, Caleb, 78

Cassville (GA), 94, *98* (map), 170n32, 170n33

Castel, Albert, 159n111

Catahoula (steamer), 76

Catton, Bruce, 117

Cedar Creek, battle of, 131

Chambersburg (PA), 125, 135

Charlottesville (VA), *115* (map), 131–132

Chase, Salmon P., 72

Chattanooga (TN), 85, 86, 91

Chickamauga, 85

Clinton (MS), 90, 169n21

Coe, Hamlin, 67

"collective responsibility," system of
     as central tenet of total war, 153n17
     as counterguerrilla measure, 15–16
     Grant's acceptance of, 162n15
     Pope's endorsement of, 25–27, 107–109, 153n14, 153n21, 171–172n16, 178n1
     Sherman and, 59–60, 72, 75–76
     in Virginia, 111, 113, 119–120
     See also assessments

colonial era, irregular warfare in, 8–10, 20, 148n4

Columbia (SC), 1–2, 102

conciliation
     Grant's early hope for, 60
     "hard war" versus, 164n35
     McClellan's approach to, 109–110, 152n8, 158n98
     Sherman's ideological transition from, 62–63

Union's abandonment of, 5, 24–25, 38, 106–107, 108, 111, 124, 141

Confederate cavalry, 3, 57, 60, 89–90, 175n97. *See also* Mosby, John Singleton

Confederate Congress, 97, 173n42

Continental (steamer), 76

Cooling, Franklin B., 59, 162n15, 164n39

Cornwallis, Lord, 9–10

Couch, Darius, 125, 135

Cox, Jacob D., 104, 118

Crook, George, 106, 111, 118, 119, 140

Cumberland River, 56

Currie, George E., 56, 81, 168n103

Curtis, Samuel R., 36–37, 40, 47, 56

Custer, George Armstrong, 131

Dade, Francis, 11

Davies, Thomas, 156n59

Davis, Edward, 136

Davis, Jefferson, 41, 92, 107–108

Dayton (MO), 31, 47, 150n50

Dayton (VA), 128–131, 135, 136, 176n100, 176n107–108, 177n127

Decatur (MS), 67, *88* (map), 90

Dederer, John Morgan, 9

Diana (steamer), 80

Donaldson, Francis A., 110

Donaldsonville (MS), 70–72, 76, 81–82, 83, 141, 165n54, 165n60

Downey, Stephen, 110

Dulany, John P., 120, 174n62

Early, Jubal, 123–124, 131

Edwards, Laura F., 174n61

Ellet, Alfred W., 80–81, 82, 168n103

Ellis, John, 3, 147n2

Ellis, Richard N., 172n25

emancipation, 4, 30, 31, 108

Emancipation Proclamation, 42, 143

Eugene (steamer), 75

Farragut, David, 57, 70–71, 72, 81, 165n54

Fauquier County (VA), *115* (map), 133, 135, 136, 160n27

Fellman, Michael
     on distinction between Missouri guerrillas and Mosby's partisans, 114

on guerrilla problem in Missouri, 26, 47, 152n6, 153n18, 154n24

on guerrillas as an intangible enemy, 22, 38, 157n74

on the Partisan Ranger Act, 158n91

on prisoner executions, 157n85, 157n87

Flagg, Samuel, 47–48

Fleagle, Amos, 65

foraging

Federal "bummers" engaged in, 89, 99

and orders to prohibit, 105

and Special Field Orders No. 120, 95, 96–97

Forrest, Nathan Bedford, 3, 60–61, 86, 89, 162n18, 163n19, 177n132

Fort Donelson, 57

Fort Henry, 57

Fort Sumter, 8

Forty-Sixth Ohio Infantry Regiment, 75

Foster, Buck T., 63, 163n28

Franklin, Freeman, 112

Frémont, John C.

and guerrilla attacks on railroads, 156n55

and guerrilla warfare in Virginia, 106, 118–119, 173n50

and Lincoln, 155n46–48

Lincoln's replacement of, 31–32, 155n43, 155n49

martial law proclamation in Missouri issued by, 29–31, 154n36, 154n38, 155n42

and Pope's punitive policies, 26, 28

French, Samuel, 87

French and Indian War, 9. *See also* Indian wars

Friar's Point (MS), 83

Gamble, Hamilton R., 23–24, 26, 154n40

General Order No. 11, 48–53, 133, 160n121, 160n127

General Order No. 17, 161n4, 165n62

General Order No. 34, 34, 38–39

General Orders 100. *See* Lieber Code

Georgia. *See* "march to the sea," Sherman's

Georgia Railroad, *98* (map)

Germantown (TN), 73–74

Gettysburg, 6, 46, 85, 142

Gladiator (steamer), 76, 78

Glatthaar, Joseph, 73, 93, 102, 166n65

Goodwin, Josiah H., 80, 167n92

Graber, Doris Appel, 153n17

Grand Gulf (MS), 69–70, 71, 76, 83

Grant, Ulysses S.

as District of West Tennessee commander, 60, 62

in the Lower Mississippi Valley, 57, 61–62, 108

Missouri's guerrilla problem and influence on, 32

as original practitioner of hard war, 162n11

popularity of, 85

postwar writings of, 162n14

rhetoric of, 63, 136, 177n130

in the Shenandoah Valley and northern Virginia, 103, 107, 120–121, 126–128, 130, 132, 174n66

and Sherman's march to the sea, 92–93, 174n62

and Union's transition to punitive war, 60, 103

Greene, Nathanael, 9–10, 148n7, 149n9, 149n11

Greenville (MS), 82

Griest, Alva G., 65, 93, 164n39

Grimsley, Mark

and Grant's postwar writings, 60, 162n14

on guerrilla attacks on railroads, 156n55

and link between guerrilla warfare and Union policies, 5, 148n8

and the moral implications of punitive war, 129

on Pope's orders, 109, 172n24

and retaliation among lower ranks, 63–64

on Sheridan, 135, 176n107, 177n127

on Sherman, 75–76, 102

on types of enemy irregulars, 3

on Union policies in Missouri, 54, 163n134

and Union restraint, 139, 144–145, 168n107, 178n5

on Union transition to hard war, 143, 158n98, 162n11, 164n35

Griswoldsville, battle of, 98–99. *See also* "march to the sea," Sherman's

Gurley, Frank, 64–65, 164n39

Guyandotte (VA), 111

Hagerman, Edward, 62–63, 163n28
Halleck, Henry Wager "Old Brains," 19, *35*
 (image), 46–47, 62, 85, 121
 assessment programs issued by, 60,
  159n114
 and criticism of Hunter's tactics, 124, 130
 and execution as punishment, 39, 41,
  156n55
 and guerrilla problem in Kansas and
  Missouri, 33–35, 37–39, 155n50,
  156n62
 and guerrilla problem in Lower
  Mississippi Valley, 56, 163n24
 and guerrilla problem in Shenandoah
  Valley and northern Virginia, 103, 107,
  118, 124–126, 175n89
 and the Lieber Code (General Orders 100),
  39, 41–46, 54, 65, 71, 157n78, 175n89
 and opposition to Pope's oath of allegiance
  order, 108
 and opposition to Sherman's march to the
  sea, 169n25
 and "reciprocity" issue, 164–165n41
 and the "severe rules of war," 124–125
 and Union's response to guerrilla warfare,
  19, 20, 48–49, 52–53, 132–133, 141
Hannibal & St. Joseph Railroad, *23* (map), 27,
 29, 153n20, 154n29
"hard war"
 antiguerrilla campaigns as groundwork for,
  6–7, 59, 161n134
 conciliation versus, 164n35
 Union leaders as practitioners of, 71–72,
  126–128, 162n11, 162n15
 Union's transition to, 143, 158n98
Harper's Weekly, 65, 85, 120
Hazel Green, (AL), 64–65
Heatwole, John, 117, 129, 173n48, 175n97,
 176n108
Hercules (steamer), 79
Hillsboro (MS), *88* (map), 90, 98, 169n21
Hindman, Thomas C., 72, 161n4, 165n62
Hitchcock, Henry M., 96, 97, 99
Hodges, James, 91
Hood, John Bell, 92, 93, 96
Hopefield (AR), 76, 79, 83
Howard, Oliver O., 94

Howard, R. L., 169n21
Hunter, David "Black Dave"
 defeat at Lynchburg, 123–124, 174n66,
  175n78
 and punitive war in Shenandoah Valley,
  31, 121–124, 126, 130, 175n73, 176n108
Huntsville (AL), 64, 68
Hurlburt, Stephen A., 27–28, 79
Hurst, Samuel, 95–96

Indian wars, 3, 148n4, 149n14, 149n16
 and guerrilla warfare, 8–9, 10–13, 20
 pacification v. retaliation in, 140
 and Pope, 109, 172n25
 See also Seminole Wars

J. H. Dickey (steamer), 76
Jackson, Claiborne, 23
Jackson, Mudwall, 117
Jackson, William Hicks "Red," 177n132
Jackson (MS), 86, 87, *88* (map), 90
James, Jesse, 22, 139, 160n131
Janda, Lance, 153n17, 157n76
Jayhawkers, 21, 35, 49, 51–52, 155n50, 156n62.
 See also Kansas-Missouri border war
"Jesse Scouts," 119
Johnston, Joseph E., 91–92, 120, 161n3
Jomini, Baron Antoine Henri, 8, 13, 17–18,
 19–20, 34, 151n46–47
Jones, Samuel Calvin, 79

Kanawha Valley (VA), 104–106, 110–111, 118,
 136, 141
Kansas-Missouri border war, 21–22, 48–53,
 152n4, 155n50, 160n121, 160n126–127.
 See also General Order No. 11; Quantrill's
  raid
Kansas–Nebraska Act, 21
Keetsville (MO), 36–37, 47
Kelley, Benjamin F., 105
Kentucky, 41, 56–57, 60–61, 111, 138
Kineo (gunboat), 69–70
King Philip's War, 9
Kircher, Henry A., 78–79
Kirkham, Ralph W., 14

Lander, F. W., 105

Lane, Jim, 49, 155, 160n121. *See also* Kansas-
    Missouri border war
Lane, Joseph, 15
Lauderdale (MS), *88* (map), 90
Lawrence (KS), 49–51, *51* (image), 52. *See also*
    Quantrill's Raid
Lazelle, Henry, 118
Lee, Robert E., 53, 93, 102, 109, 121, 136, 139
Letcher, John, 122
Lexington (VA), *115* (map), 122–123, 124, 136,
    172n23
Lieber, Francis, 41–44, *43* (image), 114,
    158n94. *See also* Lieber Code
Lieber Code, 125, 140
    death sentences addressed in, 176–
        177n116
    Halleck and, 39, 41–46, 54, 65, 71, 157n78,
        175n89
    influence of, 159n109
    "innocent" defined in, 113
    and loyalty to a legitimate government,
        158–159n103
    and Mosby's partisans, 114, 173n39
    on retaliation and reciprocity, 65, 164–
        165n41
    and rules of law, 132
    See also Lieber, Francis
Lincoln, Abraham, 96, 109, 143
    and call for Union restraint, 37, 157n71
    and Frémont's martial law proclamation in
        Missouri, 30–31, 154n38, 154–155n42,
        155n46
    and frustration with Union efforts in the
        East, 42, 158n98
    and guerrilla warfare in Missouri, 39–40, 54
    and Missouri governor's conciliatory
        proclamation, 23–24
    and punitive war, 141
    and pursuit of hard war, 162n11
    removal of Frémont from Missouri, 33–32,
        155n43, 155n49
    and reservations about Sherman's march
        to the sea, 169n25
    and Union campaign in Virginia, 103, 107,
        108, 158n98
Lincoln, Curtis, 117
Linderman, Gerald, 6, 67, 151n61

Linn, Brian M., 178–179n9
Loan, Benjamin, 40, 156n65
Lockwood, Henry, 115
Logan, John A., 74
Loudoun County (VA), 115–116, *115* (map),
    132–134, 135, 136, 160n127, 177n121. *See
    also* Merritt, Wesley
Lowell, Russell, 129, 131
Lower Mississippi Valley, 6–7, *58* (map)
    antiguerrilla policies in, 60–63, 83–84
    "collective responsibility" in, 59, 108, 113
    and emerging punitive war, 62–68, 72–79,
        84, 100–102, 166n65, 166n69
    Grant in, 57, 61–62, 108
    and guerrillas along the Mississippi River,
        56–57, 68–72, 74–76, 78–83, 161n3,
        161n5
    See also Mississippi Marine Brigade;
        Mississippi River
Lynch, Charles, 121, 122, 124
Lynchburg (VA), 123–124, 174n66, 175n78
Lyon, Nathaniel, 23, 24, 46

MacGregor, Frank, 81
Mackesy, Piers, 10
Mackey, Robert
    and categories of Union operations against
        irregulars, 167n88
    on Forrest and Morgan, 61, 163n19
    and guerrilla warfare as a Confederate
        strategy, 178n4
    and guerrilla warfare in Virginia, 130,
        171n1, 173n49, 176n108
    and guerrilla warfare link to Union
        attitudes, 5
    and the Mississippi Marine Brigade, 80,
        81, 167n99
    and Union efforts in thwarting guerrilla
        problem, 83, 139
Mahan, Dennis Hart, 18–19, 20, 151n52
Manassas Gap Railroad, *115* (map), 118, 119, 126
"march to the sea," Sherman's, *98* (map), 100
    and the burning of Atlanta, 95–96, *97*
        (image) compared to Merritt's Burning
        Raid, 134–135
    Grant's endorsement of, 92–93, 174n62
    and guerrilla attacks, 96–97, 100–102

"march to the sea," Sherman's (*cont.*),
    Lincoln's reservation's about, 169n25
    punitive war in, 93–94, 95–96, 97–99
    significance of, 100, 101, 170n51
    strategy in, 93, 94–95, 169n26
    See also Sherman, William T.
Marion, Francis, 9, 10
Marion Station (MS), *88* (map), 90
Marsh, C. C., 33, 156n57
McCarty, William, 74
McCausland, John, 125
McClellan, George B., 19, 34, 104, 109–110,
    152n8, 158n98
McCook, Robert L., 64–67, 83, 164n39. *See also*
    Ninth Ohio Volunteers
McDonald, John, 26
McNeil, John, 33, 41
McNeill, John Hanson, 117, 126, 131, 136,
    173n42
McPherson, James (historian), 162n18
    and Americans' romantic view of war, 19
    and Civil War strategy, 151n52
    on emancipation as a "morale crisis," 143
    on the "inevitable destruction of war," 142
    on Missouri guerrilla warfare, 52, 54
    on Sheridan, 128, 175n96
    on Sherman as pioneer of hard war,
        162n11, 163n30
    on Union behavior, 145
    on West Point's curriculum, 151n44
McPherson, James (major general), 88
Meade, George, 121
Meigs, John R., 128–129, 130, 175n97,
    176n107, 176n108. *See also* Dayton (VA)
Memphis (TN), 57, *58* (map), 59, 68
    and Grant's headquarters at, 60, 61
    guerrilla activity around, 62–63, 79
    Mississippi Marine Brigade operating
        near, 80, 83
    Sherman's command at, 72–73, 74–75,
        76–78, 161n8, 166n76
Meridian campaign, Sherman's, 86–91, *88*
    (map), 92, 96, 100–101, 143. *See also*
    Sherman, William T.
Merritt, Wesley, 133–135, *133* (image),
    177n119–121, 177n127

Mexican War, 8, 20, 37, 39
    guerrilla warfare in, 13–15, 17, 150n40
    and Pope, 24, 26, 152n9
    U.S. counterguerrilla tactics in, 15–17, 140
    See also Scott, Winfield
Milledgeville (GA), 95, 98, *98* (map), 99, 170n45
Mink, Charles, 160n129
Mississippi, 56, *58* (map), *88* (map)
    guerrilla warfare in, 89–90, 107, 118, 126,
        137, 139
    punitive war in, 5–6, 59, 62
    Sherman's campaign in, 78, 84, 85–91, 94,
        100–102
    See also Lower Mississippi Valley
Mississippi Marine Brigade, 79–83, 86, 167n99
Mississippi River, 47, *58* (map)
    "collective responsibility" along, 59
    guerrilla warfare along, 20, 56–57, 79, 81,
        84, 161n3, 161n5
    as key to Union victory, 56–57, 84
    and the Mississippi Marine Brigade, 79–
        83, 86, 167n99
    and Pope's capture of Island Number 10,
        31–32, 57
    punitive war along, 1, 7, 63, 68–73, 74–79,
        94, 141
    Union control of, 81, 85
    See also Lower Mississippi Valley
Missouri, *23* (map)
    assessment programs in, 25–26, 27–29, 32,
        34–35, 54, 60, 153n15, 153n21, 156n65,
        159n114
    1864 increase in guerrilla activity in, 53,
        160n130
    governor's promise on slavery in, 30,
        154n40
    habeas corpus suspended in, 34, 156n63
    Halleck's approach to noncombatants in,
        37–39, 157n74, 157n76
    and the Lieber Code, 44, 158n102, 158–
        159n103, 159n107
    Lincoln's removal of Frémont from, 30–
        31, 155n43
    Lincoln's view on, 155n49
    martial law in, 29–31, 154n36, 154n38,
        155n42

noncombatants' powerlessness in, 27,
   154n24
and Order No. 11, 49–53, 54, 159n111,
   160n127, 179n24
postwar guerrillas from, 53, 160n131
prisoner executions in, 32–33, 40–41,
   156n54, 157n85
punitive policies in, 27, 31–32, 108, 153–
   154n23, 178n1
railroad attacks in, 24–27, 37–39, 138, 141,
   154n25, 154n29, 156n55
Schofield in, 46–48, 50, 159n113
Union restraint in, 35–36
and Union transition to hard war, 53–55,
   161n134
Union troop behavior in, 154n30, 156n62
See also Kansas-Missouri border war;
   Pope, John
Missouri State Guard, 22, 31
Mobile (AL), 86–87, 121
Mobile & Ohio Railroad, 86, *88* (map), 89
Moore, Thomas, 57
Moorefield (VA), 105
Morgan, John Hunt, 3, 60–61, 138, 162n18,
   162n19
Morrison, James L., 18–19
Mosby, John Singleton, 104, *117* (image), 131
   battlefield celebrity of, 116–117
   and guerrilla characterization, 114–115
   and the war's end, 136, 177n132
   See also Mosby's Confederacy; Mosby's
      irregulars
Mosby's Confederacy, 115–117, 121–122, 131–
   135, 177n121. *See also* Merritt, Wesley
Mosby's irregulars
   collective responsibility in dealing with,
      119–120
   and the Lieber Code, 114, 173n39
   Partisan Ranger Act and, 114, 173n42
   railroad attacks by, 126
   in Shenandoah Valley and northern
      Virginia, 114, 115–116, *116* (image),
      118–120, 174n62
   Sheridan's contests with, 127
   See also Mosby's Confederacy
Mudd, Joseph A., 152n4

Naglee, Henry, 111–112, 172n35
Napoleon, 19, 39, 115, 123–124. *See also*
   Jomini, Baron Antoine Henri; Mahan,
   Dennis Hart
Napoleon (AR), 81, 82, 167n100
Neely, Mark E., 5
   on Dayton's burning, 176n107
   and Frémont in Missouri, 30, 155n46-47
   and the Lieber Code, 44, 159n107
   on Merritt's Burning Raid, 135, 136
   on Sherman's and Grant's rhetoric, 63,
      177n130
   on Union conduct in Missouri, 54
   and Union restraint, 142, 144–145,
      168n107, 179n12, 179n24
New Market (VA), *115* (map), 121, 122
New Orleans (LA), 57, *58* (map), 59, 68–69,
   71, 77–78
Newtown (VA), *115* (image), 122, 130, 135,
   177n127
New York Herald, 80, 103, 166n76
Ninth Ohio Volunteers, 64–67, 164n35, 164n39
North Missouri Railroad, 24–26

Oates, Stephen B., 21, 152n2
Okeechobee, battle of, 11–12. *See also* Indian wars
O'Neil, Charles, 69–70
Order No. 11
   displacement of civilians by, 160n127
   in response to Quantrill's raid, 49, 50–51
   severity of, 52–53, 54, 133, 145, 159n111,
      160n129
   See also Quantrill's Raid; Schofield, John M.
Owen, E. K., 86

Paine, Eleazer, 32
Paint Rock (AL), 67–68
Palmyra (MO), *23* (map), 27–30, 33, 41,
   154n30
Partisan Ranger Act, 41, 46, 105, 114, 117–118,
   158n91, 173n42
partisan rangers, 3, 114. *See also* Mosby, John
   Singleton
Pea Ridge, battle of, 37
Pemberton, John C., 85
Peninsula Campaign, 103, 106–107, 110, 158n98

Pensacola (FL), 157n71

Petersburg (VA), 92, 93, 102

Philips, Pleasant J., 98

Platter, Cornelius C., 94, 96

Polk, Leonidas, 86, 88, 89, 90–91

Pope, John, *28* (image)
  antiguerrilla policies of, 152n9
  assessment programs in Missouri issued
    by, 27–29, 60, 27–29, 153n21, 153n23,
    153–154n23
  and collective responsibility, 25–27, 71,
    107–109, 153n14, 153n21, 171–172n16,
    172n24, 178n1
  in the Indian wars, 109, 172n25
  as key to Union transition to total war, 54,
    158n98
  legacy of failure in Missouri, 31–32
  McClellan's attitude v. that of, 109, 110
  as punitive war champion in Missouri,
    24–29, 52, 156n55
  as punitive war champion in Virginia,
    107–109, 122, 130, 172n24
  on secessionists, 152–153n11

Porter, Albert Quincy, 87

Pottawatomie Creek (KS), 21, 152n2. *See also*
  Brown, John

Powell, William H., 131

Price, Sterling, 22, 23, 31, 37, 53

Prucha, Francis, 12

Quantrill, William Clarke. *See* Quantrill's
  Raid

Quantrill's Raid, 49–53, *51* (image), 159n118.
  See also Lawrence (KS); Order No. 11

Randolph (TN), 179n24
  and collective responsibility system, 113
  Grimsley on, 75–76
  Sherman's order to burn, 1, 75–76, 77, 78,
    81–82, 83, 99, 130, 141, 145, 166n69

Reichelm, E. Paul, 81, 167n100

Richmond (VA), 1–2, 41, 100, 106, 111, 121

Robinson, James, 95–96

Roe, F. A., 71

Rolla (MO), 29, 33

Royster, Charles, 4, 19, 62, 63, 86, 91, 101, 142,
  179n12

Savannah (GA), 92, 94, 96, *98* (map), 100, 102.
  See also "march to the sea," Sherman's

Schofield, John M., *48* (image)
  assessment programs of, 156n65, 159n114
  on guerrilla threat in Missouri, 46–47
  Missouri depopulation enforced by, 76,
    126
  and Order No. 11: 48–53, 133, 160n121,
    160n127
  See also Quantrill's Raid

Scott, Winfield
  and call for restraint in Civil War, 19–20,
    151n59
  and Mexican War, 13–15, 16, *16* (image),
    17, 19, 39, 150nn34, 37
  and Second Seminole War, 11, 13

Second Manassas, 24, 109

Seddon, James, 57, 161n3

Seminole Wars, 11–13, *13* (image), 26, 149n23

Seventh Kansas Cavalry. *See* Jayhawkers

Shenandoah Valley, *115* (map)
  Cedar Creek, battle of, 131
  Grant's plan for, 121, 174n66
  guerrillas in, 113–114, 116–118, 125–126,
    131–132, 136–137, 173n48
  Hunter's punitive war in, 31, 121–124,
    126, 130, 175n73, 176n108
  and Merritt's Burning Raid, 133–135,
    177n127
  Mosby's irregulars in, 114, 115–116, *116*
    (image), 118–119, 120, 174n62
  New Market, battle of, 121, 122
  Sheridan in northern Virginia and, 103,
    107, 126, 127–128, 175n96, 176n107,
    177n130
  topography of, 174n64

Sheridan, Phillip, *127* (image), 140, 144–145
  and the burning of Dayton, 129, 130
  and Cedar Creek battle, 131, 132
  and civilian disloyalty, 135–136
  and "God in Israel" decree, 132–133
  Grant's orders to, 126, 127–128, 132
  as hard war practitioner, 127
  and link between guerrilla war and
    punitive war, 131–132, 141–142
  and Merritt's Burning Raid, 127, 133–135,
    160n127, 177n119–121

and punitive war in Virginia, 103, 107, 175n96, 177n127, 177n130

and retributive burning, 129–131, 176n108

subordinates' views on, 129–130, 176n105

and "war is punishment" belief, 137

Sherman, Ellen, 87

Sherman, William T., *73* (image), 144–145, 169n17, 177n132

and burning of Randolph, 75–76, 78, 81, 130

"campaigns of terror," 102, 171n57

and capture of Atlanta, 91–92, 95–96, *97* (image), 160n127, 170n45

and collective responsibility, 59–60, 72–76, 108, 161n8, 166n65, 166n69

and ideological move from conciliation to punitive war, 32, 60, 62–63, 72, 78–79, 83–84, 141–144, 162n11

in the Indian wars, 140, 149n23

and Jomini influence, 5, 151n54

"march to the sea," 92–100, *98* (image), 100, 133, 134–135, 169n26, 170n51, 174n63

Meridian campaign of, 86–91, *88* (image), 92, 96, 100, 101, 143

Missouri guerrilla problem and influence on, 32, 47, 48–49, 54

as modern warfare progenitor, 85–86

and punitive war in Lower Mississippi Valley, 55, 59, 72–79, 81, 84, 99–101, 102, 113, 166n65, 166n69

rail lines as target of, 91–92, 93, 98, 134–135

rhetoric of, 63, 102, 136, 163n30, 177n130

and "rules of war," 124–125, 126

sanity questioned, 85, 168n2

Shiloh, battle of, 6, 60, 64, 67, 142, 162n14–15, 168n2

Sibley (MO), 47–49

Sigel, Franz, 107, 121–122, 126

Simpson, Brooks D., 60, 162n15

Skelton, William B., 10

Slade, A. D., 176n100

slavery, 21–24, 143, 144, 154n40

Slocum, Henry W., 95

Smith, George Gilbert, 165n54

Smith, Horace, 131

Smith, Howard Malcolm, 177n121

Smith, John E., 94

Smith, W. Wayne, 153n15

Smith, William Sooy, 89, 169n17

Southern Railroad, *88* (map), 89

Southwestern Railroad, *98* (map)

St. Louis (MO), *23* (map)

assessments in, 34–35, 61

Union command in, 23, 24, 32, 46, 168n2

Stanton, Edwin M., 68–69, 126, 157n71, 173n50

Staunton (VA), *115* (map), 121, 122, 124, 130, 131

Stevenson, James H., 133

Stevenson, John, 133–134

Stiles, T. J., 22

Stout, Harry T., 45

Stuart, J. E. B., 173n42

Sumter, Thomas, 9, 10

Suter, John P., 123, 124

Sutherland, Daniel, 54, 108, 158n98

Swamp Dragoons, 104, 171n2

Taylor, J. P., 111

Taylor, Zachary, 11–13, 14–15, 16

Tennessee River, 56–57

Thomas, George H., 65, 66, 92–93, 96

Thomas E. Tutt (steamer), 78–79

Thompson, James D., 36, 174n73

Thompson, M. Jefferson, 30, 155n45

Toland, John T. (Toland's Raid), 112–113

Twiggs, David E., 15

U.S. Navy, 70–71, 79, 86. *See also* Mississippi Marine Brigade

Vicksburg (MS), 81, 85, 86, *88* (map)

Vicksburg & Selma Railroad, 86, *88* (map)

Virginia

collective responsibility in, 111, 113, 119–120

guerrilla problem in, 104–106, 113–114, 116–118, 125–126, 131–132, 136–137

Pope's orders in, 107–110

punitive war in, 102, 103–104, 107, 120, 135

retaliatory burnings in, 111, 112

Southern women in Union's punitive war in, 120, 174n61

Union efforts to combat guerrilla threat in, 173n49, 173n50

See also Crook, George; Kanawha Valley;
    Shenandoah Valley
Virginia Central Railroad, 174n66

Waghelstein, John D., 8, 11, 13, 150
Walcutt, Charles C., 75–76, *77* (image),
    166n69. *See also* Randolph (TN)
Walters, John Bennett, 59, 75, 78, 161n8
Washington, George, 10, 149n10
Watson, P. H., 39–40
Watson, William G., 122, 123, 174n73
Weigley, Russell F.
    on conventional tactics against the
        Seminole, 11, 12, 149n14
    on Grant and the guerrilla threat, 60,
        162n16
    on Jomini, 17–18, 151n46
    and progression of a "war against peoples," 4
    on Sherman's "campaign of terror," 100,
        102, 171n57
    and unconventional war, 9, 10, 149n11
    on Union destructiveness and morality, 144
    on unprepared military leaders, 8, 148n2
    on western Virginia's local guerrillas, 104

Weiser, Charles, 79
Westervelt, William B., 87, 90, 169n21
West Point, U.S. Military Academy at
    Civil War leaders as alumni of, 17, 24, 46
    curriculum of, 41, 151nn44, 52
    Jomini in curriculum at, 17–19, 34
    See also Jomini, Baron Antoine Henri;
        Mahan, Dennis Hart
Wheaton, Lloyd, 179n9
Wheeler, Joseph "Fighting Joe," 96
White, Elijah, 117
Wilcox, Alfred G., 95
Wilkin, William Porter, 1
Williams, Thomas, 69–70
Wills, Charles, 94, 163–164n33, 170n33
Wilson's Creek, 31, 46
Winfield, John Q., 117
Woodson, Buck, 117
Woodworth, Steven E., 64
Wool, John E., 15–16, 26
Worth, William J., 12, 13, 15, 26
Wytheville (VA), 112–113, 121, 179n24

Young, Henry, 119